First World War
and Army of Occupation
War Diary
France, Belgium and Germany

24 DIVISION
Headquarters, Branches and Services
Royal Army Medical Corps
Assistant Director Medical Services
21 August 1915 - 29 March 1919

WO95/2196/1

The Naval & Military Press Ltd
www.nmarchive.com
Published in association with The National Archives

Published by

The Naval & Military Press Ltd

Unit 10 Ridgewood Industrial Park,

Uckfield, East Sussex,

TN22 5QE England

Tel: +44 (0) 1825 749494

www.naval-military-press.com

www.nmarchive.com

This diary has been reprinted in facsimile from the original. Any imperfections are inevitably reproduced and the quality may fall short of modern type and cartographic standards.

© **Crown Copyright**
Images reproduced by permission of The National Archives, London, England, 2015.

Contents

Document type	Place/Title	Date From	Date To
Heading	WO95/2196/1		
Heading	Asst Dir. Medical Services Aug 1915-1919 Mar		
Heading	24th Division HQ. 24th Division Vol I Aug & Sept 15 Dec 18		
Heading	War Diary Of A.D.M.S. 24th Div Covering Period From August 21 1915 To September 30 1915		
War Diary	Blackdown Aldershot	21/08/1915	24/08/1915
War Diary	Blackdown	25/08/1915	30/08/1915
War Diary	Boulogne	31/08/1915	31/08/1915
War Diary	Royon	01/09/1915	22/09/1915
War Diary	Bomy	22/09/1915	22/09/1915
War Diary	Busnes	23/09/1915	24/09/1915
War Diary	Bethune	25/09/1915	25/09/1915
War Diary	Sailly Labourse	26/09/1915	28/09/1915
War Diary	Si Hilaire	29/09/1915	29/09/1915
War Diary	St Hilaire	30/09/1915	30/09/1915
Miscellaneous	24th Division-XIth Corps		
Miscellaneous	No 72 Field Ambulance 24th Division		
Miscellaneous	No 73 Field Ambulance 24th Division		
Miscellaneous	Battle Of Loos No. 74 Field Ambulance 24th Division. O.C. Capt A.N. Rose R.A.M.C.		
Heading	24th Division H.Q. 24th Division A.D.M.S. Vol. 2 Oct 15		
War Diary	St Hilaire	01/10/1915	02/10/1915
War Diary	Steenvoorde	03/10/1915	05/10/1915
War Diary	Steenvoorde Reninghelst	06/10/1915	07/10/1915
War Diary	Reninghelst	07/10/1915	31/10/1915
Heading	H.Q. 24th Div, A.D.M.S. Vol 3 Nov 15		
War Diary	Reninghelst	01/11/1915	22/11/1915
War Diary	Tilques	23/11/1915	30/11/1915
Map			
Heading	A.D.M.S 24th Div Vol 4 December 1915		
Heading	War Diary Of A.D.M.S. 24 Division From Dec. 1st To Dec 31st 1915 Vol 4		
War Diary	Tilques	01/12/1915	31/12/1915
Heading	A.D.M.S 24th Div Vol 5 Jan 1916		
Heading	War Diary Confidential A.D.M.S. 24th Division Vol 5- January 1916 With Map		
War Diary	Tilques	01/01/1916	07/01/1916
War Diary	Reninghelst.	08/01/1916	31/01/1916
Map			
Heading	A.D.M.S. 24th Div Feb 1916		
Heading	War Diary A.D.M.S 24 Division Feby. 1916 Vol VI		
War Diary	Reninghelst.	01/02/1916	29/02/1916
Heading	War Diaries Of A.D.M.S 24th Division For March April 1916		
Heading	A.D.M.S 24th Division Vol VII March 1916 Vol 7		
War Diary	Reninghelst.	01/03/1916	31/03/1916
Heading	A.D.M.S 24 Division Vol VIII April 1916 Vol 8		
War Diary	St Jans Cappel	01/04/1916	24/04/1916

War Diary	Bailleul	25/04/1916	30/04/1916
Heading	A.D.M.S 24th Division May 1916		
War Diary	Bailleul	01/05/1916	31/05/1916
Map			
Heading	A.D.M.S. 24 Division Vol X June 1916		
War Diary	Bailleul	01/06/1916	30/06/1916
Heading	A.D.M.S. 24 Division. Vol XII. July 1916		
War Diary	Bailleul	01/07/1916	03/07/1916
War Diary	Locre	04/07/1916	13/07/1916
War Diary	Bailleul	14/07/1916	19/07/1916
War Diary	St Jans Cappel	20/07/1916	25/07/1916
War Diary	Cavillon	26/07/1916	31/07/1916
Heading	A.D.M.S. 24 Division Vol XII August 1916 August 1916		
War Diary	Corbie	01/08/1916	02/08/1916
War Diary	Happy Valley	03/08/1916	09/08/1916
War Diary	Citadel	10/08/1916	19/08/1916
War Diary	Citadel	20/08/1916	22/08/1916
War Diary	Forked Line Camp	23/08/1916	24/08/1916
War Diary	Buire	25/08/1916	31/08/1916
Map			
Heading	A.D.M.S. 24 Division Vol XIII September 1916		
War Diary	S Of Albert E. 11. Central	01/09/1916	03/09/1916
War Diary	(Albert) E. 11. Central	04/09/1916	07/09/1916
War Diary	Ailly	08/09/1916	19/09/1916
War Diary	Bruay	20/09/1916	29/09/1916
War Diary	Comblain L'abbe	29/09/1916	30/09/1916
Miscellaneous	A Form Messages And Signals.	20/09/1916	20/09/1916
Miscellaneous	Preliminary Medical Disposition 24 Division On Taking Over Line	20/09/1916	20/09/1916
Heading	24th Division A.D.M.S. Oct 1916		
Miscellaneous	D.A.G. 3rd Echelon.	01/11/1916	01/11/1916
Heading	A.D.M.S. 24 Division Vol XIV October 1916		
War Diary	Camblain L'Abbe	01/10/1916	28/10/1916
War Diary	Bruay	28/10/1916	29/10/1916
War Diary	Braquemont	30/10/1916	31/10/1916
Map			
Operation(al) Order(s)	RAMC Operation Order No 81 By Colonel F. R. Buswell A.M.S. Adms 24th Div	22/10/1916	22/10/1916
Operation(al) Order(s)	R.A.M.C. Operation Order No.83 by Colonel F.R. Buswell A.M.S., A.D.M.S 24th Divn.	23/10/1916	23/10/1916
Heading	A.D.M.S. 24th Division Nov 1916		
Heading	War Diary. A.D.M.S. 24 Division Vol XV November 1916		
War Diary	Braguemont	01/11/1916	30/11/1916
Map	To Accompany Medical Diary 24 Division November 1916		
Heading	A.D.M.S 24 Division. Vol XVI. December 1916		
War Diary	Braquemont	01/12/1916	31/12/1916
Heading	A.D.M.S. 24th Division Jan 1917		
War Diary	Braquemont	01/01/1917	31/01/1917
Heading	A.D.M.S. 24th Division Feb 1917		
Heading	ADMS 24 Division Vol XV February		
War Diary	Braquemont	01/02/1917	14/02/1917
War Diary	Labeuvriere	15/02/1917	28/02/1917

Type	Description	Date From	Date To
Operation(al) Order(s)	R.A.M.C. Operation Order No 101 By Colonel F. R. Buswell C.M.G. A. M. S. Adms 24th Divn	10/02/1917	10/02/1917
Operation(al) Order(s)	R.A.M.C. Operation Order No 102 by Lieut Col Amrose DSO. R.A.M.C. For A.D.M.S. 24th Division.	26/02/1917	26/02/1917
Miscellaneous		28/02/1917	28/02/1917
Heading	A.D.M.S. 24th Division Mar 1917		
Heading	A.D.M.S 24th Div Vol XIX March 1917		
War Diary	Labeuvriere	01/03/1917	11/03/1917
War Diary	Barlin	12/03/1917	31/03/1917
Operation(al) Order(s)	R.A.M.C. Operation Order No 102 By Lieut Col Amrose DSO. RAMC For ADMS 24th Division	26/02/1917	26/02/1917
Heading	ADMS 24th Div Vol XX April 1917		
War Diary	Barlin	01/04/1917	03/04/1917
War Diary	Braquemont	04/04/1917	20/04/1917
War Diary	Norrent Fontes	21/04/1917	24/04/1917
War Diary	Bomy	25/04/1917	30/04/1917
Miscellaneous	B.E.F. Summary Of Medical War Diaries Of 24th Division.		
War Diary	Moves	03/04/1917	03/04/1917
War Diary	Operations Enemy	06/04/1917	06/04/1917
War Diary	Med. Arr.	07/04/1917	07/04/1917
War Diary	Operations	12/04/1917	12/04/1917
War Diary	Evacuation		
War Diary	Casualties	13/04/1917	13/04/1917
War Diary	Operations Enemy	14/04/1917	14/04/1917
War Diary	Operations & Med. Arr.	15/04/1917	15/04/1917
War Diary	Evacuation		
War Diary	Military Situation		
War Diary	Med. Arr.		
War Diary	Evacuation Terrain & Ops. Enemy	16/04/1917	16/04/1917
War Diary	Military Situation & Med. Arr.	19/04/1917	20/04/1917
War Diary	Moves & Transfer	20/04/1917	20/04/1917
War Diary	Moves	24/04/1917	24/04/1917
War Diary	Med. Arr.	30/04/1917	30/04/1917
War Diary	Health of Troops		
War Diary	Appendices		
War Diary	Moves	03/04/1917	03/04/1917
War Diary	Operations Enemy	06/04/1917	06/04/1917
War Diary	Med. Arr.	07/04/1917	07/04/1917
War Diary	Operations	12/04/1917	12/04/1917
War Diary	Evacuation		
War Diary	Casualties	13/04/1917	13/04/1917
War Diary	Operations Enemy	14/04/1917	14/04/1917
War Diary	Operations & Med. Arr.	15/04/1917	15/04/1917
War Diary	Evacuation		
War Diary	Military Situation		
War Diary	Med. Arr.		
War Diary	Evacuation Terrain & Ops. Enemy	16/04/1917	16/04/1917
War Diary	Military Situation & Med. Arr.	19/04/1917	20/04/1917
War Diary	Moves & Transfer	20/04/1917	20/04/1917
War Diary	Moves	24/04/1917	24/04/1917
War Diary	Med. Arr.	30/04/1917	30/04/1917
War Diary	Health of Troops		
War Diary	Appendices		
Miscellaneous	D.D.M.S. I Corps 72 Fld Ambce	15/04/1917	15/04/1917

Type	Description	Date From	Date To
Operation(al) Order(s)	R.A.M.C., Operation Order No. 105 By Colonel F.R. Buswell C.M.G., A.M.S., A.D.M.S. 24 Divn	18/04/1917	18/04/1917
Miscellaneous	Medical Arrangements.	17/04/1917	17/04/1917
Operation(al) Order(s)	R.A.M.C. Operation Order No. 104 By Colonel F.R. Buswell C.M.G. A.M.S. A.D.M.S. 24th Divn	07/04/1917	07/04/1917
Operation(al) Order(s)	R.A.M.C. Operation Order No. 103 By Colonel Fr Buswell C.M.G. A. M S Adms 24th Division	29/03/1917	29/03/1917
Operation(al) Order(s)	R.A.M.C. Operation Order No. 104 By Colonel F. R. Buswell C.M.G. A. M S.A D M S 24th Divn	07/04/1917	07/04/1917
Heading	A.D.M.S. 24th Division May 1917		
Heading	A.D.M.S 24th Division Vol XXI May 1917		
War Diary	Bomy	01/05/1917	09/05/1917
War Diary	Norrent Fontes.	10/05/1917	12/05/1917
War Diary	Winnezeele	13/05/1917	15/05/1917
War Diary	Brandhoek	16/05/1917	31/05/1917
Heading	A.D.M.S. 24th Div June 1917		
Heading	A.D.M.S. 24th Div Vol 22 June 1917		
War Diary	Reninghelst	01/06/1917	13/06/1917
War Diary	Micmac Camp	14/06/1917	30/06/1917
Miscellaneous	Summary Of Medical War Diaries Of 24th Div. 10th Corps, 2nd Army.		
War Diary	Operations	03/06/1917	03/06/1917
War Diary	Ops. Enemy	04/06/1917	04/06/1917
War Diary	Casualties		
War Diary	Operations	05/06/1917	05/06/1917
War Diary	Decorations	06/06/1917	06/06/1917
War Diary	Operations		
War Diary	Operations	07/06/1917	07/06/1917
War Diary	Casualties		
War Diary	Medical Arrangements		
War Diary	Operations Enemy	08/06/1917	08/06/1917
War Diary	Casualties		
War Diary	Casualties, R.A.M.C.		
War Diary	Casualties	10/06/1917	10/06/1917
War Diary	Moves	13/06/1917	13/06/1917
War Diary	Operations	14/06/1917	14/06/1917
War Diary	Casualties		
War Diary	Evacuation		
War Diary	Operations Enemy. Casualties, R.A.M.C.	17/06/1917	17/06/1917
War Diary	Operations enemy. Casualties	18/06/1917	18/06/1917
War Diary	Sanitation	20/06/1917	20/06/1917
War Diary	Casualties Gas, R.A.M.C.	21/06/1917	21/06/1917
War Diary	Operations enemy	22/06/1917	22/06/1917
War Diary		26/06/1917	26/06/1917
War Diary		28/06/1917	28/06/1917
War Diary	Moves	30/06/1917	30/06/1917
War Diary	Casualties, R.A.M.C.		
War Diary	Appendices		
Miscellaneous	Summary Of Medical War Diaries Of 24th Div. 10th Corps. 2nd Army.		
War Diary	Operations	03/06/1917	03/06/1917
War Diary	Ops Enemy	04/06/1917	04/06/1917
War Diary	Casualties		
War Diary	Operations	05/06/1917	05/06/1917
War Diary	Decorations	06/06/1917	06/06/1917
War Diary	Operations		

War Diary	Operations	07/06/1917	07/06/1917
War Diary	Casualties		
War Diary	Medical Arrangements.		
War Diary	Operations Enemy	08/06/1917	08/06/1917
War Diary	Casualties		
War Diary	Casualties R.A.M.C.		
War Diary	Casualties	10/06/1917	10/06/1917
War Diary	Moves	13/06/1917	13/06/1917
War Diary	Operations	14/06/1917	14/06/1917
War Diary	Casualties		
War Diary	Operations. Enemy	17/06/1917	17/06/1917
War Diary	Evacuation		
War Diary	Casualties, R.A.M.C.		
Miscellaneous	24th Div. 10th Corps. 2nd Army A.D.M.S.		
Heading	A.D.M.S. 24th Division July 1917		
Heading	ADMS 24th D.W Vol 23 July 1917		
War Diary	Lumbres	01/07/1917	19/07/1917
War Diary	Steenwoorde	20/07/1917	23/07/1917
War Diary	Zevecoten	24/07/1917	31/07/1917
Miscellaneous	B.E.F. Summary Of Medical War Diaries Of 24th Div 10th Corps 2nd Army		
Miscellaneous	24th Div. 10th Corps. 2nd Army.	05/07/1917	05/07/1917
Miscellaneous	Summary Of Medical War Diaries Of 24th Division.		
Miscellaneous	24th Div. 2nd Corps, 5th Army.	01/07/1917	01/07/1917
Miscellaneous	Summary Of Medical War Diaries Of 24th Div. 10th Corps 2nd Army		
Miscellaneous	24th Div. 10th. Corps. 2nd Army.	05/07/1917	05/07/1917
Miscellaneous	B.E.F. 24th Div. 2nd Corps, 5th Army.	01/07/1917	01/07/1917
Heading	A.D.M.S. 24th Division Aug 1917		
Heading	A.D.M.S. 24th Division Vol. XXIV August 1917		
War Diary	Zevecoten	01/08/1917	31/08/1917
Miscellaneous	B.E.F. Summary Of Medical War Diaries Of 24th Division.		
Miscellaneous			
Miscellaneous	B.E.F. 24th Div. 2nd Corps, 5th Army.	01/07/1917	01/07/1917
Miscellaneous	Weather & Evacuation.		
Miscellaneous	B.E.F. 24th Div. 2nd Corps, 5th Army.		
Heading	A.D.M.S. 24th Division Sept 1917		
Miscellaneous	B.E.F. Summary Of Medical War Diaries Of 24th Div. 10th Corps.		
Miscellaneous	B.E.F. 24th Div. 10th Corps 2nd Army.		
Miscellaneous	B.E.F. Summary Of Medical War Diaries Of 24th Div. 10th Corps.		
Miscellaneous	B.E.F. 24th Div. 10th Corps 2nd Army.		
Heading	A.D.M.S. 24th Division Vol XXV September 1917		
War Diary	Zevecoten	01/09/1917	23/09/1917
War Diary	Beugny	24/09/1917	26/09/1917
War Diary	Peronne	27/09/1917	30/09/1917
Heading	A.D.M.S. 24th Division Oct 1917		
Heading	A.D.M.S. XXIV Division Oct 1917 Vol 26		
War Diary	Nobescourt Farm	01/10/1917	07/10/1917
War Diary	Nobes Court	08/10/1917	31/10/1917
Heading	War Diary Of A.D.M.S 24th Div for Nov 1917 Vol XXVII		
War Diary	Nobescourt	01/11/1917	30/11/1917

Heading	Vol XXVIII War Diary A.D.M.S. 24th Div Dec 1917 Vol 29		
War Diary	Nobes Court	01/12/1917	08/12/1917
Miscellaneous	A.D.M.S. 24th Div 1917		
War Diary	Nobes Court	09/12/1917	31/12/1917
Heading	A.D.M.S. 24th Div. Jan 1918		
War Diary	Nobescourt	01/01/1918	31/01/1918
Heading	War Diary (Original) A.D.M.S 24th Div February 1918 Vol XXX		
War Diary	Nobes Court	01/02/1918	05/02/1918
War Diary	Nobes Court Farm	05/02/1918	13/02/1918
War Diary	Nobes Court	14/02/1918	28/02/1918
Heading	Original War Diary A.D.M.S 24th Div March 1918 Vol XXXI		
War Diary	Nobes Court Farm	01/03/1918	02/03/1918
War Diary	Merau Court	03/03/1918	12/03/1918
War Diary	Bouvincourt	13/03/1918	24/03/1918
War Diary	Rosieres	25/03/1918	25/03/1918
War Diary	Demouin	26/03/1918	28/03/1918
War Diary	Castel	29/03/1918	29/03/1918
War Diary	Cottenchy	30/03/1918	31/03/1918
Heading	Original War Diary Adms 24th Div April 1918 Vol XXXII		
War Diary	Cottenchy	01/04/1918	05/04/1918
War Diary	La Boutillerie	06/04/1918	06/04/1918
War Diary	St Valery	07/04/1918	16/04/1918
War Diary	La Thieuloye	17/04/1917	30/04/1917
Heading	Original War Diary ADMS 24th Division For May 1918 Vol XXIII		
War Diary	La Thieuloye	01/05/1918	02/05/1918
War Diary	Sains-En-Gohelle	03/05/1918	31/05/1918
Heading	Original War Diary A.D.M.S. 24th Divn June 1918 Vol XXXIV		
War Diary	Sains-En-Gohelle	01/06/1918	30/06/1918
Heading	War Diary ADMS 24th Division July 1918 Vol XXXV		
War Diary	Sains-En-Gohelle	01/07/1918	31/07/1918
Diagram etc			
Heading	Original War Diary A.D.M.S. 24th Divn August 1918 Vol. XXXVI		
War Diary	Sains-En-Gohelle	01/08/1918	30/08/1918
Miscellaneous	Dysentery Chart. Aug. 1918		
Heading	War Diary A.D.M.S. 24th Divn September 1918 Vol XXXVII		
War Diary	Sains-En-Gohelle	01/09/1918	30/09/1918
Heading	ADMS. 24th Div Oct 1918		
War Diary	Lucheux	01/10/1918	06/10/1918
War Diary	Moeuvres	07/10/1918	07/10/1918
War Diary	Cantaing	08/10/1918	08/10/1918
War Diary	Nine Wood	09/10/1918	09/10/1918
War Diary	Mont Sur L'Oeuvre	10/10/1918	10/10/1918
War Diary	Cambrai	11/10/1918	13/10/1918
War Diary	Avesnes Les-Aubert	14/10/1918	18/10/1918
War Diary	Cambrai	19/10/1918	26/10/1918
War Diary	St. Aubert.	27/10/1918	31/10/1918
Miscellaneous	Casualties 24th Division		

Heading	Original War Diary Of A.D.M.S. 24th Divn For Nov 1918 Vol XXXIX		
War Diary	St Aubert	01/11/1918	03/11/1918
War Diary	Bermerain	04/11/1918	04/11/1918
War Diary	Sepmeries	05/11/1918	05/11/1918
War Diary	Wargnies-Le-Grand	06/11/1918	08/11/1918
War Diary	Bavai	09/11/1918	18/11/1918
War Diary	Masny	19/11/1918	26/11/1918
War Diary	Sameon	28/11/1918	30/11/1918
Heading	War Diary ADMS 24th Division. December 1918 Vol XL		
War Diary	Sameon	01/12/1918	11/12/1918
War Diary	Rongy (Belgium)	12/12/1918	12/12/1918
War Diary	Rongy	13/12/1918	17/12/1918
War Diary	Tournai	18/12/1918	31/12/1918
Heading	War Diary Of A.D.M.S. 24th Division For January 1919 Vol XLI		
War Diary	Tournai (Belgium)	01/01/1919	31/01/1919
Heading	War Diary Of A.D.M.S 24th Divn For February 1919 Vol XLII		
War Diary	Tournai (Belgium)	01/02/1919	28/02/1919
Heading	War Diary For March 1919 24 Div Vol XLIII		
War Diary	Tournai	01/03/1919	29/03/1919

was 95/2196/1

24TH DIVISION
MEDICAL

ASST DIR. MEDICAL SERVICES
AUG 1915 - DEC 1918
1919 MAR

151/7083

24th Division

H.Q. 24th Division A&hd.
Vol I

Aug & Sept 15
Dec '18

Summarised for not copied.
Dec 1917

Aug. 1915 S/51
Sept "

Confidential

War Diary of A.D.M.S.
24th Divn
Covering period from August 21. 1915
to September 30. 1915,
both dates inclusive.

24th Division
A D M S   Army Form C. 2118

WAR DIARY
INTELLIGENCE SUMMARY
(Erase heading not required.)

Place	Date	Hour	Summary of Events and Information	Remarks and references to Appendices
Blackdown	1915 August 21		Rumours of early departure of the Division abroad	
"	22nd		Advanced parties of the 3 Field Ambulances arrived - 72nd, 73rd, 74th	
"	23rd		Main bodies of the Field Ambulances arrived	
"	24th		The Division returned to CHOBHAM COMMON for Trench Warfare. D.A.D.M.S. visited the 74th Ambulance requesting put in again to ascertain requirements for winter ambulances for them. Told to apply at once to W.O. direct. Sent a driver and company clerk of Division of each Transport N.C.O. saying 21 motor ambulance wagons and 3 motor cycles needed.	
"	25th 26th		Visited the 74th Ambulance on Bulswater Common. There is a hitch over the drawing of their Ordnance Equipment from the A.O.D. and they send down without saying what it was. They is evidently some delay for the A.O.D. accounter will not come in. This is knocking about. I gave his point, all is planned for 26th inst. Our grazing finds leave to all M.O.S. Troops returned from CHOBHAM COMMON.	

WAR DIARY
or
INTELLIGENCE SUMMARY.
(Erase heading not required.)

Army Form C. 2118

Instructions regarding War Diaries and Intelligence Summaries are contained in F. S. Regs., Part II. and the Staff Manual respectively. Title pages will be prepared in manuscript.

Place	Date 1915	Hour	Summary of Events and Information	Remarks and references to Appendices
Aldershot	Aug 25		Weather very favourable. Sir J Cowans paid for the 3rd & 4th Ambulance trips may arrive from Bois. The great bulk of the Division appears to have arrived.	
	26	—	Completion of equipment of 7th Ambulance progressed today. Visited 7th Ambulance units & c.c. all seem anxious as making no tonight.	
	27		All ambulances still present	
	28		Advance parties starting	
	29	—	Left with Adv. H.Q. by troop train from FRIMLEY at 5.50 pm. Embarked at Folkestone about 9.30 pm. Landed BOULOGNE about midnight. Spent the night there	
	30	—		
Boulogne	31st		Left 9.45 am by motor car for concentration area. Arrived at ROYON which is Divl. Hd Qrs — in a chateau.	
Royon	Sept 1st	—	Concentration of troops in progress. Visited ETAPLES to see advance almost disposed of by units of the Division.	
	2nd		Visited Abbeville and had interview with D.M.S. L.C.	
	3rd		Rain all night. Visited No 1 Canadian General Hospital to see of the dentists. Rain all day.	
	4th		Have had any division work.	
			Went all round Divl area with Col A.Q.M.G. My Stevens visitor the Field Ambulances which have just arrived.	
	5		Sunday. Drew some medical Stores from ETAPLES	
	6		Had a long ride on horseback to various locations of Troops. General per no Substitution of alleged anthrax from an MAREMAS.	
	7		Many fresh arrangements in preparation of transfer North. Cold, true though. Horse ain lo fresh inexperience	

WAR DIARY

Army Form C. 2118

A.D.M.S. 24th Division

INTELLIGENCE SUMMARY

Place	Date	Hour	Summary of Events and Information	Remarks and references to Appendices
Royon	8/9/15		Spent all day with General HAKIN - Corps Commander. Visited 74° F¹ Ambulance 107° & 109° Brigades R.F.A. Went out of our area, on the march. Sent a motor ambulance with them.	
"	9/9/15		Visited 72nd 7th Ambulance, & my Dressers until the 73rd Dressn. run met stores.	
"	10/9/15		Lectured on anti-gas methods. Visited all the 7th Ambulances with Divng Comdr.	
"	11/9/15		Went our on field day to see the wounded arrangements.	
"	12/9/15		Sunday. Went to Etaples & 72nd 7th Ambce. Sick now being received by 7th Ambces.	
"	13/9/15		Inspected 74° 7th Ambce. Accompanied G. O.C. Division to Etaples to see wounded.	
"	14/9/15		Went our on Divl. Field Day. Visited 73rd F¹ Ambulance in afternoon - inspected it.	
"	15/9/15		Inspected 72nd F¹ Ambulance.	
"	16/9/15		Divgday morning. Busy in getting in forms returns.	
"	17/9/15		Preparing for night march.	
"	18/9/15		Started at 3 A.M. for tactical exercise. Back 11 A.M.	
"	19/9/15		7th Ambulance changed billets to get into their own areas. 2 sections of each 7th Ambce.	
"	20/9/15		Chapel 7th Ambce. Whilst completed instructions in Regards M.O.s. fresh at 73rd 74th & 7th Ambces. Whilst skying in tour J (Col. S.F. Clan, A.D.M.S.) fell down a trench & injured my ankle (right). The Dressing wears today. My foot is worse and I went up to hospital at ETAPLES for X-ray examination and rest. Made all necessary arrangements for the S.F. Coll. Cd. A.M.S.	/sa
"	21/9/15		march with D.A.D.M.S. who was away on various	/sn
"	22/9/15		Assumed duties temporarily. Wrote Capt. Rand. Division moved from ROYON to BOMY. Lt Col Blair arrived & took over duties A.D.M.S. during rest of Division from BOMY to BUSNES	

Army Form C. 2118

WAR DIARY
or
INTELLIGENCE SUMMARY.
(Erase heading not required.)

Instructions regarding War Diaries and Intelligence Summaries are contained in F. S. Regs., Part II. and the Staff Manual respectively. Title pages will be prepared in manuscript.

Place	Date	Hour	Summary of Events and Information	Remarks and references to Appendices
BOMY	22.9.15	5.30 p.m	Joined the 24th Division and took over duties of A.D.M.S as a temporary measure in accordance with orders received from D.M.S.	G/OM 69 of 21.9.15 from D.M.S XIth Corps
BUSNES	23.9.15	6 p.m	Visited 72nd 73rd 74th F. Ambulances and issued instructions with regard to transport arrangements. Ordered each unit to reduce its establishment to 100 each. Saw A.D.M.S. re smoke helmets, supply & resprayings. Arranged that resprayings should be done by F. Ambulances	
	24.9.15	6 p.m.	Accompanied by D.A.D.M.S attended conference at LILLERS. Received orders to move to BETHUNE and left for that place abt 6.30 p.m.	
BETHUNE	25.9.15	6 p.m	This morning had a conference with O.C. 72-73-74 F.A. after making arrangements for Ap.R. 1 XI/9/4/75. Visited said Ambulances & sent them heavier Motor Ambulances & am reinforced. Followed by their horsed ambulances began work on wounded between 6 & 7 a.m. & after Aeu. followed by their horsed ambulance began work at a place between occurrences also arrived ? Red Cross Gend and the 2nd Troop & 1 Plat [illegible] - [illegible] - 140 Gen 172 & 174 moved to F 20 And 343 the detach by C.C. Field Ambulances. These Gen & Motor transport with had to stand for [illegible] - about 1.30 140 Gen 172 & 174 [illegible] & 9th the wounded & [illegible] heavy been received from 73rd Field Ambulance Company & 9th the wounded had been sent to proceed into La [illegible] at 8.30 knowledge had not now news to proceed into BETHUNE being cut off from [illegible] and Dressing stations about BEUVRY. During the day and BETHUNE [illegible] communications with the H Qn 9 F.A. ultimately succeeded in getting information as to my move of [illegible] heavy units.	
SAILLY-LABOURSE	26.9.15	6 p.m.	Arrived & self moved in [illegible] 25-26 To ST [illegible] LABOURSE undertook [illegible] & report [illegible] position with a view to making disposition at several hundred & advanced report[illegible] concentration with a view the same Division often had wer at ALCOAS [illegible] - [illegible] 72 & 73 [illegible] and inform [illegible] [illegible] that the same Division often had wer at ALCOAS [illegible] Hydrams [illegible] Hd On Rau as they now [illegible] to advance further	

1577 Wt.W10791/1773 500,000 1/15 D.D.& L. A.D.S.S./Forms/C. 2118.

Army Form C. 2118

WAR DIARY
or
INTELLIGENCE SUMMARY.
(Erase heading not required.)

Instructions regarding War Diaries and Intelligence Summaries are contained in F.S. Regs., Part II. and the Staff Manual respectively. Title pages will be prepared in manuscript.

Place	Date	Hour	Summary of Events and Information	Remarks and references to Appendices
SAILLY-LABOURSE	26/9/15	6 p.m.	General HAKING in which their importance during the morning during the 4th p.m. Cavalry were lectured in 72nd F. amb. Sent Sergeant with the Div. to reconnoitre a position for receiving the Cavalry reported that the available building at LE RUTOIRE was already occupied by another Field, ordered FC 74 FA to open a dressing station on any available building he could find in VERMELLES and also if many casualties to keep from 72nd FA Lieutenant on RC 85, 72nd FA Post. They moved off their horses Frisians and trucks with their beds and led they had resumed support from 74 Div. Out the many cases of a military clearing 73rd FA and their detachment of 73rd FA attached to FC 74 FA. On the 3 men of military detn. ordered to do duty at SAILLY-LABOURSE were put incharge of non other 2 torches LEZ-VERMELLES	(Memo 25/9/15)
SAILLY-LABOURSE	27/9/15	6 p.m.	Moved at 8 pm. 16.50 received report informed improvements that moved evacuation 26 1/2 were brought into and Dressing Station at LA RUTOIRE. Relieved the 72 FA and at 6 am told not to then Relieved - OP when reporting 72 FA A dressing station to have been established at VERMELLES 3 1/2 of GF. 3, 4 to GS supporting 72nd FA to & evacuating from LA RUTOIRE and some of the men from VERMELLES to FA to evacuate the wounded of their divisions at SAILLY LABOURSE, others received in and sent to SAILLY LABOURSE received instructions empowered by and the continued concerned ad 6:45 went to tell them the 2 at 74th and had 1 get instructions instructions informed the books attention of FA at VERMELLES and 72 FA at LE RUTOIRE At 12.20 p.m. received wire from 74 2 A stated 20 sitting on lying awaiting evacuation hospital Divl. & army FCs 74 F M & C, 74th F M & C stated OCs 72nd 74 FAs to have a final consult made of the area recently fought on by their respective Brigades No. 5 of the VERMELLES - HULLOCH road. Also to continue to admit casualties from any formation with those D.Ss and failed to report to the tomorrow morning while the area is being cleared of 24th Division Casualties.	
SAILLY-LABOURSE	28/9/15	6 p.m.	Having been informed by FC 73rd and 74 Sh Ambulances for the area are on which their Bearer Divisions had been working nor clear of all wounded of 24 Division retired from to close their D.S. and report their F.Qs. D. Q.M.S. XI Corps office. The opt FC had been done to the further instructions. Orders received to leave. 93 F.A. reported division orders received for the Div to move to ST Hilaire, principally by rail Mr all men ordered had been evacuated.	

Army Form C. 2118

WAR DIARY
or
INTELLIGENCE SUMMARY.
(Erase heading not required.)

Instructions regarding War Diaries and Intelligence Summaries are contained in F. S. Regs., Part II. and the Staff Manual respectively. Title pages will be prepared in manuscript.

Place	Date	Hour	Summary of Events and Information	Remarks and references to Appendices
SAILLY-LABOURSE	26.9.15	6 p.m.	Transport to arrive. Waiting for the night at ANNEZIN. Saw G.S.O.T and A.A. & Q.M.G and arranged to meet 74 F.A., M.A.W. Unit and SANITARY SECTION independently. Issued orders repeatedly to have units left SAILLY LABOURSE at 8.15 p.m. and proceeded to ST HILAIRE via BETHUNE and admitted my office this at 9.30 A.M. on	
ST HILAIRE	29.9.15	6 p.m.	Saw belonging officers 72-73-74 F.A. and showed him their area. 2 fm Secondam to afford French Division offer having one of large photograph taken of Gl Clark Sent car for 23 O'clock Bliss —	DDMS 1st Corps MS A 29/9/15
ST HILAIRE	30.9.15	6 p.m.	Proceeded to G.H.Q. as ordered at 11 a.m. & received instruction from DDS. to hold 3 ind officers + 150 men in readiness to proceed from I.C. to Casualty Clearing Station if necessary. Wrote J.A. + told O.C. to have 3 officers + 50 men for J.C. ready as ats. Received news & prepared 2nd f Divison to STEENVOORDE probably road — men by rail.	

1577 Wt. W10791/1773 500,000 1/15 D. D. & L. A.D.S.S./Forms/C. 2118.

(1)

BATTLE OF LOOS

24th DIVISION - XIth CORPS

A.D.M.S. Col. S.F. Clark. A.M.S. till 21/9/15; Lt Col E.W. Bliss RAMC performed duty till 29/9/15 when Lieut Col F.R. Buswell RAMC took up the appointment.

D.A.D.M.S. Major F.J. Weston.

Note. During the last few days of August the division concentrated at Blackdown Aldershot. The Field Ambulances were stationed on Bullswater Common and were busily engaged in fitting up with equipment etc. D.H.Q. embarked at Folkestone on the 30th August and landed at BOULOGNE on the 31st. ROYON was the concentration area of the division where the F.As arrived on the 4th September. The next fortnight was occupied with field days, gas instruction, etc. On one of these the A.D.M.S. had an accident to his horse and injury to his own foot, necessitating his evacuation on the 21st September before the Division marched into 1st Army area. All medical arrangements were made for the march and the D.A.D.M.S. was instructed to carry on. On the following day Lieut Col. Bliss arrived from No.9.F.A. to perform the duty of A.D.M.S. temporarily. The D.H.Q. arrived at BUSNES on the 23rd, and left on the evening of the 24th for BETHUNE.

THE BATTLE

September.

25th

Location D.H.Q. - BETHUNE.

Conference. At A.D.M.S. Office with the Os.C.F.As.

Med Arr. Ordered that each F.A./BD should move in rear of its respective Bde and that each F.A. should a TD in readiness to move and open. H.Qs. and MAWs to stand fast in BETHUNE with the F.A.W.U. Later in the day H.Q. 72nd and 74th F.A. moved to F.20.(36b)

Mil Sit. Orders for the 73rd Bde to be attached temporarily to the 9th Division. 73rd F.A. ordered to move under orders of the G.O.C. 73rd Bde.

26th

Move ADMS. Office with that of AGMG moved to SAILLY LABOURSE.

Med Arr. Found that the BDs of 72 and 74 F.As had established D.Ss at VERMELLES. They were unable to proceed further towards HULLUCH owing to heavy shell fire. THE D.A.D.M.S. with the two Os.C. went on to Le Rutoire to reconnoitre for any suitable buildings as A.D.S. but the only available were already in occupation of medical units. Ordered 74th F.A. to open in any suitable bdgs in VERMELLES and get any assistance he required from No.72.F.A. Instructed Os.C. that they must get in touch with Bdes and ascertain locations of any R.A.Ps in operation.

27th

Move ADMS. Office moved at 8 p.m. to NOYELLES les VERMELLES.

27th

Casualties Informed by ADMS 1st Div at 10-50 that many casualties of 24th Div were being admitted to A.D.S. of his division at Le RUTOIRE.

Med Arr. 74.F.A. D.S. at VERMELLES - G.8.a.3. 72nd F.A. sent forward a TSD and established D.S. at Le Rutoire. Remainder of unit prkd at Sailly Labourse.

Evacuation. 3 MAWs of 72 and 74 F.As were evacuating back from Le Rutoire and No.7.M.A.C. was evacuating from VERMELLES.

Move ADMS. Move at 11-30 p.m. to SAILLY LABOURSE.

Mil Sit. p.m. division placed in reserve.

Med Arr. ordered 72 and 74 F.As to make sure before moving that all 24th divl casualties had been collected.

28th

BATTLE OF LOOS

No.72.FIELD AMBULANCE - 24th DIVISION

O.C.Capt W.C.Nimmo RAMC.

Note. Unit arrived at HAVRE on the 2nd September 1915. It proceeded on the 3rd to the Divl concentration area, being billetted at NEUVILLE. On the 23rd September the unit moved to BERGUETTE and on the 24th to BETHUNE.

THE BATTLE

25th

Conference. At office of A.D.M.S.

Move F.A. BD sent off with the 72nd Bde. Remainder of unit moved to F.20.d.2.3. and parked. Unit apparently did not nothing practical - the O.C. being mainly engaged running about and looking for his BD or the A.D.M.S.

26th

Location BD. Message received that they were in VERMELLES.

Ops RAMC. 1 BSD had attempted to work its way along the HULLUCH Road, but had to turn back through shrapnel fire.

Casualties RAMC One staff-sergt and 7 men wounded.

Ops RAMC. BD proceeded to Le Rutoire Ferme after dusk and cleared from the Bde.

Evacuation. The HAWs operated from Le Rutoire and the MAWs were engaged clearing to CHOCQUES.

Med arr. In the evening some bell tents were pitched for the resting of cases that were walking to the C.C.S.
Orders had come from the ADMS during the absence of the O.C. (he was away from his HQ for 3 hours) to move to LONE TREE and open. The O.C. could not find this spot on the map so he halted the unit at PHILOSOPHE and apparently again went to find the A.D.M.S. Orders were then received to open one TSD with 3 officers at Le RUTOIRE. The remainder of the unit to return to SAILLY LABOURSE

27th

Ops RAMC. Bde area North and South of the HULLUCH Road well searched for wounded.

28th

Move F.A. TSD and BD rejoined HQ and late p.m. the unit moved to OBLINGHEM.

Casualties. During the time that the D.S. was open, 166 cases were treated there.

One would gather the impression from this diary that too much time was spent running about looking for the A.D.M.S. Not much initiative was shown by the O.C. The unit certainly had had no experience of active service but even with that being allowed for the O.C. would have done better to have stayed with his H.Q., done what was ordered him and waited for further orders to arrive.

BATTLE OF LOOS.

No. 73. FIELD AMBULANCE - 24th DIVISION

O.C. Capt W.G.Mayden R.A.M.C.

Note. This unit had received its preliminary training at EASTBOURNE. It joined the division at Bullswater Camp on the 24th August. On the 2nd September it landed at HAVRE, and on the 4th Sept concentrated with the Bde at AIX en ISSART. On the 19th the unit moved to LEBRIZ. and on the 21st began the march to the 1st Army area. On the 23rd they arrived at La MIQUILLERIE and early a.m. on the 25th at BETHUNE.

THE BATTLE

25th.
    Move F.A. Ordered at 12-30 p.m. to proceed to NOYELLES. Arrived at 3-30p.m. BD ordered to get in touch with the Battns of 73rd Bde which had been attached to 9th Div.

    Ops RAMC. Casualties were collected - the work was very trying to the raw bearers but they stuck it well and behaved with great courage.

26th
    Med arr. C/TSD was ordered forward to the A.D.S. of 29th F.A.

    Ops RAMC. Hard work owing to the distance of the carry.

    Casualties RAMC. 1 SB killed and one wounded.
27th
                    one SB wounded.

    Move Det. B/TSD relieved C/TSD.
28th
              A/TSD relieved B/TSD.

    Move F.A. p.m. marched to SAILLY LABOURSE and on the following day to ANNEZIN and on the 30th to NORRENT FONTES.

(1)

BATTLE OF LOOS

No.74.FIELD AMBULANCE - 24th DIVISION.

O.C. Capt A.N.Rose R.A.M.C.

Note. The unit arrived at the Divisional concentration area - Bullswater Camp - from EASTBOURNE on the 24th August. It arrived at HAVRE on the 2nd September and at NEUVILLE sous MONTREUIL on the 4th Sept. Until the 21st the time was spent in lectures and divisional exercises etc. It then moved BETHUNE arriving ~~nyxxkkxx24th~~ early a.m. 25th.

THE BATTLE

25th

Move Det. BD moved with the Bde towards VERMELLES with the HAWs. TD with remainder of transport and MAWs moved to BEUVRY.

26th

Med arr. B/TSD opened D.S. at VERMELLES. A & C /TSDs remained in reserve.

Evacuation. MAWs sent forward to VERMELLES.

Casualties. "Many" wounded treated.
RAMC. - 2 SBs wounded.

27th

Ops RAMC. The whole BD engaged collecting wounded - B/BSD over 9th Divl area, and remainder over the 71st Bde area.

Casualties. Total treated in D.S. = 300 from various divisions.

28th

Move. Left BEUVRY at 8-30 p.m. arrived at ANNEZIN at 11-30 p.m.

121/7431

24th November

H.D. 2 & 2 Divisions Adms.
Vol: 2

Oct 15.

Oct 1915.

Army Form C. 2118.

WAR DIARY
or
INTELLIGENCE SUMMARY.
(Erase heading not required.)

Instructions regarding War Diaries and Intelligence Summaries are contained in F. S. Regs., Part II. and the Staff Manual respectively. Title pages will be prepared in manuscript.

Place	Date	Hour	Summary of Events and Information	Remarks and references to Appendices
ST. HILAIRE	1st Oct 1915	6 p.m.	Visited J.O.s and told C.O.s arrangements for march. Ordered all Motor Vehicles to be in at H.Q. by 10 a.m. tomorrow at "4".	
ST HILAIRE	2nd Oct 1915	6 p.m.	Left ST HILAIRE for STEENVOORDE — All motor vehicles of J.As, M.W.U, & Sanitary Section passed under O.C. M.W.U. & road. Opened office at 8 p.m. at	
STEENVOORDE	3rd Oct 1915	6 p.m.	Saw Brig. Genl. Milford taken in sick last night. D.D.M.S. & D.A.D.M.S. VI Corps visited H.Q. the morning — A.S.C. & mail F20 & collect sick. Major General G.J. Ramsay left for England. Major General Capper took over Command of Division.	
STEENVOORDE	4 Oct 1915	6 p.m.	General Milford improved in health. Sent O.C. 41st Sanitary Section to 71st Brigade area near PROVEN to report on water supply. Read "Shallow wells" which rapidly pumped dry. D.M.S. 2nd Army visited H.Q. 14th Division.	
	5th Oct 1915	6 p.m.	Attended at office of D.M.S. V Corps in the morning — Proceeded to REMINGHELST & saw A.D.M.S. 17th Division & took its list behind by this Division. Also arranged to lend out Attachment of 41st Sanitary Section to water areas.	
STEENVOORDE REMINGHELST	6th Oct 1915	6 p.m.	Proceeded to REMINGHELST & opened office at 12 noon. Lt. Col. F.R. Buswill R.A.M.C. arrived as A.D.M.S. Division. Took over A.D.M.S. Division. Lt. Buswill H.E. Rome.	
"	7 Oct 1915		Attended conference under D.D.M.S. 5th Corps re. ambulance trains and vacancies for loss of sick stores, of tables & form of Light. Posts not beyond Dept. on ambulance & Group Clearing. Men will give Lg per man for the 4 days they will occupy the trenches. Railway van for premanent scavenging of trem water. G.E. S Section. Visited 6 D Station La Clytte, 1 Nov. 20 OR. 725 Id Amb. detailed for Inst. etc. 2,8 to Fd Amb. g 2. Fin	

Army Form C. 2118.

WAR DIARY
or
INTELLIGENCE SUMMARY.
(Erase heading not required.)

Instructions regarding War Diaries and Intelligence Summaries are contained in F.S. Regs., Part II. and the Staff Manual respectively. Title pages will be prepared in manuscript.

Place	Date	Hour	Summary of Events and Information	Remarks and references to Appendices
REMINGHELST	7th Oct/15	6 P.M.	I.m. Officer one tent detachm in 74th Fd Amb. detailed to proceed to BOESCHEPE tomorrow morning to take over Batho & Rest Station, pending arrival of Fd Amb. Visited Bdes HQ & 74 Fd Amb.	Apps.
"	8th Oct/15		Visited Battns with view to disposal of med units & Relief of 8000 gallons on and daily. Saw General PORTER D.M.S. 2nd Army visited 74th Amb encampment.	Apps.
"	9th Oct/15		Saw DDMS 5th Corps upon routine matters	
"	10th Oct/15		Saw DDMS & H.Q. 9th Div. into conference. Saw ADMS 9th Div. re medical arrangements for reliving med & wounded from our Posts W. of Canal. To be shown by 9th Div. to A DMS taken over at 9 a.m.	
"	11th "		Jo. O.V.D.R. A.D.M. C.R.O. & LAITGRIE ADS.	
"	12th Oct/15		hastily experience DDMS 5th Corps ABEELE; visited Rest Station POPERINGHE	
"	13th "		completed arrangement of taking over from ADMS 9th Div.	
"	14th Oct/15		Saw ADMS 9th Div. by whom details for tr. en: of the front line Kruis leaving over 17th Bde. 6th Div. from him tra. (Rem 2 Battalions) in place of 71st Inf. Bde.	

WAR DIARY or INTELLIGENCE SUMMARY

Army Form C. 2118.

Place	Date	Hour	Summary of Events and Information	Remarks and references to Appendices
REINGHELST	Feb/15	15th	73rd Fd. Amb. reports taking over area from 9th Div. Fd. Ambulances. Got two hospitals. 72nd & 73rd Fd. Amb. Reported medical arrangements to forward area to G.O.C.s 5th Corps. Saw A.A. & Q.M.G. note of same. Re ambulances, hospitals &c.	
	16th		Visited position of advanced aid posts with G.O.C.s 5th Corps. Saw S. 2nd Army. Inspected 72nd Fd. Amb.	
	17th		Saw 2 L Middleton. No. 1/c 12th Advanced Dressing Station. Sent to 12 C.C.S. Hazebrouck. Jaundice.	
	18th		Visited Brigade Hq and Posts. with 12, 73rd Fd. Amb. Found either recommendation re wounded into dug out for personnel.	
	19th		Conference at Hq.s 5th Corps. Lt. Playfair. Run C. 73rd Fd. Amb. evacuated to Base. Ophthalmia. Lt. Williams, Lt. Macmillan & Playfair.	
	20th		Inspected 74 B. Fd. Amb. Received Rest Station. Bathe. & Special hospital &c. Surg. inflicted injuries at BOESCHERE.	
	21st		Visited Regtl aid Posts of Brigades VOORMEZEELE and huts the camel with trains 5th Corps. Case of Cerebro Spinal Fever reported from 2 cases in Regt. of 8th Queens Regt. which arrived there 18th but are entrain. requested lepingation.	
	22nd		Held sanitary inspection of Rest Camp & division.	

Army Form C. 2118.

WAR DIARY
or
INTELLIGENCE SUMMARY.
(Erase heading not required.)

Instructions regarding War Diaries and Intelligence Summaries are contained in F.S. Regs., Part II. and the Staff Manual respectively. Title pages will be prepared in manuscript.

Place	Date	Hour	Summary of Events and Information	Remarks and references to Appendices
REMY SIDING	23rd		Received St. Johns Ambulance book consigt. of 1st October for report.	
	24th		Routine work.	
	25th		D.D.M.S. 8th Green Regt. inspect ambulance car convoy. Also spare & contents. Car sent with plasmoden to St Omer.	
	26th		Visited isolation camp. Attended conference LtCol. S. 4th & 5th Corps.	
	27th		Capt Colev. Ram C reported for duty posted to 12th stationary Section	
	28th		Received wire Inspector C.S.O. anys the air dryness influenza.	
	29th		Routine work	
	30th		Routine work	
	31st		LtCol. S. attended tents conference. 1st Corps at H.Q. 9.2 &c weather inclement during past week	

M S [signature]
ADMS

H.D. 24th Divn:
Adjnd.
Vol: 3

121/7624

Nos 15.

Nov 1915

Army Form C. 2118

ADMS
2nd Div

WAR DIARY
or
INTELLIGENCE SUMMARY.
(Erase heading not required.)

Instructions regarding War Diaries and Intelligence Summaries are contained in F. S. Regs., Part II. and the Staff Manual respectively. Title pages will be prepared in manuscript.

Place	Date	Hour	Summary of Events and Information	Remarks and references to Appendices
REMINGHELST	Nov/15			
	1st		Routine. Weather bad.	
	2nd		Attended Conference Vth Corps. Sth A.D.M.S. accompanied G.O.C. at inspection of recently arrived draft. Captain BIDER v.M. R.A.M.C. att 2nd Lieuts Rifts. sick to 12. P.B.	
	3rd		Routine. Strength 7th Ind to 31st Oct. 904 Officers. 16168. O.R. billeted in Rininmal [?]	
	4th		Indiv.	
	5th		ADMS. & St Omer, attend lecture on antigas measures.	
	6th		Inspected 7th & Field Amb. & advanced dressing station 73rd Fld Amb. OVERDOM.	
	7th		DMS 2nd Army inspected Divisional baths etc.	
			Took over Advanced dressing station at BEDFORD house 1.26.A.6.4. Map 28.40 SW ──── Belgium	
			from 9th Division, no an front has been constructed N. of Canal. 19 iron tunnels just being made	
	8th		Took at BEDFORD house. 2 Officers 20 O.R. in two bilicules [?] & new splinter proof shelters	
	9th		had instruction from DMS 7th Corps, Re-cable arrangements at OVERDOM and ROUENDHELST for reception & treatment of the sick & wounded of 100 men 3rd Cavalry divn in my dug a dug in in defence works.	
			Attended Conference Vth Corps H.Q.	
	10th		Routine.	
	11th		Routine.	

Army Form C. 2118

WAR DIARY
or
INTELLIGENCE SUMMARY.
(Erase heading not required.)

Place	Date	Hour	Summary of Events and Information	Remarks and references to Appendices
REMINGHELST	NOVEMBER 12th		Sent map showing scheme of medical arrangement for collection & evacuation of sick & wounded from this area to S.D.M.S. V. Corps.	
	13th		Routine	
	14th		Visited Divisional Rest Station 74th F.A. Amb. at Boeschepe with G.O.C. Division. S.A.D.M.S. to baton conference. 70 cases of trench foot admitted during the week. 39 belonging to 24th Division & 31 to other divisions	"
	15th	9.30am 4pm	Visited Advanced dressing station. Reviewed collecting station & the Regimental aid posts to accompanied by S.a. & Y. Sgng very belligerent & enemy giving considerable shelling. In the evening at Ridge wood & just South of BEDFORD house. Evacuated No 72 — to Conv. & reliened additional officer & O.R. to stand by for lectures learned.	
	16th		Attended Conference at V. Corps H.Q.	
	17th		A.D.M.S. & S.A.D.M.S. 3rd Division called with reference to relief of Division in 3rd Division. Supplied maps of medical arrangements for the various areas in the area.	[signature]

Army Form C. 211

WAR DIARY
or
INTELLIGENCE SUMMARY.
(Erase heading not required.)

Instructions regarding War Diaries and Intelligence Summaries are contained in F. S. Regs., Part II. and the Staff Manual respectively. Title pages will be prepared in manuscript.

Place	Date	Hour	Summary of Events and Information	Remarks and references to Appendices
	November /15			
REMINGHELST	18th		Lecture upon abdominal Surgery at BOESCHEPE by Sir A. Bowlby. Large attendance.	
"	19th		Received revised table of moves	
"	20th		Visited CSM of 3rd Divn in lyarding some alteration in billets. 73rd Fd Amb. proceeded to billets at EECKE to land of 73rd Fd Amb. upon relief by 142nd Fd Amb.	
	21st		Preparations for move.	
	22nd		MO of NO 7 Fd Amb placed in escort by Sergeant. accused made Escape 40. At 2:45 pm H.Q. left REMINGHELST having handed over to 3rd Divn in. Moved to TILQUES & established office there at 6:45 pm. Received report from A & B Secs. that being remainder of him were reported falling out on the march from 73rd Bde.	
TILQUES	23rd	4:30pm	No 73rd Fd Ambulance reported on arrival & that he had had only 5 detention & had seen in Stragglers. Followed as motor ambulance cars to detention & report to 67 & 74 Fd Ambulance to assist in carrying casualties if necessary.	
	24th		Visited g. H. g. in medical arrangements in the new area. Walked to EBERLECQUES to visit 73rd Fd Amb. Installed in large farm with S'Consult accommodation for patients.	
	25th		4 NCOs + 22 men. Rank & File received reinforcements for the 3 Fd Ambulances	MMB

#353 Wt. W2544/T454 700,000 5/15 D.D. & L. A.D.S.S./Forms/C. 2118.

Army Form C. 2118

WAR DIARY
or
INTELLIGENCE SUMMARY.
(Erase heading not required.)

Instructions regarding War Diaries and Intelligence Summaries are contained in F. S. Regs., Part II and the Staff Manual respectively. Title pages will be prepared in manuscript.

Place	Date	Hour	Summary of Events and Information	Remarks and references to Appendices
TILQUES	NOVEMBER/15			
	26th		Routine hard front. Leave allotment to Div in future.	
	27th		Return received that Major W.C. NIMMO Ranc. will have on command of No. 72 to hand to Captain G.B. Edwards Ranc on arrival & proceed to Rigdes & report to A.D.M.S. By order of D.M.S. 2nd Army. Communicated confidential reports to temp. W.C. NIMMO Ranc — Captain G.B. Edwards Ranc reported arrival.	
	28th		Tinat conference. Leave opened for division.	
	29th		Tinat arrangements for Lectures. Chemical advice p'try on the subject of the Chemistry of gases used in trench operations. All available M.O's of Ranc to attend.	
	31st		Got Divisim signified his intention to deal with the case of the H.H.C. Ranc. No. 72 Fd. Amb. placed in arrest on 22nd Nov. 15. Visited No. 72 Fd Amb. at NORDAUSQUES. " " " Château de la VIERGETTE. 74 do do " HOULLE. 73 do do " "	
			Major W.C. NIMMO Ranc. reported his departure for Staples.	

Wulaud MBrowniw
Wins x.1.15

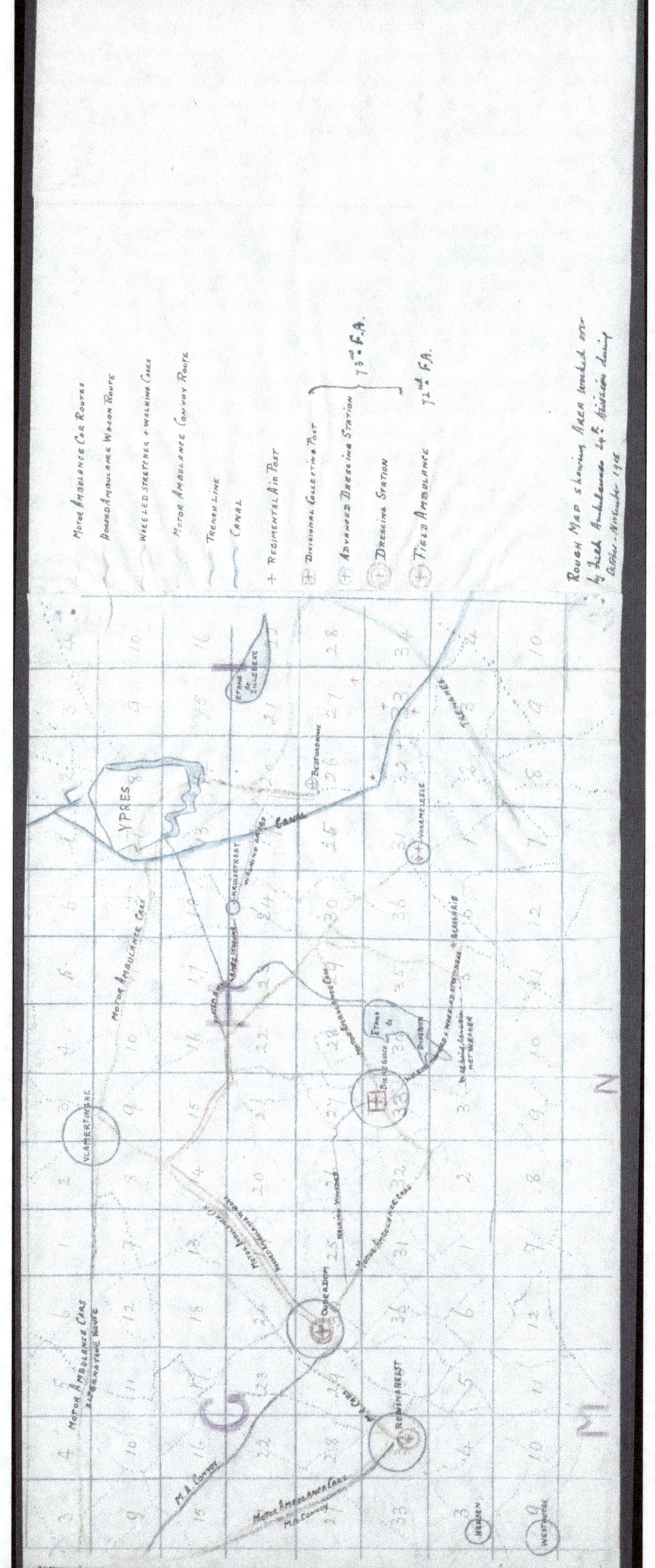

Asking 24th the Division.
pl: 4

9608/12/

F/41/11

December 1915

CONFIDENTIAL

War Diary
of
A.D.M.S. 24 Division

From Dec. 1st to Dec. 31st 1915

Vol. 4.

VOL. IV.
Army Form C. 2118

WAR DIARY
INTELLIGENCE SUMMARY.
(Erase heading not required.)

A.D.M.S.
24 Div.

Place	Date	Hour	Summary of Events and Information	Remarks and references to Appendices
TILQUES	1st		Captain T.H. SCOTT. R.A.M.C. who is to assume the duties of D.A.D.M.S. division. General routine.	
	2nd		Brig. General R. PORTER visited the division drew attention to the want of dry cloth. Inspection by M.O. kinds for cases of frostbite, & to the provision of hot items for the destruction of lice eggs in clothing, also care of the men's feet. Attended lecture in the chemistry of gases, had in building operations by Capt. BARRETT R.E. & Capt. BARRETT R.A.M.C.	
	3rd		Major O.T. Violin R.A.M.C. having handed over the duties of D.D.M.S. to Capt. T.H. SCOTT R.A.M.C. reported his departure.	
	4th		Very hot. Visited 2nd London and 9th East Surrey Reg. Inspecting lines considered unfit to withstand the rigours of the trenches during the winter. The 9th East Surrey Reg. badly affected with lice.	
	5th		Lieut. Colonel Dick hutchinson sent by D.D.M.S. Sanitary G.H.Q. at work in the 9th Regt. Inverse Reg. clothing. Saw the system working with D.D.M.S. Sanitary G.H.Q.	
	6th		General routine.	
	7th		Visited 9th Rl. Sussex Regt. Inspected 13 men considered unfit for service in the trenches. Also visited No. 74 ½ ft Amb.	
	8th		Lieut. Colonel Nicholas ADS Inspection. to look in the clothing of the 9th East Surrey Regt.	NWB

Army Form C. 2118.

② A.D.M.S
24 DIV.

WAR DIARY
INTELLIGENCE SUMMARY.
(Erase heading not required.)

Place	Date	Hour	Summary of Events and Information	Remarks and references to Appendices
TILQUES	December/16.			
	9th		Lt Col J.M Bruarth Ram.C. departed with eight days leave to England. Major Maydew Ram.C. to town acting A.D.M.S. Case of measles occurring in depth. 9th Royal Sussex Regt. all precautions taken.	
	10th		General routine.	
	11th		"	
	12th		Acting A.D.M.S. inspected billets of 1/1st Regt Fusiliers and 3rd Regt Rifle Brigade.	
	13th		Sa.M.S. Visited Hq. 48th Div. re billets improvements.	
	14th		Sa.M.S. again visited Hq. 49th Div. 3 Fd - Am. - sent also to report on the 3 Field Ambulances sites and divisional billets. Reports very clean and bright.	
	15th		General routine.	
	16th		Lt Col J.M Bruarth Ram.C. returned from leave.	
	17th		Sa.A.M.S. departed on expeditionary leave.	
	18th		Second case of measles in contact 9th Royal Sussex Regt. reported.	
	19th		General routine.	

Army Form C. 2118.

③

A.D.M.S.
24 DIV.

WAR DIARY
~~INTELLIGENCE SUMMARY.~~
(Erase heading not required.)

Instructions regarding War Diaries and Intelligence Summaries are contained in F. S. Regs., Part II. and the Staff Manual respectively. Title pages will be prepared in manuscript.

Place	Date	Hour	Summary of Events and Information	Remarks and references to Appendices
TILQUES.	December 1915.			
	21st		Visited 6th Corps. H.Q. & informed Genrl. & inspecting Officer the 3 Fd. Amb. & 49th Div. Amb. & arranged to try and continue in chg. of front & start everywhere. Arrangements at the Ambulance quite good.	
	22nd 23rd 24th } 25th 26th 27th 28th		Completed arrangements for the Divn. Capt. Eden, F.H. Scott, arrived, wanted to see Hers evening all order for the approaching Divn. was cancelled. General Leave 1 Divn. to represent from 8th R. West Kents. both Fd. Amb. holding themselves ready at the Stn. Ambulance in the morning.	
	2		A.D.M.S. 17th Div. visited H.Q. at 3 p.m. & another conference. Visited all the Fd. Amb. again with him and obtained all particulars of the Ambulances of the Div. & Fd. of the M.U. of the 17th Divn.	

TMB

WAR DIARY
INTELLIGENCE SUMMARY.

Army Form C. 2118.

A.D.M.S.
24 DIV.

(4)

Place	Date	Hour	Summary of Events and Information	Remarks and references to Appendices
TRAMES.	December 1918.			
	29th	-	A 3rd case of T.B. occurring in the 12th Royal Fusiliers. Closing the hands. A investigation returned	
"	30th	-	The Role of ORs. More than usually. Motor Ambulance Cars Activities. M. 72 and 76 Coys to visit N.50th Fd. Amb. to move. Fine bright day.	
"	31st	-	A.D.M.S. 17 Div. and O.C. Sanitary Section visited 24 Div. area re impending move. Received free written particulars of Medical arrangements of 17th Fd. Amb. in exchange of them of the Division area. Heavy rain and strong wind.	

Gerhard R. Brownell. Col.
A.D.M.S. 24th Div.

A.Shd. 24 D Div.
Vol. 5

F/41/2

24 DIV.

Jan 1916
5

WAR DIARY - CONFIDENTIAL

A.D.M.S.

24th DIVISION.

- VOL. 5. - JANUARY 1916 -

WITH MAP

CONFIDENTIAL

Army Form C. 2118.

A.D.M.S.
24th Division
VOL. 5.
Page 1.

WAR DIARY
INTELLIGENCE SUMMARY.
(Erase heading not required.)

Place	Date	Hour	Summary of Events and Information	Remarks and references to Appendices
TILQUES	1st			
	2nd		General routine. A.D.M.S. 17th Division arrived here to take over the following units, are arranged. No 72 Fd Amb. will relieve No 51 Fd Amb. 6.1.16 at POPERINGHE. and various outposts. No 74 Fd Amb will relieve No 53 Fd Amb at — on 7.1.16. No 73 Fd Amb will relieve No 5 2 Fd Amb. at — on 7.1.16. forming the Divisional Rest-Station, and furnishing Staff for the Divisional baths at P. Advance parties of all the Fd Amb will leave on 5.1.16 to take over the 41 Station and the O i/c here will relieve them opposite numbers on the 7.1.16. There has been an exchange of visits between the O.C. of all the medical units of both Divisions.	

/JMS

Army Form C. 2118.

WAR DIARY
or
INTELLIGENCE SUMMARY.
(Erase heading not required.)

Instructions regarding War Diaries and Intelligence Summaries are contained in F.S. Regs., Part II. and the Staff Manual respectively. Title pages will be prepared in manuscript.

Place	Date	Hour	Summary of Events and Information	Remarks and references to Appendices
TILQUES	January, 1916		General routine.	
	3rd			
	4th		A case of measles reported from the 9th E. Surrey Regt. at present in Tilques in 25th Contracts the Regt. in Tilques has for 16 days after the departure of known case in relief. Transport of 72nd, 74th & L.F. Amb. proceeded by train to relieve. Case of Cerebro spinal meningitis reported 2nd Canadian F.B. 13 Middlesex Regt. who died at No. 7 General Hospital. Great difficulty is being experienced in getting certain important spares of the Siddeley motor ambulances. replace	
	5th		Another case of measles from among the contacts 9th E. Surrey Regt.	
	6th		72nd Fd. Amb. left NORDAUSQUES. for forward area by rail. Transport 73rd L. Amb. left for forward area. Hqrs. Offrs. closed TILQUES at noon. Left 3 pm for STEENVOORDE. Billeted the night.	

WAR DIARY or INTELLIGENCE SUMMARY

Army Form C. 2118.

Place	Date	Hour	Summary of Events and Information	Remarks and references to Appendices
REMINGHELST.	January 1916.			
	8th		Arrived & opened office 11.30 am.	
	9th		Visited all the Fd. Ambulances in their new locations. The 72nd Fd Ambulance with H.Q. at POPERINGHE and accommodation for about 100 patients, has by 2 Sections, an advanced dressing station at the Asylum W. of Ypres in the cellars with a strength of 2 Officers & 20 O.R. with an advanced post at the Lille cellars in the MENIN Road behind the Officers & 6 men present at night. E. of Ypres in the MENIN Road behind the left sector of our front. The ambulance owns the left sector of our front. The 73rd Fd Amb. acts as the Divisional Rest station on the POPERINGHE - BOESCHERE Road. RESY. Siding. accommodate about 200 to 250 patients & is at present in the hands of the Vth Corps R.E. who are putting up huts later. The ambulance also runs the Divisional baths at POPERINGHE. which are to be taken in hand by the R.E. & much improved. The 74 Fd Amb. is in the POPERINGHE - REMINGHELST. Road in a field & has been for patients housed in tents. can be & will be very much improved by building huts etc. Also an A.D. Station at KRUISTRAAT in 3 days. 2 Officers 12 O.R. and 2 cars with & wounded of lighting duties & other activities. HMB	

Army Form C. 2118.

WAR DIARY
or
INTELLIGENCE SUMMARY.
(Erase heading not required.)

Place	Date	Hour	Summary of Events and Information	Remarks and references to Appendices
RENINGHELST	January 1916			4
	10th		Visit to 58th F.A. V Corps Fins Dt test camps on OUDERDOM ROAD. Staging and Subsidiary. Very dirty condition. Left the R/Os vis at work cleaning up. The weather is more favourable. Making arrangements for waterproof bags to bring dirty socks from billets up to battalion in the trenches, also to keep men's feet well. There is no doubt that the numbers of Trench Feet can be very much diminished by careful attention to the provision of dry socks, foot massage, dry putties, exercise & hot food.	
	11th		Capt Kinioch visited all the Fd Ambs. & latrines. S.M.S. Advice, a dissertation on the various latrines to be adopted for the extermination of body lice by an entomologist expert.	
	12th		General routine.	
	13th		Visited 74th & 72nd & 2nd Fd Ambulance. When with 6 Infs & ...... also latter POPERINGHE. & A.D.S. BRANDHOEK	JMB

WAR DIARY
INTELLIGENCE SUMMARY

Army Form C. 2118.

Place	Date	Hour	Summary of Events and Information	Remarks and references to Appendices

January 1916

REVINNGHELST

14th — To OUDERDOM HUTS. Visited camps with arrangements for sanitation & improving. To POPERINGHE 72nd F.A., 73rd F.A., 91 Cavalry & Infantry Div. with reference to future water supply, the present arrangement of separate small sites being very liable to fuel & running machinery stop & labour.

15th — Heavy shelling by enemy in vicinity of 74th General Institution. No casualties to Brit. A.T.S. BRANDHOEK, Asylum. W of Ypres. To 72nd Ld Amt. Represented ad. Pos 15 at the MILL MENIN to the three regimental A.Ps. Ar to fix up the Ypres & Goute point. Represented A.P. au to switch the firing line dry rots in switches commun eating trenches to be made if possible. to hem WITTEPOORT from as soon as possible.

16th —

Leonce Contout

17th —

MWB

Army Form C. 2118.

WAR DIARY
or
INTELLIGENCE SUMMARY.

(Erase heading not required.)

Place	Date	Hour	Summary of Events and Information	Remarks and references to Appendices
REMINGHELST.	January 1916			6.
	18th		Conference at S.D.M.S.: Abeele. Visited A.D.S. BRANDHOEK. to inspect chief of 9th East Surrey Regt. reported by O.C. as not up to standard. Very unfit & ill.	
	19th		Present Routine.	
	20th		do	
	21st		do. The question of the water supply for the troops quartered in Ypres is difficult. The old water supply from DICKEBUSCH lake is greatly in jeopardy by gunfire along the banks of the DICKEBUSCH BEEK. No share pipe has changed the pipes in several places. The proper calibre [water?] has now is longest up in water-carts. At present available. The situation in general.	
	22nd			
	23rd		In a Conference under Col. Kinnis at R.A.H.Q. YPRES. 2½ hours discussion in various points in starting new A.D.S. on Grand Stand close into place in the vaults in the MENIN Road. was taken & temporary to view dug outs at Railway west from the culvert under the MENIN Rd.	

[signature] JMB

WAR DIARY
INTELLIGENCE SUMMARY

Army Form C. 2118.

Place	Date	Hour	Summary of Events and Information	Remarks and references to Appendices
REMY LHERT	January 1916			
	24th		Arrangements being made for a effort to trace at the Asylum YPRES to give the working parties some employment in their return from the front line by the 72nd Fd Amb. There will be very beneficial in breaking off our fatigue parties. Capt Barkshire RAMC S.E. to exp. conference at ABEELE.	
	25th		with SMO 7th Corps. re draft of 9th E	
	26th		A DS BRANDHOEK with SMO to their station from these trenches Swing Myst. in to inter Braid. at H.Q. 50th Div. SO SMI S. to inter Braid	
	27th		General routine.	
	28th		General routine. Stations to Asylum Ypres & small MENIN Rd. is now A.D.S.	
	29th		Worrick. General routine.	
	30th		Conference at ramparts Ypres. Looked into I basis amongst other things the insanitary condition of some of the front line trenches due in of insanitary supports tck.	

MW6.

WAR DIARY
or
INTELLIGENCE SUMMARY

Army Form C. 2118.

Vol. 5.
Page 8

Place	Date	Hour	Summary of Events and Information	Remarks and references to Appendices
RENINGHELST	January 1916			
	30th		Case of mumps amongst B Company amongst 12th Division & Kingston. Suspected case of Cerebro Spinal Meningitis in the 8 & 2 Interborough Battalion. All precautions taken.	
	31st		Heavy frost - fires at 2.30 to 3.30 this morning & 11am to 1pm on our side. Coke & Frosty. General intense. Soup Kitchen & coffee bar run by O.C. 72nd Fd Amb opened at the Asylum Ypres, Tuesday about 10.30 pm on the way back from the refreshment of working parties & I regard this as most beneficial, as there has been an often but through my time & with no chance of obtaining hot food at returning to camp. Help attached of Divisional Medical Unit distribution.	Julian Brownless Col. Ans. 24 W. Kin...

A.D.1908. 24th Dec.

February
5

CONFIDENTIAL

WAR DIARY
A.D.M.S. 24 DIVISION

Feby. 1916 - Vol. VI

Army Form C. 2118.

WAR DIARY
or
INTELLIGENCE SUMMARY.

A.D.M.S.
24 DIVISION
VOL VI.

(Erase heading not required.)

Place	Date	Hour	Summary of Events and Information	Remarks and references to Appendices
REHINGHELST.	February 1916			
	1st		To A.D.M.S. to 8th Corps. Conference. To Lattoo POPERINGHE les 72o 73o & 74o Field Ambulances. Soup Kitchen for dyeing parties of Asylum Orphan doing well.	
	2nd		General Lintene very cold frosty, with high wind.	
	3rd		At the Bough Rouse C. reported his arrival for duty with 8 C.A. West Kent Rgt. New Lt PASCALL to ETAPLES. held at A.D.M.S. at higher to No.1. A.E.S. Asylum & Coffee train. also visited A.E.S. in the prison at POPER hands by Mr Kim. Very starry cold. Sir Arthur Sloggett hut Laws. Total Seconds of Cases of French frost bite in 4.5 for the month of January. G.O.C. Divisions inspected the Field Ambulance & the latter POPERINGHE & expressed himself very satisfied with the progress made since the Division moved up into the line. The improvement of the billets is very good, especially the arrangements for the keeping of duty & clean clothing. Separate than preventing vermin reinfection.	
	4th			

Army Form C. 2118.

WAR DIARY
or
INTELLIGENCE SUMMARY.
(Erase heading not required.)

Place	Date	Hour	Summary of Events and Information	Remarks and references to Appendices
REMINGHURST	February 1916.		General Routine.	
	5th			
	6th	11 a.m.	To hairdressers Ypres at 11 a.m. for inspection. Germans dropped 5·9 shells near Lully front & Lille gate). Conference lasted over 3 hours. Very few points of practical interest raised.	
	7th		Making arrangements for ambulance instruction for 1 N. E. O. per Company & 2 N. C. Os per Co. Ambulance. Battery at the technical school POPERINGHE of the division supervised by W.O.'s The Ambulance who have had a short course in the subject at the Gas School at ONELAIRE. Class commences on 10th instant & lasts 5 days. Lectures 5th STHS. 6 to 11. Tu battler at OUSTADEN. Quite good. 3 p.m. Office & to tea. & tea to duty. Also the orders of men in the trenches are too thin, damp, very unfit.	
	8th	10	O.C.'s & Corps conference at STM S. Office. Case of paratyphoid B in S.R. Kent Vents notified by S.G. W.S. (This man was admitted at WORDHUYPHE 2.1.12.15. When the division was in rest) Case of measles. 9. R. Cameron Rgt. Old precautions taken.	
	9th		Another case of measles in & East Lancashire Battn.	
	10th		I. WOSLER. BRANDHOEK with Stf STM. S. inspected dugouts 1st N. Stafford Rgt. 8 men. Re man from P. U. to POPERINGHE was being shelled had to wait about 30 minutes.	JMB.

WAR DIARY
INTELLIGENCE SUMMARY

Army Form C. 2118.

(3)

Place: REMY SIDING

Date: February 1916

Date	Hour	Summary of Events and Information
11		General routine.
12		Gun alert & very heavy shelling to the Northward this afternoon. Guns in standing to. Our boys on the line 2 patrols.
13		To transport lines. Conference from shelling. Here to H.Q. Visited Stretcher bearers Grenade wounded from BROOKE Trenches. Asked to open to 5th & 74th to have to proceed in motor ambulance to asylum Ypres thence to Chwike party using all night & removed stretchers along MENIN Rd.
	5 pm	No 90 Coee. St DMS visited Muth. Capture. BRANDHOEK A.D.S. Removal of wounded continued this morning. 4 Stretcher bearers Cos 74 & 72 lent borrowed by Strafinck Motor amb cars lie here run with 15 minutes interval. Visited held MENIN Rd. & D.S. BRANDHOEK by 72nd Fd Amb. S.B.
14	5.30 pm	Order to Div "to stand to". Cancelled at 8.5 pm. Capt WM BIDEN Rame attd 2nd Leins to Rgt. wounded in the head at Chill MENIN Rd.

MW

Army Form C. 2118.

WAR DIARY
or
INTELLIGENCE SUMMARY.
(Erase heading not required.)

Place	Date	Hour	Summary of Events and Information	Remarks and references to Appendices
NEUVE EGLISE	February 1916			
	15		All hand for B.H.Q reported. To BNS engineers Rond-T-S. MITCHELL Rnm.C. 7th Ld. Amt. Comp at 9.R. Sherwood Regt. in killed in WEST LANE Communication trench with his orderly by shrapnel in the head. Buried at Cemetery M6.VIV.R.D. 1.9.D.4.6. Sheet 28. BELGIUM. Strong gale of wind g.w.	
	16		Surgeon General O'DONNELL & PORTER visited the office this afternoon re rendering assistance to 17th Div. at BRANDHOEK in case of need. Much less activity.	
	17		To ADS. BRANDHOEK. To meet SDMS V th Corps re site for additional huts at that place & to take POPERINGHE & 7th to Aug. at H.C. for T.C. Name. wounded re help for the temporarily 6, 7th & 8th to Aug to leave collecting & forward walls.	
	18		Zeppelins dropped many bombs in neighbourhood at 0.30 am. Aeroplane dropped 6 bombs at 8 am.	

MWB

WAR DIARY
INTELLIGENCE SUMMARY

Army Form C. 2118.

Place	Date	Hour	Summary of Events and Information	Remarks and references to Appendices
OMINNEHOLST	February 1916			(5)
	19th		General routine. Gas alert reported from IV 9 at about 8 pm. notified all the Battn's. Aeroplane bombs dropped at 7 am in vicinity.	
	20th		To Companies at the Pope Hop Rampants Ypres. Sanitation of Ypres considered some shelling. Visited all the billets in Ypres with Capt Davies in Gas alert at 11 am.	
	21st		Visited OC's v 2nd in Interstaff Ms. In handing over must arrange of the left sector of our front. Decided to shout the MILL MAISON R.D. with the 5th Divn in alignment out post	
	22nd		To A.D.M.S. 5th Corps to Inform him — his views — his concern as to when we to usual re view of warden of trench fit in the climin. There was due to this exceptional military situation of the ypres week. Gas alert at 6.10 pm. Very cold lurid front & snow.	
	23rd		General routine.	
	24th			
	25th		D.D.M.S. V Corps to ADMS 14th Div. visited these office.	
	26th		Aeroplane dropped bombs at 7.30 am morning in own field in the office. Killed men & 3 animals in rest field & wounded two others.	

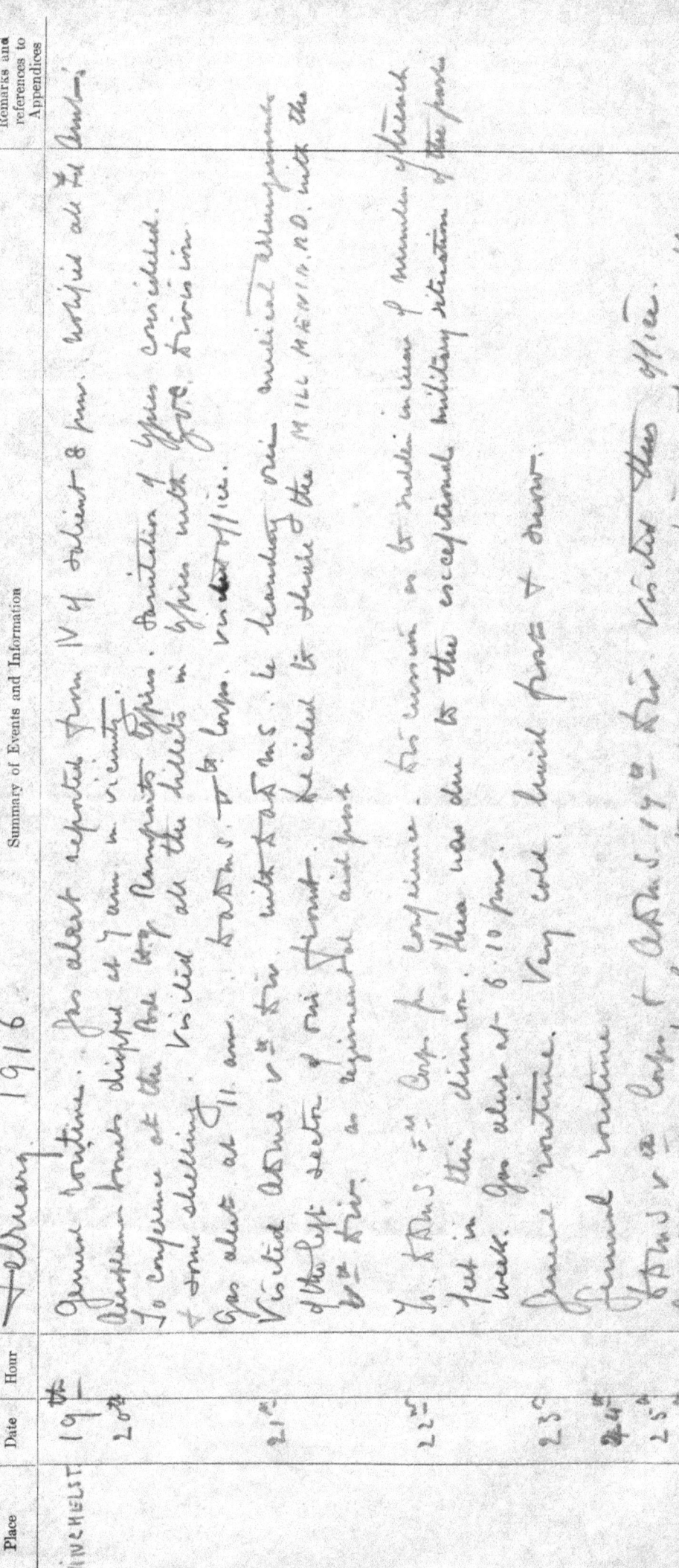

Army Form C. 2118.

(6)

WAR DIARY
or
INTELLIGENCE SUMMARY.
(Erase heading not required.)

Place	Date	Hour	Summary of Events and Information	Remarks and references to Appendices
MENINGHEST	February 1916 27th		Conference at Bde Hdq. at 11 am. General interior claim.	
	28th		Lieuts W.B. BRANDHIGH Smith 8th and 6th Cope be 6 men of 9th R. Seaners. impt on improvements. Gas alert 5- to 8 pm.	
	29th		The understand Officers Reinfts. joined the Division during the month. Lt. Ho COUCH TC. 3/16 to 8 R. West Kents (revised 25/16 shrapnel) Lt. W.C. FOX TC. 17/16 to 2nd Inniskilling Battalion Capt. S.W. McLAY TC. 22/16 to 2nd Innis. relieving Capt. BIDEN, wounded shrapnel Dr. V.E. CARTWRIGHT TC. 22/16 to 9th Sussex. C.S.M. H.H. CARTER TC. 22/16 to 12 Fd. A.C.A. Lieut S.S. to Conference at Ecoivres at HQ 85th Bde at Acheux.	

Signed: [signature] Lieut.M.Burnell Lt. to Bde O.C. 3rd Bde.

War Diaries

of

A.D.M.S. 24th Division

for

March } 1916
April

September 1916

COMMITTEE FOR THE
MEDICAL HISTORY OF THE WAR
Date 9-JUN

WAR DIARY
or
INTELLIGENCE SUMMARY.

Army Form C. 2118.

CONFIDENTIAL DIARY.

Vol. 7

A.D.M.S.
24 DIVISION
VOL. VII
MARCH 1916.

WAR DIARY
INTELLIGENCE SUMMARY

Army Form C. 2118.

A.D.M.S.
24th DIVISION
VOL. VII.

March 1916

Place	Date	Hour	Summary of Events and Information	Remarks and references to Appendices
REHINGHELST	1st		R. 74th to Cant. wired to Winifred A.D.S, KRUISTRAAT, & 1 N.O. & S.O.R. with adequate supply of kits, dressings, rations etc. O.C. 72nd Fd Amb. ordered to reinforce A.D.S Asylum YPRES. with additional personnel & material to hold road & holding room of the 3rd & 17th Division in view of impending attack. Dressing station BRANDHOEK also reinforced to provide extra divisional casualty evacuation positions along the Bluff. Heavily bombarded from 4.30 & 4.45 pm & 5 pm & 5.45 pm.	
	2nd		Heavy bombardment 4.30 a.m. & Infantry assault & BLUFF carried. Casualties in order treated at A.D.S Asylum YPRES, 72nd Fd Amb. 3rd Division 215 wounded. 20th Division 1 wounded. 17th Division 78 do 50th do 1 do. 3 line bayonet wounds. Lt.Col PORTER visited office today.	
	3rd		Casualties still continue to arrive at the A.D.S Asylum Ypres. 3rd Div 43., 17th Div 41. German counter attack failed. O.C A D.S 17th Div. Fd. Amb. Fr the assistance rendered by the 72nd Fd. Amb. in dealing with Casualties during the attack on the BLUFF.	
	4th		Services routine. Heavy snow during the night.	

Army Form C. 2118.

VOL. VII.   (2)

WAR DIARY
INTELLIGENCE SUMMARY.
(Erase heading not required.)

Instructions regarding War Diaries and Intelligence Summaries are contained in F. S. Regs., Part II. and the Staff Manual respectively. Title pages will be prepared in manuscript.

Place	Date	Hour	Summary of Events and Information	Remarks and references to Appendices
	March 1916.			
REMMELST	5th		Conference at Bde. Division. The Brigade to be taken over on our right from 50th Division. This means that then down in into take in the ADS. at MAPLE COPSE	
	6th		With StOsMJ to Hy. 50th Division re taking over the resuscitation of line To 74th Amb when will take over MAPLE COPSE. 12th & Hunt 28 BELGIUM.	
	7th		To ADMS. 5th Corps Conference. Arranged the taking over from the 50th Division in the night. 9/10. 1 off in & 2.0 O.R. with be lensed equipments to ADS. KRUISTRAAT. H.Q. & T.O. will be lensed over to the 50th Division at a future date. Lieut G. McLaity R.A.M.C. reported for duty & posted for [?] instruction to Lt 72nd Tb Amb. Heavy snow.	
	8th		General routine.	
	9th		Lieut V.E. Cartwright R.A.M.C. admitted to hospital T.B.?. Took over ADS. MAPLE COPSE. from 50th Div. 1 O. 2.0.O.R. 74th Fd Amb.	
	10th		Strs.Brs. to H.Q. 50th Div is handing over of ADS at KRUISTRAAT.	MWB

WAR DIARY

INTELLIGENCE SUMMARY

Army Form C. 2118.
VOL. VII. (3)

Place	Date	Hour	Summary of Events and Information	Remarks and references to Appendices
REMY CHAUST.	MARCH 1916.			
	11th		General routine. ADMS 3rd Canadian Division came to inspect horse to rear area	
	12th		Inspection of Ramparts at LILLE gate by PAGS. ADMS & ADC & SPPMS visited office & men.	
	13th		To ABEELE. Conference at ADMS office. Tried & men.	
	14th		General routine.	
	15th			
	16th		With ADMS 3rd Div. to 1st Canadian Corps area. Saw all the situation of Field Ambulances during station advances during station changes. Baths & water supply. The knew report written from PM.S. 2nd Army with a view to dealing with the question of minimum standards in the absence of a travelling steam disinfector, but as the minimum is on the move he sees himself to avoid over close of his schemes.	
	17th		ADMS 3rd Canadian Division visited office to inform by me.	
	18th		General routine	
	19th		72nd & 1st Aust. Div. on the return of BRANDHOEK and Asylum (Ypres) relieved by No I Canadian Fd Amb. 72nd Fd Amb to METEREN with 73rd Bde. BRANDHOEK Asylum F.S. relieved, Relief completed at 4.30 pm 19/3/16	

Army Form C. 2118.

VOL VII (4)

WAR DIARY
INTELLIGENCE SUMMARY
(Erase heading not required.)

Place	Date	Hour	Summary of Events and Information	Remarks and references to Appendices
MEWIMEHURST			March 1916.	
	20th		Staff. O.C. Coys visited office. & more.	
	21st		H.q. 24th Div. left for Cassell. Rest area at FLETRE. 74th Fd Ambulance relieved by No 5 Canadian Fd Amb. & proceeded with 72nd by Bde. to BERTHEN. O.C. visited Adv.H.q. 1st Canadian Div. to hire. Very cold & snow. Visited No 72nd & 74th Fd Amb.	
	22nd			
	23rd		Lieut V.E. CHATWRIGHT R.A.M.C. reported for duty from a.g.hospital at the Base. A.D.Ms. 3rd Canadian Div. No. 2377/15/24.	
	24th		Heavy firing during this night. To STRAZEELE with D.T. g/m. & is taking over school known to Ambulance accommodation.	
	25th	am	General routine	
	26th	10	General routine	
	27th	am	One of Centres opened morning & updates from 8. O.C.S. Left Ypres. No 77.06. O.V.S. attached 24th Div Amb. at GODWAERSVELDE. All private tax taken contacts sent to his Mobile Laboratory. To BAILLUL with ADMS to see ADMs 1st Canadian Div & Canadian Div in Corduroy Camp at T. 20.2 not 26. 73rd Fd. Amb. hrs & billets, to STRAZEELE & A.D.J. Then WULVERGEM. Visiting 1st Canadian Fd Amb. In conference at ADMs to Capt. ROGERS and to STRAZEELE with our typing & Div. Hd Quarters	
	28th			
	29th			
	30th		Fd.Bn. moved to H. ans CAPEL. 72nd & 74th Fd Ambulances moved to B.DSSIVE in Chief 1st Canadian Fd Ambulance.	
	31st			

Colonel M.B. Boswell
ADMS 24th Div.

1577/0/ N.C.W. 6791/1773 500,000 4/15 D.D.&L. A.D.S.S./Forms/C. 2118.

Army Form C. 2118.

WAR DIARY
~~INTELLIGENCE SUMMARY~~
(Erase heading not required.)

A D M S 24 D
Vol 8

A.D.M.S.
- 24 DIVISION -
VOL VIII.
APRIL - 1916 -

Instructions regarding War Diaries and Intelligence Summaries are contained in F. S. Regs., Part II. and the Staff Manual respectively. Title pages will be prepared in manuscript.

Place	Date	Hour	Summary of Events and Information	Remarks and references to Appendices

Army Form C. 2118.

WAR DIARY
or
INTELLIGENCE SUMMARY.
(Erase heading not required.)

A.D.M.S.
2^A DIVISION.
VOL. VIII. (1)

Instructions regarding War Diaries and Intelligence Summaries are contained in F.S. Regs., Part II. and the Staff Manual respectively. Title pages will be prepared in manuscript.

Place	Date	Hour	Summary of Events and Information	Remarks and references to Appendices
St. JnCAPPEL	April 1916.			
	1st		To D.D.M.S. 2nd Army HAZEBROUCK. and D.A.S. BAILLEUL.	
	2nd	A.G. 17. 15.	Govt. trained Conference. Situation of aid posts. Advance advisory Stations & Orders of Evacuation discussed. A.D.M.S. to A.D.S. & D.S. 7th Field Amb. and reported	
			Quarters 3rd R. Bde. and 7th Fd Amb.	
	3rd		Visit F.D.M.S and O.C. beds & Sanitary station to Brig. 17. Inf. Bde. & Sanitation of Transport lines which were left in very dirty condition by those preceding. New site suggested. To battn & inspected water supply BUSFORD Camp. Very liable to Contamination. A.D.M.S. to B N A W O U T R E. 78th Fd Amb. & bathrs. Visit Hercules, R.A. & BRIDGMAN.	
	4th		R.D. N.A.M.C. Contracts confirmed, to England. General routine. A.D.M.S. visited A.D.S. 73rd Fd Amb. W U L V E R G H E M.	
	5th		Visit F.D.M.S. visited 73rd Fd Amb. and A.D.S. W U L V E R G H E M. Candidate shelling A.D.S. situated in farm in NEUVE EGLISE — WULVERGHEM Rd. for commnication. drew front they are not hostile, very liable be shelled.	
	6th 7th 8th		General routine. To 72nd Fd Amb. & F.D.M.S. O.C. Corps. & F.D.M.S. 9. R. Div.	

General routine.

WAR DIARY
or
INTELLIGENCE SUMMARY

Army Form C. 2118.
VOL VIII (2)

Place	Date	Hour	Summary of Events and Information	Remarks and references to Appendices
Mjan Cappel			April 1916	
	9th		To watch conference at Strand. 2nd Corps C/C. CE providing. Various units into the Corps & Schemes promoted to move into training areas. Shun is a difficult intelligence in this area. Attention water especially difficult.	
			Issues to Bdy. Ex conference. GOC visited No 72 & 74 Fd Ambulances & arranged relief of	
	10th		ROMARIN Farms inspected and inspected reports and Fuels. Water is tested & advance organization. Inspection thus the BFCS not than to have present-situation Farm at E of Berceaux.	
	11th		Glass. 73rd Fd Amb. Very crowded in STRANOOTRE, will have to have another site suggested. G.O. of I Kemmetting Corps. Cases of Typhoid reported in 24 & 3rd Sig Co.	
			& have Explains in 7 N Hants Regt.	
	12th		general Routine.	
	13th		Visited to C. 72 Fd Amb. to select site for new division and new station & 73. A very good site found in two fields off main road, being favourable & there. just beside Farm at Stroobin. Line 5 N. & 2.8 & CAMP. Company also the stall the site later & approved of it. It will be based him heavily. When surprised in a house in the town. Heavy cases & have to remove being sanitary in the theatre. Satisfied about the division. ole for the prevention of them.	WW

Army Form C. 2118.

VOL VIII (3)

WAR DIARY
or
INTELLIGENCE SUMMARY.
(Erase heading not required.)

Place	Date	Hour	Summary of Events and Information	Remarks and references to Appendices
Wym Lyppl	April 14th		KB led I BROWN. D.Corps troops in [inspecting] [...] of KMS. Brit 2nd Army for stated that a certain [...] of cases [...] to take in mags so we ought to have the [...] C.C.S. of war-stream against the strain [...] evacuated. there will invariably aid in the [...]. The KMS will temporarily move to St Jean Cappel until the new site also mentioned is being opened up.	
	15th		With a supply train now site for STMS BROWN, BROWN, E BRUYETRE + others. The [...] steam disinfector left by the 1st Canadian Divn has been received here returned to them by 15th Corps. This is a great loss to the KMS line dress station. Through the [...] thundered our lot [...] in return we are not [...] so efficient. The head of [...] beside a great clear-up here.	
	16th		I luckily [...] Conference for division d. to KMS. ROMARIN. Stations. to new site STMS BRUYETRE held at 9.30 the cords. A [...] Sterilizing [...] is being installed by the 41st Sanitary Section at the [...] Effluent from the laundry portion to my [...] about 600 gallon daily of the [...] [...] to my [...]. the water from the baths flows to [drainage] but cool.	

MWB

WAR DIARY
INTELLIGENCE SUMMARY

Army Form C. 2118.

VOL VIII (4)

Place: Septans April

Date	Hour	Summary of Events and Information
April 17th		Visited H.Q.S. & H.Q. Rein Corner. 2nd Trench dug out, nearly finished, some hay protection to be made in front of dim which is open to road. Demolition to be made. To BULFORD Camp, & bath. The latter very cramped & ill designed, requires a lot of improvements. Arrangement for disposal of laundry water taken.
18th		H.Q. moved to BAILLEUL. Conference at SSN 3, 7th G. Corps. (Arrangement from own Telegr. have been introduced by Australian Corps.)
19th		Stadac. to him into SNS & bathe BRAIVOUTRE, where some pump penetrating earth are being erected.
20th		To Infantry Camps. KORTE PVP. Incineration defect km until in movement to be established. Demirio. Also BULFORD. Would be much improved since my last visit.
21st		SNS. 2nd Army visited 74th & G. Cont. Gas alert at 11 p.m.
22nd		With Stand. To Corps. to visit new site for SNS. This regent now proposed lying on a bad road to the fair East.
23rd		H.Q. Train in Conference at 11 a.m. at 73rd F.A. H.Q. To STANOVTRE Latter sharing sheds & NEUVE EGLISE latter, built Cpl G in interstellar atmosphere. Also visited 103 Coy. RE. incinerator of excreta of these divisions being well carried out.
24th		Surrey Shuffled about 20 trucks on town, utterly destroyed, leaving many orders & damage others. 7 other civilian ghosts. A. Emery at the Asylum Farm. Not much damage attained.

M.B.

Army Form C. 2118.

VOL. VIII (S)

WAR DIARY
or
INTELLIGENCE SUMMARY.
(Erase heading not required.)

Instructions regarding War Diaries and Intelligence Summaries are contained in F.S. Regs., Part II. and the Staff Manual respectively. Title pages will be prepared in manuscript.

Place	Date	Hour	Summary of Events and Information	Remarks and references to Appendices
BAILLEUL	25th		General Routine.	
	26th		Conference at H.Q.M.S. & G. Corps	
	27th		7th M.D. LODGE Pits 63 with H.Q.M.S. & Corps. to incinerators trestle supply. BUFORD Camp water supply burning plant. Large well being cleared out with petrol pumps. additional. To road near water supply at FORT. To see new Convalescent Hospital at 73rd Fd Amb. & 74th Fd Amb. & STRAMEUTREL &	
	28th		Ambulances respectively. To new site for 73rd Fd Amb.	
	29th			
	30th		At about 12.30 am Enemy made gas raid opposite left sector of our front. gas lasted 15 minutes & was followed by small infantry attacks, which we repulsed. Later the 338. Cases of gas poisoning received & 190 wounded. Very heavy artillery bombardment. Immediately commenced. Collection & evacuation carried out by the 78th & 74th & 76th Ambulances. Very satisfactorily. The gas is considered to be the same as that used in former attacks on these front.	

Signed N.B. Burnell Col
A.D.M.S. 25th Div

MAY 1916.

A.D.M.S 24th Division

COMMITTEE FOR THE
MEDICAL HISTORY OF THE WAR
Date 26 JUN. 1915

Army Form C. 2118.

A.D.M.S.
24 DIVISION — Vol IX.

WAR DIARY
or
INTELLIGENCE SUMMARY
(Erase heading not required.)

Remarks and references to Appendices: Vol 9 ①

Place	Date	Hour	Summary of Events and Information
BAILLEUL	May 1916 1st		Up to 9.30 am today 344 Officers & men had been admitted to the 3 Casualty Clearing Station here, belonging to this division, and of these 27 had died & more lies dying. Of the 73rd Field Amb. STANOUTRE 10 cases had died in the town of BAILLEUL itself, a great deal of the population in civilian population in the town have been hard hit & showers of gallons of &c. The effects are very great apparently. The young lives hang all shrivelled up & fallen off. Some place entirely escaping. Many people in the town are suffering with slight headache symptoms & the result of the gas.
	2nd		Conferences at the H.Q. of 2nd & 3rd Corps. In care, Containers to be administered. The effects being very severe delayed, remarks to 2nd Cavalry Division & London. Additional wells have been put in. The army sent about 100 sure new hammocks to reserve Field Ambulance from in Ambulance wagon together hammocks to reserve Field Ambulance from in Ambulance wagon together hammocks used in their own transport. In each is to reside & medicals to it. Them marches back & details of some this midst only.
	3.		Water supply at BOLFORD is becoming scanty, & additional supplies are being sought for. Incinerators are being put up wherever practicable & permanent standing men left in the various camps. It seems certainly to be above a of which does as VMB

Army Form C. 2118.

VOL. IX (2)

WAR DIARY
or
INTELLIGENCE SUMMARY.

May 1916

Place	Date	Hour	Summary of Events and Information	Remarks and references to Appendices
BOEUVE	3rd		Much to render sanitary measures futile in the Salvaging Warfare.	
	4th		Gas cases continue to come in, in smaller numbers. Weather hot + close.	
	5th		Total number of Gas cases = 6 Officers + 304 O.R. fatal. Wounded = 16 Officers + 226 O.R. "	
	6th		The new P.H.C. gas helmet is difficult to put on, causing delay, & the eye-pieces are much too far apart, enduring rain very difficult. The frame separates later my hat, but an my Ambulance having smelling lights could be a great improvement here & Brad a P.B. at 74th Fd. Amb. as my O.R. & steam supply. Coples & stoning. Eight Cars of inspected entire, occurring in the 8th Corps but Rest Depôt, an Island to 2 legates. Number fairly moderate.	

Army Form C. 2118.

WAR DIARY
or
INTELLIGENCE SUMMARY.
(Erase heading not required.)

VOL IX (3)

Instructions regarding War Diaries and Intelligence Summaries are contained in F. S. Regs., Part II. and the Staff Manual respectively. Title pages will be prepared in manuscript.

Place	Date	Hour	Summary of Events and Information	Remarks and references to Appendices
BAILLEUL	8.5.16		A.D.M.S. proceeded on leave – weather cold with some rain. Lieut FULTON, R.A.M.C. allotted 13th MIDDLESEX Regt. & posted 21st STEWART 13th FA in relief	
"	9.5.16		Routine.	
"	10.5.16		Afternoon A+QMG, D.C. Sanitary Section & D.A.D.M.S. & BULFORD camp to inspect new well & pile of latrines. Visited NEUVE EGLISE baths. New wells West of NEUVE EGLISE – BAILLEUL road. A.D.M.S. & D.R.S. ST JANS CAPPEL	
"	11.5.16		A.D.M.S. & 74th FA	
"	12.5.16		Gas alert received 6.35 PM all FA's & SANITARY Section warned, night cloudy, very little wind	
"	13.5.16		Heavy rain in early morning. Inspected water tank near DRANOUTRE also drawing station etc.	
"	14.5.16		A.D.M.S. & D.A.D.M.S. & new D.R.S. Huts almost completed. Mortar wet and running.	
"	15.5.16		D.A.D.M.S. to new D.R.S. and inspected water supplies at NEUVE EGLISE. Lt. DUMMERE 74th F.A. evacuated to train from No 2 C.C.S. young ENTERIC FEVER. 2 relief ordered for early Lieuts WALTON and CLARK R.A.M. 2 (TC) reported for duty from ETAPLES. Pte(?) to 74th FA	
"	16.5.16		Report from Mr. F.R.W.F. KENT Regt. a suspected CEREBRO SPINAL MENINGITIS. attached	
"	17.5.16		AFAS returned from leave.	
"	18/5/16		Routine – Weather must warmer. General waters	
"	19/5/16		D.A.D.M.S. proceeded on leave. Visited 74th FA Fire Centre.	
"	20/5/16		Visited right section. Hill 63. A.D.S. 74th FA Levels and posts. 1st A.B. & Rd LODGE. At latter place minnesota alleged to have driven shell fire & his entrance injuring later much from shelling in PROSTREET – ROMARIN Rd. Pro Garrett here finds duckboard under at 74th & Dugouts ROMARIN. Conference at Sir H.G. Sec at D.D.M.S. D.D & L. Necessity of water in firing line area. All possible sources to be provided down & tapped.	
	21/5/16			[signature]

A.D.S.S./Forms/C. 2118.

Army Form C. 2118.

WAR DIARY
or
INTELLIGENCE SUMMARY
(Erase heading not required.)

VOL. IX (4)

Instructions regarding War Diaries and Intelligence Summaries are contained in F.S. Regs., Part II. and the Staff Manual respectively. Title pages will be prepared in manuscript.

Place	Date	Hour	Summary of Events and Information	Remarks and references to Appendices
BAILLEUL	22ⁿᵈ		To 74ᵗʰ Fᵈ Amb to see fly proof latrines, constructed by O.C. To 73ʳᵈ Fᵈ Amb. gun situation. off main road, near the town of post reconnoitered in huts & tents. great improvement on the STRAZEELE site. Very wet & rafny this morning. Changing to cooler after thunder storm. Orderly me[e]t[in]g. Conference at DM.S. to 6.15pm.	
	23ʳᵈ			
	24ᵗʰ		With D.D.M.S. known to St James Chapel, to visit the temporary F.R.S. 74ᵗʰ Fᵈ Amb. then to 73ʳᵈ Fᵈ Amb. S.D.S.O.(12)and to Chauring Station at DRANOUTRE. and the Rue wood buffer (the troops supplying showers with Colonels of lines but nothing quite so well. no wonder the roads from the laundry road preng in scarcity of water being very difficult to deal with.) & then back to 74ᵗʰ Fᵈ Amb, in the Rue de Bultein. the R.A.P. arrangements very much field with the troops of the Fᵈ Ambulance in.	
	25ᵗʰ		Routine.	
	26ᵗʰ		To hill 63 map 28. to select site for the & an extra training in evacuation from the position of 3 battalion in camp on the hill. a good deal of work in hearing down on providing splinter proof shelters. & additional men for the A.D.S.	
	27ᵗʰ		Routine.	

2353 Wt. W3544/1454 700,000 5/15 D.D. & L.   A.D.S.S./Forms/C. 2118.

WAR DIARY
INTELLIGENCE SUMMARY

Army Form C. 2118.

VOL. IV. (5)

Place	Date	Hour	Summary of Events and Information	Remarks and references to Appendices
BAILLEUL	28th		Routine.	
	29		Capt Platt Reade 51st Div returned from leave having been held up in Boulogne 24 hrs owing to train starting a few minutes before the train arrived. (a bad arrangement.)	letter
			To STRAZEELE to 72nd I.B. a. J. Scheme. for annoying the enemy.	
			Lieuts W. C. SOUTHEY. A.S.C. 74th Para C. left for England Contracts expired.	
			Lieuts C.A. Whittaker (SR). C. HARRIS (TC) & W. DIXON (TC) R.A.M.C. Arrive as Replacements.	
	30th		Lieut M.J. KERWE (TC) R.A.M.C. reported his arrival. Conference at 5 pm at Capt. Openshaw of the history of one horse, by having its gas helmet continuously rolled up on the his forearm for a short period, application of Vaseline has been the net effect Capt. Openshaw of Vaseline covered will be frequently to see.	
	31st		General Routine. Map of area occupied by this division by Captain Th Scott. Names & nos. is attached.	

Frederic McBurnell Col
A.D.M.S. 2nd Div

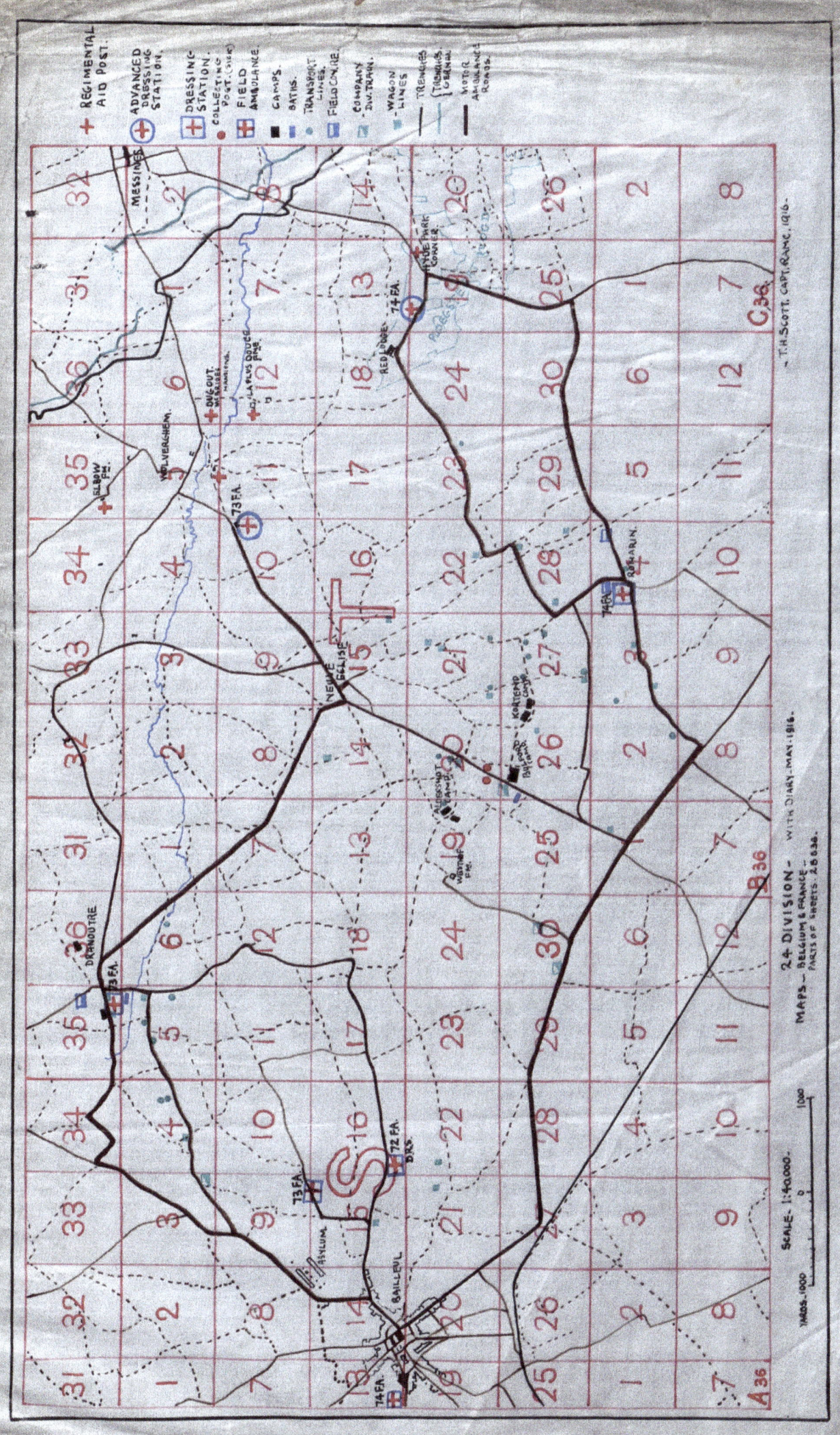

ADMS 24/D23
Army Form C. 2118.
Vol 10.

WAR DIARY
~~INTELLIGENCE SUMMARY~~
(Erase heading not required.)

Place	Date	Hour	Summary of Events and Information	Remarks and references to Appendices

A.D.M.S. 24 DIVISION.
VOL X — JUNE
1916

COMMITTEE FOR THE
MEDICAL HISTORY OF THE WAR
Date 31 AUG 1915

Army Form C. 2118.

WAR DIARY
or
INTELLIGENCE SUMMARY. A.D.M.S. 24 DIVISION   VOL. X

(Erase heading not required.)

Instructions regarding War Diaries and Intelligence Summaries are contained in F.S. Regs., Part II. and the Staff Manual respectively. Title pages will be prepared in manuscript.

Place	Date	Hour	Summary of Events and Information	Remarks and references to Appendices
BELLEU.	1st		Routine.	
	2nd		Ams 2nd Army, DDMS Vth Corps visited this office with reference to certain scheme. Visited new SDMS working party camp. Field approx. half rounded with buildings. Rooms with No 1 Coy. to NEUVE EGLISE baths, to have drainings & catchment area of own new wells. Recommend change of site but shall stand by 2nd Corps verdict office, to payment of men working incinerators at BUCQUOY camp.	
	3rd			
	4th		To STANDORTE & shortage of teaching notice, also water supply now to being abandoned. Into contaminated by sewage of 1.A.R.C.	
	5th		Talk DDMS & DADOURS. To inspect men of ration draft unfit to serve in this theatre. Also to ADS ROMARIN. Heavy showers fell.	
	6th		To Conference with SDM S Vth Corps. No of drafts schedules required for a division in 21 supported.	
	7th		Visited Rest Station at last present to been site 5.16.c.4.4 from the convent chateau at St Jans Cappel. No 72 & 74. To ambulances with SDM S.D.D.	
	8th		Corps Commander his talks.	
	9th		Corps to inform us times of planes with this arrangements. Lt. Kirkpatrick Rum C 109 R.Fd. left for England. Return not expected.	

Army Form C. 2118.

VOL X. (2)

WAR DIARY
or
INTELLIGENCE SUMMARY.

(Erase heading not required.)

Place	Date	Hour	Summary of Events and Information	Remarks and references to Appendices
BAILLEUL			June. 1916.	
	10th		General routine.	
	11th		Conference at Hd. Division. Question of constantly having the steel helmets in the Front Trenches was decided to continue during do. Very cold, wet rain.	
	12th		Emerging hearer water supply to brewery STRAZEELE. Officer in charge 6th Canadian Labor Coy. stated that all Belgian lines contain. B. Coli.. he particulars SNY/1006 noted from consumption of the same. Returns to BUFORD CAMP re repairs of the Thieu incinerators. Wet + cold.	
	13th		Wet + cold. Memorial service for the late Lord Kitchener. General routine.	
	14th		Letter from G.O. visit A.D.M.S. 50th Division in morning of 73rd Bde into new billets arranged by 50th Division. A.D.S. at LINDENHOEK been occupied by 50th Div arranged to take over right sector. The left being Sheet 28. N. 27. C. 10.5. for the evacuation of our right sector. The left being handed through the 50th A.D.C. at KEMMEL to LOCRE (to amb. in the Asylum). To officers hospital. 50th Div. at MONT NOIR. Very indifferent station + accommodation	
	15th		Sn 7th & Bn of 2nd Cavalry Division is to take over the area occupied by 73rd Bde of 25th Division. Returns to H.Q. 50th Div. to arrange to move.	
	16th		Returns to A.D.S. LINDENHOEK and been inspected by A.P. WAKEFIELD F BADAJOS huts at LOCRE. By Coopers at A.D.S. to Corps re improving events.	194

Army Form C. 2118.

VOL X (3)

WAR DIARY
or
INTELLIGENCE SUMMARY.

Place	Date	Hour	Summary of Events and Information	Remarks and references to Appendices
BEUVIL	16th		Gas alert at 6.20 p.m. About 11.30 p.m. gas released by enemy all along lines and from Very Lights	
"	17th		Considered by no one. Stand to relieved at 1.8 a.m. 1.10 to 7.3. Gt. Guns heard for 2 an. L3 shortly in relief reported 50 gas cases arrived. General at HDQ visited GMSA at 5.10 a.m. M.T. care sent for. Consulted reports to him 17.6.16. in visited of this division. General 144. Evacuated 138. Visited CCS No 8 & 12 Canadian. At No 8 CCS Cases were mostly deaths of the worst type. very distressing to witness at No 1 Canadian some of the later cases were not so serious. started to evacuate D.S. & ADS. and requested outposts at 11 a.m. to open the ciermin. go report which the affected were not so serious.	
	18th		General Cam continue to come in. Arrangements effected when had been made. were taken in motor cars to avoid excitement during last night (17th). Field Cars up to date = 5 Officers and 57 other ranks. (DEAD.) Total admissions. 13 Officers + 425 Other ranks up to 4 p.m. Left Pte. Dragon & No 6 Amb. Lt. Corp. R.E. arrived. also 1 Section No 1 Sect to use Reconnaissance Est. Collecting Post. NEUVE EGLISE - POP ENTIERES.	798
	19th			

Army Form C. 2118.

WAR DIARY
or
INTELLIGENCE SUMMARY.
(Erase heading not required.)

VOL X (b)

Instructions regarding War Diaries and Intelligence Summaries are contained in F.S. Regs., Part II. and the Staff Manual respectively. Title pages will be prepared in manuscript.

Place	Date	Hour	Summary of Events and Information	Remarks and references to Appendices
BAILLEUL			June 1916.	
	20th		Escort. HRS. 74 Fd Amb & light motor transfer to view new Park for Lysenmobile cars & with SE. at Specelin to new Camp at LUCAS. — WARFIELD — BADAJOS. Every sanitary arrangements will be necessary.	
	21st		With G.O.C. 8AMB & OE IXth Corps to inspect BTS. 72nd Bde. for any extent of the sanitary arrangements of any kind being excellent. To Kemmel Shelters & various camps in vicinity of LUCAS.	
	22nd		BATHS, LAT. Laundry, Doctor to BEDFORD Camp, to note supply latrines incineration. & green traps. All baths leaking. Water supply defective.	
	23rd		BATHS 2nd ANZAC Corps to office. I found Div also to taking over. BATHS. IX Corps Offices & round STEAM VIATAC one with SATNS. then train in to late Lieuprised Shelley to IX Bde Grps. Captain R.E. HOOPER Rant. Transport from 2nd & to 41st Division. Heavy shelling of own front line during the night.	
	24th		ADMS & STDMS 2 Hague RN to office. Custom to MONRO RAMC. I.C of 3rd R.B. to LUCAS. India order. BMS in Camp.	
	25th		To NJ 74 Fd Amb. Inspected & seen Inspect for charge at the Front. Recommend to have defects.	
	26th		Will STDMS to Kemmel Shelters & villages of Kemmel where there is a good old STDMS Clearing Station to begin & collect at present used by 50th Div. Will Park will be taken in shortly by us.	[signature] MWB

Army Form C. 2118.

VOL X. (5)

WAR DIARY
or
INTELLIGENCE SUMMARY.
(Erase heading not required.)

Place	Date	Hour	Summary of Events and Information	Remarks and references to Appendices
BAILLEUL			June 1916	
	27		To Conference at D.H.Q. Corps Hq. Details of entire equipment to be attained.	
	28"		Forwards for future events especially ration Blankets 1000, Stretchers 250 etc etc. Returns for A.D.S. Kemmel & R.A Posts in new line. Lieut Stedman & Cpl. J. W.? Le Cault to accompany him to Kemmel Hgts. to accommodation reconno- troops for huts/lines. Recommended new site for Fst Aid at LOCRE.	
	29"		Sent returns with VCs. 72 & 74 Fd Amb to inspect new sites. Plans to receive W. 10.4.0. An either shortly of Command.	
	30"		Sat Evans, Lt. Col Evans & Col H.Q. to Talking Pns ADS at Kemmel. Crest showing Weather. Gas was used by us & the enemy. A height of 28/29, dense cloud. Hun seen to pass on the German trenches in a height of 29/30. Very heavy cannonade by enemy in retaliation on 28/29. Bright 10 German prisoners were taken. 3 of them were wounded.	Both 132 Casualties Allenyon Trench were brought in

WAR DIARY
INTELLIGENCE SUMMARY.
(Erase heading not required.)

Army Form C. 2118.

24 / ADMS, 24 Div

July

Vol II

A.D.M.S.
24 DIVISION
VOL. XII - JULY -
- 1916 -

COMMITTEE FOR THE
MEDICAL HISTORY OF THE WAR
Date 5 - SEP. '15

Army Form C. 2118.

VOL XI. (1)

WAR DIARY
or
INTELLIGENCE SUMMARY.

A.D.M.S.
2nd DIVISION

Place	Date	Hour	Summary of Events and Information	Remarks and references to Appendices
BAILLEUL	July 1916 1st		74th Fd Amb moved to, 2 S.M. 26 a 9.9 being relieved by 7th Aust. Fd Amb. & the 73rd Fd Amb. relieved personnel of 72nd Fd Amb at LINDENHOEK. A.D.S. This A.D.S. is not frost-protected & requires a considerable amount of work done on it. C.R.E. consulted. 72nd Fd Amb sent advance party to new site at 2 S.M. 23 a.7.9. n LOCRE-KEMMEL RD. 41st Fd Ambn also sent advance party to 2 S.M. 29 a 8.9. Same time 72nd Fd Amb to KEMMEL village to inspect cellar accd & capacity of cellars in lining with view to further strengthening.	
	2nd		General routine.	
	3rd		With STAS, I×C Corps & STAFFS. to KEMMEL-village. Exhaustive survey of A.D.S. & having cellars. The enemy dropped a sting range into the hard house & adjoining grounds, while we were in the vicinity. At 10 pm tonight there them in persist under the command of the 1st C. Corps.	
LOCRE	4th		Hq. moved from BAILLEUL to LOCRE. Heavy thunder storm. Closed 3/12 at 3 pm 5th B. & reported down here at LOCRE. Captain AVELING, R.A.M.C. reported arrival for shortly.	
	5th		Stand by H.Q. 50 km to taking over A.D.S. KEMMEL and made election the cistin 74th Fd Amb. to METEREN to take on a number of buildings. 72nd Fd Amb hand front 97. St P.C. Cam. to 74th Fd Amb. at METEREN. preparatory to moving.	
	6th		72nd Fd Amb. moved to 2 S.M. 23. b. 7.9. & took on A.D.S KEMMEL village. Inst. station at KEMMEL SHELTER & LOCRE-BAILLEUL Rd. taken over from 50th Fd Amb. 6th Australian. 72nd handed over Stn Station to 6th Australian Fd Amb.	

1992

Army Form C. 2118.

VOL XI (2)

WAR DIARY
or
INTELLIGENCE SUMMARY.
(Erase heading not required.)

Place	Date	Hour	Summary of Events and Information	Remarks and references to Appendices
LOCRE	July 1916.			
	6th		Captain Caden Rounce att 12th Lincolnshire transferred for duty with IX Corps Cavalry. Captain WELLING M.R.M.C. posted to 12th Lincolnshire Royston.	
"	7th		About 6.30 7a.m. Enemy Aeroplane to 7th R. Brent at MONT NOIR. Shots & Went in unsuccessful in the site of the hill on a grass airing. & very hostile observation. Surrounding fires. View of the surrounding plains. also to METEREN. where he 7n to Brent into demonstrations & sections to open up buildings and temporary acts. O.P.s but not in action.	
"	p.m.		From that the division will be a part entered division to forces present of H.Q. when to BAILLEUL. WESTRN. to those. Anga m. Corps. & the Arthis 2nd Australian & 47th	
			1st Australian division is handing of taken over	
			by 72nd Lt. Brent to return to its Original S.P.S. being 8 on fr the 6th Australian. Lt Amb. & the 73rd Lt Amb. will take on the HQT. of Kandahar Farm	
	9th		72nd Brent leave on H.Q.T. Kummel village to 50th Division.	
"	10th		H.Q. Division moved from LOCRE to BAILLEUL. All medical units back to Original Stations. Ot.	
"	11th		Special lecture:	
"	12th		Att. LINDENHOEK. Personnel again applied to 72nd Lt Amb.	
"	13th		General Lecture	

#353 Wt. W2544/T454 700,000 5/15 D.D. & L. A.D.S.S./Forms/C. 2118.

Army Form C. 2118.

VOL XI (3)

WAR DIARY
or
INTELLIGENCE SUMMARY.
(Erase heading not required.)

Place	Date	Hour	Summary of Events and Information	Remarks and references to Appendices
BAILLEUL	July 1916.			
	14th		Captain P.J. McDonnell Reno. R.A.M.C. S.R. placed in arrest - in charge of thosaKearnan. Lt. 74th tt Canat. been entrusion with you to take place shortly. Made all arrangements for dealing with extra casualties.	
	15th		Expected that so in probably between the Kemmel line shortly. Went - work to started in the lining KEMMEL village, with a view to backing up Mouchester. Scouts from shell fire. the A.D.S. will take 120 cases in the cellars. This morning with Bdr.Grls h.b. MAYOUTA. D.S. and LINDENHOEK. A.D.S. 72nd ft Lunk. Saw & recommendaeis at the little place, let - the clay onto rather flimsy. V. Unprotected. Propose to line 3. Splinta proof Lance shelves deep ones to hold about 100 casualties. on the A.D.S. with probably be a very important front in a division, showing a heavy engagement. The hearty shelled all "round" sunrounded a tonal by Genus visited front lines brenches & Regimental Aud Post. held by 12th Royal Tushlirus. The and Pat. Injuries a great deal of strengthening. Visible destruction of left water brenches by bomine super bricks.	
	16th		Bde. Conference at 72nd Bde. Hq. hear Eugene's farm.	
	17th		Jennie Laatint	

[signature]

Army Form C. 2118.

VOL XI. (4)

WAR DIARY
or
INTELLIGENCE SUMMARY.
(Erase heading not required.)

Place	Date	Hour	Summary of Events and Information	Remarks and references to Appendices
BAILLEUL	July 1916.			
	18th		2 Lt. A.J. S. 5th Corps. Conference + discussed matters concerning preparation for active operations.	
	19th		Recent orders to move to list area at once. Handing over Att. LINDENHOEK to 50th Divn in P.O.V.R & 9.11.54 Rost to 29th Divn also STANDYNTRE + divn station POORP & 11.54 Rost to 29th Divn. also 72" 73" + part of 74th Siege Bties. to 20th Divn. & Divns 20th & 50th to divide to après la mer.	
			To Span Cappel this evening	
St-Jans Cappel	20th		To Auth 6th heavy of METEREN and to 72nd, 73rd to Auth Fr Tanks which in turn all its front FLETRE respectively. To 74th Fr Tanks. L.O.H tin s'Dins = to Corps stations voided NOIR. To Army L.O.H tin s'Dins = to Corps stations voided both at L.A. BESACE. N q METEREN. and at X.20.D. that 27.	
			When in an endeavor to lend the regiment in the vicinity.	
	21st		Fr Corps will entrain on Sunday 24th July.	

/MK

Army Form C. 2118.

VOL. XI. 5

WAR DIARY
or
INTELLIGENCE SUMMARY.
(Erase heading not required.)

Place	Date	Hour	Summary of Events and Information	Remarks and references to Appendices
St JANS CAPPEL	July 1916			
	22		Relieved 74th Fd Amb. to move fm MT. NOIR & METEREN.	
	23rd		General C.M. held inspn of gun Capper & Capt P.J. Westmuir Frank	
			6 Sisters & Cooks 74- & 75th Fd Amb at METEREN and	
			79th Fd Amb at CAPPEL h. 2nd Division. 8 in number.	
			2 Ambulance cars fm 2nd Amb. left this morning for the South. We at	
			delivering of equipment of receiving.	
			72nd Fd Amb. entrained at Bailleul heut. 28.28. 73rd Fd Amb at Ontreourir rest	
			at 28.30. & 74th Fd Amb. at BAILLEUL ended at 22.28.	
	24th		Remarks of Ambulance Cars left in Convoy at 5am fm the South. Route. Hazebrouck	
			ST VENANT, ST POL - DOULLENS - VIGNACOURT - PICQUIGNY - PICQUIGNY. of the last named	
			there were this was & CAVILLON. 24 & D.M.G. three to the 3. Fd Amb locations	
			72nd Fd Amb to OISSY. 79th Fd Amb to MOLLIENS VIDAME. & 74th to	
			CAVILLON. tons officer closed at 10 am and reopened at 4 pm at CAVILLON.	
			41st Sanitary Section being left at 11 am. Personnel entraining at BAILLEUL rear at 17.28.	
			72nd & 74th Fd Am. & 41st San Sec detrained at LONGUEAU & 73rd Fd Amb detrained at	
			SALEUX. In the vicinity of AMIENS.	

Army Form C. 2118.
VOL XI. (6)

WAR DIARY
or
INTELLIGENCE SUMMARY.
(Erase heading not required.)

Place	Date	Hour	Summary of Events and Information	Remarks and references to Appendices
CAVILLON			July, 1916	
	26th		Visited 74th Fd Amb at CAVILLON where bivouacs have pitches for about 20 sick in an orchard. also to 72nd Fd Amb quartered at OISSY where also the drum hounds of Corps can be accommodated.	
"	27th		Bn S.M. Capt visited the offices then proceeded to No 39. C.C.S. ALLONVILLE. near AMIENS. very cold & dull. Sun shone in RAMC Very damp. Field damp. many deer hot so cold. Lent Capt Wright to BOVES who was at laundry both for the Division.	
"	28th		To Villein BOCAGE to see D.Dus 18th Corps.	
"	29th		General routine.	
"	30th		Orders received that Division to train in 2nd Army on 31.7.16 to XIII Corps area in CORBIE-SAUVRS Fd Amb to be divided into Bivvie & Post division, the former to be attached to & move with their Brigades. Conference of Cts, Fd. Amb. at the Office. 6 pm. Finding of G.C.M. on Captain M. L. McConnell RAMC S.R. promulgated. Sentence to be discussed down a. The transport proceeds tonight.	/MMS.

#353 Wt. W2344/1454 700,000 5/15 D. D. & L. A.D.S.S./Forms/C. 2118.

Army Form C. 2118.

VOL XI (7)

WAR DIARY
or
INTELLIGENCE SUMMARY.
(Erase heading not required.)

Place	Date	Hour	Summary of Events and Information	Remarks and references to Appendices
CORBIE.	31st		July 1916	
			72nd F.A. entrained at AILLY. 73rd entrained at HANGEST 8 am	
			74th F.A. entrained at PICQUIGNY 9.10 am.	
			72nd F.A. detrained MERICOURT f. { MORLAN COURT Been stu / Sur Upper COPSE Tent stu }	
			73rd F.A. detrained VECQUEMONT f. { SAILLY-LE-SEC Been stu / Sur ins COPSE Tent stu }	
			74th F.A. detrained MERICOURT f. { Bois du Taillis Been stu / Sur Lower COPSE. Tent stu }	
			Adms. office closed 10 am. CHIPILLON reopened CORBIE same time. Report to Sur COPSE, the main clearing station for the XIII Corps, a large place, with the tent divisions of 10 & 12 Fd Ambs.	

Edward P Burroughs Col
ADMS 24th Div
31.7.16.

24 Army Form C. 2118.

WAR DIARY
INTELLIGENCE SUMMARY.
(Erase heading not required.)

A.D.M.S
24 DIVISION
VOL. XII - AUGUST
1916

August 1916.

COMMITTEE FOR THE
MEDICAL HISTORY OF THE WAR
Date -5 OCT 1916

Army Form C. 2118.

WAR DIARY

INTELLIGENCE SUMMARY

— ADMS 24 DIVISION —
VOL. XII.

Place	Date	Hour	Summary of Events and Information	Remarks and references to Appendices
CORBIE	August 1916			
	1st		By car to DIVE COPSE. To be arrangements of main dressing station. Came by Hqrs XIII Corps at ETINEHEM. Saw ADMS explained ops. and Corps requirements. Joined division Hqrs L73 & L74. Spoke to take over the Chateau at CORBIE as the Corps rest station. Completed this system. Very hot though. Rising to great heights & deepness.	
"	2nd		Visited C.R.S. Left CORBIE at 3 pm for L2808 (Happy Valley) past 62 D. where part of the H.Q. is to be quartered. Very dry and dusty. Intense bombardment during night 2/3rd to E & camp accompanied apparently by destruction of some ammunition depôts (French). To ADS at Sappers Corner. Held L & Nests. Saw three or 4 motor ambulance exchanges. Considerably matters FDSM & Citadel. Hqs 2nd & 5th Divisions to be arranged. Examined collection of casualties. Much shelling during the night. Visited 72nd.	
HAPPYVALLEY	3rd		To General Review of Sandpits - Huns de collin Hqs 73rd Bde in Happy Valley Camps. Good site. Much cleaning up. 72nd & 73rd	
	4th		Rain here. Citadel, to MDS, who received about the remnant of wounded dead at BERNAFA of TRÔNES wood. to the depressing effect upon young soldiers. 7th xiii Corps about this same when they proceed to gain orders to the stream in line & lovely the	
	5th			

Army Form C. 2118.

WAR DIARY
INTELLIGENCE SUMMARY.
(Erase heading not required.)

VOL XII - (2)

Place	Date	Hour	Summary of Events and Information	Remarks and references to Appendices
Happy Valley	5th	—	To XIV & 5th Corps to see Gl. 7 & 5 Lt Wood about making inspection for digging practice to wear. Contradictions in garage and eucalyptus examples inside of every minute of hope. 200 trench & stand-up & then running to Kitspons etc. I'm sent up to THOMAS hunt. The XIII Corps were trying to see if any of the old nets in powder an ethnic cable & put them up to the trench in the hut run to travel long generation of quick lines also stand up. This divn is keen in trains as unable to be kind up at the front at present. 2 Cavalry Chatline trees Corps but Station. This place requires a Cat charge to side coin at all completed there an an plate known & jerks to any Compres where an extensive front divn & two trunch wire Station. The constant change of units building it, about in to carry ten days present continuity of scheme. The disposal of excreta deep trenches in bad. Incinerator little built at once. Full benefit to own to from itts.	[signature]
Happy Valley	6th	—	Very fine. To Citadel & XIII Corps Hqr. To see APM & 2nd Div. about talking over rate of sandpits to see 72nd & 74th Bdes Divisions.	

WAR DIARY
INTELLIGENCE SUMMARY

Army Form C. 2118.
VOL XII (3)

Place	Date	Hour	Summary of Events and Information	Remarks and references to Appendices
HAPPYVIEW	August 1916			
	7	a	To OATNOY. H.S.S. recaptured by 2nd Division. Fruit stand bent hughe the enemy dropped a few 5.9. shell directly on letter bag & dump station, they set on — which was a dugout & two prisoners. He no injured but one cap of steel helmet. Through day of various raids & perhaps one bright alarm. The bay of day intense. Too flimsy, Owing to shining channel. This H.S. cam. shell & made very good with a little attempt at ease. Good shelling by our artillery themselves to bright prepare trench known as QUIESMONT, by 2nd & 5th Div. the of m brigades the 17th will move tomorrow with a view to taking over from the 2nd Div.	
	8		The 3 bean Division relieved to BRONFAY farm when 72nd & 73rd will remain in reserve. While the 74th sent up an advanced party to BERNAFAY hurt. To train preparatory attack one at 2 p.m. tomorrow. 72nd To find T.E.N.T. Div. turn up advanced party to OATNOY. H.S.S. clear of division at taken over H.G. Fappin Corner (of St CARNOY at 2 pm tomorrow. HQ. 72nd to last with le et Fappin. Circuit I will supply all hursetails overland telenphs etc. for stores.	

Army Form C. 2118.

VOL XII (A)

WAR DIARY
INTELLIGENCE SUMMARY.
(Erase heading not required.)

Place	Date	Hour	Summary of Events and Information	Remarks and references to Appendices
	August 1916			
HAPPY VALLEY	8th		All orders for relief cancelled owing to circumstances. Is do not take over from the 2nd Lieut. 55th Division the arrangement has been taken in entirely change of disposition. Cancelling orders dispatched to all concerned.	
"	9th		Relief of 58th Bn. Kept 9/10th Medical Arrangements to be made almost as under 58th Ku. K.O.S.B.s at 10.30 a.m. to H.Q. 5th Division. O/C saw Lieut. Col. Billson O/C heads. Personnel. Officer at Unit C.O. Billson prior to workers. O.P. 45 — he came to do the same thing concerning the working of the journal there same with regard to working of B.M. Station, finding definite instruction from other officer. Very quiet today but much change.	
CITADEL	10th		Office moved to CITADEL at 9 a.m. A.D.S. BERNAFAY was taken over by 'Berion Division 74th Field Amb. Fr. 72nd Amb. Fr. STIVES' COPSE & SAPPER CORNER took on A.D.S. at C.A.N.V. SAPPER CORNER w/c burst insanitary condition will be improved. Burial division of 72 & 73 Field Ambs. encamped at BRONFAY prior.	
"	11th		Visited H.Q. at MINDEN POST F.18 C.3.4. the A.D.S. at C.A.N.V. where the wounded in they evac. have been released & those cleared by the M.E. along the C.A.N.V-MONTAUBAN Rd. to MINE ALLEY. All the new German trenches in left-hand side of road going N. & detachment of 4 Bom & Beer & House Grade calls to local sick. Very firm & accommodation & sequence dwellings.

HWMS

WAR DIARY

INTELLIGENCE SUMMARY

Army Form C. 2118.

VOL XII (5)

Place	Date	Hour	Summary of Events and Information	Remarks and references to Appendices
CITADEL	August 1916			
	11th		Went to TRONES WOOD. Wood still in a horrible condition with innumerable dead & fragments of humanity. The stalking of the wood both day and night there very dangerous. No suitable spot to use ground for ADS or Regtl aid posts. Communication trench to WATERLOW from my Hd Q exceedingly cramped. No cover. Aid post at the farm can put up about 50 walking & sitting. Very difficult for stretchers. Also ADS at BERNAFAY wood.	
	12th		Sanitary Section moved to CITADEL. As CRE to arrange for evacuation of wounded from our trenches station of the line. Three present arrangements of bringing them lighted down to KUBLIN TRAMWAY the ADS of the Division. A new light railway being constructed to BRIQUETERIE for to be collected together & given a rough clump. Visited CCS Station at CORBIE CHATEAU. Considerable improvement. The Royal Red Cross Huts very materially assist in making the place more comfortable. Also the deep trench latrines have been constructed. Also inside the place have been somewhat improved. The place is not ideal for a CCS station. It has been used as from its position very great. The Area taken over.	
	13th		To ADS. Appre Corbie kept G.B. Island. To Amt Ham made great sanitary improvements in Cooperation with the French Government of BRQY. The sanitary state to be to Sands than the CCS at Heniest. The insanitary condition of former Camp mainly to excrete drainage with filth & maggots visual on a latrine by the adjacent French trench which appears the Commandant promises to get latrine dealt to the French troops.	

2353 Wt. W 25141/1454 700,000 5/15 D.D.&L. A.D.S.S./Forms/C. 2118.

WAR DIARY / INTELLIGENCE SUMMARY

Army Form C. 2118.
VOL XII (6)

Place	Date	Hour	Summary of Events and Information	Remarks and references to Appendices
OT & DEL	August 1916			
	13th		the & smallest amount necessary if judging from the appearance of the ground the pits are very abundant. It is remarkable that the men lie down in a few days become immune. To Batt. 575th Co at Mont Peronne. Lorry of gout ende landays given by Lord Cur. Through HARDECOURT which in attempts advanced up to Batts. BERNAFAY WOOD, which is in fair deep dug out formed sign which is very heps in Bn. 9/16 in a huge dugout contacts shelter the Bn. for car is in a very bad condition which made the removal of the wounded very difficult. Dug out very dark but provided with outer lamps of men. Very wounded and severely buried lorries laying about & fell victim of enemy description. The lines of ctrin wire a very dangerous during at the instant of this ammunition which is lying about in great quantities.	
	14th		At MINDENPOSTE Batt C.M. MOIR to some ammunition & high explosives of the 8th Rev situs an been dumped at the dive of the dressing station. by B R.N.F.N. from Batt. Apple Corner. Then afterwards Batt D.M.3/IN-TRENCH no. occupied Mo. 652 to Killed & IMD wounded, also Lieut W.G. Knight Rem C. 73rd to Brit. who was awaked had his members fragmin. Porce in the very burst occurred which 1 Sgt ten killed & me private wounded of the 73rd W. Imp.	

Army Form C. 2118.

VOL XII (7)

WAR DIARY
or
INTELLIGENCE SUMMARY.
(Erase heading not required.)

Place	Date	Hour	Summary of Events and Information	Remarks and references to Appendices
CITKASEL			August 1916	
	15th		To BRONFAY FARM & MINDEN POST. Issues to Att BERNAFAY WOOD sent to front line then to maintain. Gun pits section of trenches it end of TRISH ALLEY handed to infantry? Working parties of L.S. Regt C. Coy of brass turned on to construct RST to rapidly & further used RE Infantry. Increased for use in T.S.S dug outs. Very heavy trains during the night. French steel dugouts drawn at RE dump despatched to new RTO. at Carlepont. T. Edmonds. Recent appreciation of situation issued of F.C.M.	
	16th		7th to 9th Septmts for gallant conduct in attack on Ridge 12/13. August 74th to 92nd to ditto in attack on enemy trenches. Many casualties in respect of 16/17.	
	17th		To Supper Corin Bridges from CARNOY & MINDENPOST. Ridges to extern the 3rd division adjacent to R on on at CARNOY. On large numbers of casualties they be expected if the 2nd division does not receive the ... Art. with them to CARNOY. the holes in known to enemy to supply reinforcements to Att. in BERNAFAY & BRIQUETERIE. Blnd on Canal works of the 3rd Division ... T CANNON at lock 26.45.	

WAR DIARY
INTELLIGENCE SUMMARY
(Erase heading not required.)

Army Form C. 2118.
VOL XII (8)

Place	Date	Hour	Summary of Events and Information	Remarks and references to Appendices
CITADEL	17th		August – 1916. Capt. F.J. WAVER came att. 1st N. STAFFORDS. Killed by shell at Bn. H.Q. at TREUI BOISS. Lt. Kane Browne detailed in relief.	
"	18th		Enemy attack in enemy position at 4.45 p.m. Capt. H.M. NEWRID signed at 8.30 p.m. Succeeded in pushing our attempt to BERNAFAY wood H.B.S down the ripples. Enemy's M.G. & M.G.E shut the delay. In 3 or 4 hours were fully occupied all the Infts 18/19, and further hours for the upwards had full retirement to the entry in my different 4 P/Cs & 5 S6 O.R. balky rounds of the line in from strength BRUNFAY from ave 18 6. Dan 19th - Piers Commencement of operation. Rein O. Brown in Killed 1 O. wounded 30. O.R. Killed 3, wounded 22.	
"	19th		To A.D.S. CHAMAS when they have been very busy during the night. Capt. S.M. McLAR, R.A.M.C. att. 2nd LEINSTERS wounded. To assist him believes early this morning to go & permit to R.D.S.S. How assistance began. & convoy evacuation and did very good service in clearing the BRIQUETTERIE. A.D.S. Bernafay wood by noon.. BRIQUETTERIE functional later.	

Army Form C. 2118.

VOL XII (1)

WAR DIARY
INTELLIGENCE SUMMARY.
(Erase heading not required.)

Place	Date	Hour	Summary of Events and Information	Remarks and references to Appendices
BITRTEL	August 1916		To CRANSY MIRDEN POST. Quiet day after the attack.	
"	21st		Air battle started at 4.30 p.m. today. Made all arrangements for heavy casualties. During the attack the name of personnel at R.A.P. BERNAFAY wood of 2.0. & 42 O.R. was increased to 0.4. O.R. 108. & at the A.D.S. Briqueterie fm 0.2. O.R. 48 increased to 0.3 & O.R. 108. Evacuation about 110 O.R. prisoners, all disposal. Asked 107 Fd Amb 20th Fd Amb to come to office to that division. At 10 p.m. telephone message that reinforcements of 100 stretcher was urgently needed. Sending writer to O.C. 72nd Fd Amb also in similar telegr for Bernafay farm.	8.30 pm
"	22nd		Down in the relieved by 20th div in today. Evacn b. A.D.S.S. former my place cleaning Casualties. The army lorries during the night for Brigade was greatly exaggerated. The casualties were eventually small up to 12 noon being 0.4. O.R. 176 only were reported from Bernafay farm (W.W) + known dressing station town opere. (Stretcher cases.) The X M.O.C. failed to evacuate Bernafay wood A.D.S that was cleared by wheeled stretcher & horse ambulance to on the plenum mearim. I don't but was obtained on the shed when the stretcher case await the cars. O.R. 2. killed 74— Sgt Rent — to me pakent. Unst Unknown.	

#353 Wt W4544/1454 700,000 5/15 D.D.&L. A.D.S.S./Forms/C. 2118.

Army Form C. 2118.

VOL XII (10)

WAR DIARY
or
INTELLIGENCE SUMMARY.
(Erase heading not required.)

Place	Date	Hour	Summary of Events and Information	Remarks and references to Appendices
Forked Tree Camp	23rd		August — 1916.	
			Division Hqrs. moved to Billa Camp this morn. Brot.	
			Evacuation from Aug. 12th to 19th — O.79. OR 17.30	
			Sick evacuation " " " O.12. OR 99.	
	24th		To hosiers. Col detailed for duty with X M.A.C. from 72nd Fd Amb.	
BUIRE	25th		Div Hqrs. moved to BUIRE — D.26.a.8.5. & Adv H.E. 13.14.(62d) at 9.30 am. hrs in 16th Corps area. Visited 57 and 14th Corps. & the test division of the Div Fd Ambs at CORBIE & DIVE Copse. All detachments to report units at ask.	
"	26th		In SRD & XV Corps at HEILLY — to new area SRDNI. to SRD NS 14th Div. is taking over 72nd Fd Amb. Reported have complete at 8.15 pm. & SRD NS at D.30.a.(62d)	
"	27th		SRDNS. to the O.C. 44th Fd Amb. to take pre on its forward area at LOUVENCOURT. Visited Buire & reprimanded and Posts at Crucifix & A.D.S. at Querrey. Very heavy rain & considerable shelling.	
"	28th		Visited HPnS XIV div. re taking over. and Pole camps with Autyonts in the afternoon. Condition of camps rapidly improving. Shelter & baths to A ward latrines being the chief. Considerable amount of diarrhea about. Squadron of Hies. during the stat. Ambulance to ennuy disposition to charge flu M.S.

Army Form C. 2118.

VOL XII (11)

WAR DIARY
INTELLIGENCE SUMMARY
(Erase heading not required.)

Place	Date	Hour	Summary of Events and Information	Remarks and references to Appendices
BOIRY	29th		He also took over the 33rd Div. part of the line, stationing the 33rd Div. be hvre. the tent but division from each ambulance sent to XV Corps main dressing station for duty.	
"	30th		Bdn. provided in relief of 14th & 33rd Divisions the 2 ambulances viz. 72nd & M47572 MONTAUBAN Rd F.G.A. 3.D. with A.D.S. at Quarry S.22.c.0.5. & Rly train pass at Crucifix S.230.6.7. & Green DMP. relieving 44th Div. Amb. The 78th Fd. Amb. relieving 48 Fd Amb. at F.7 d.9.8. & 74th Fd. Amb. will relieve 42nd Fd Amb. at E.5.d.00. Weather dry but torrents of rain. So 33rd H.Q. to As.Ams. S. le Mere. Our div. in takes over from 14 & 33rd divn.	
"	31st		Hq. Div. moved to E.11. Quesnil Late Hq. 33rd Div. Vindlui 73rd Fd Amb. at Walking wounded dressing station, while there the enemy dropped about a dozen 4.5 shells about 100 yards rear & encrust the D.S. he comalties whate considering the traffic was unnrable. A map by Captain TH. Scott Nam C. Staff S. Div of the govint of the levent approximation of the 12th to the 22nd August is enclosed.	

Lieut Colonel AMBrowell 2d o RM

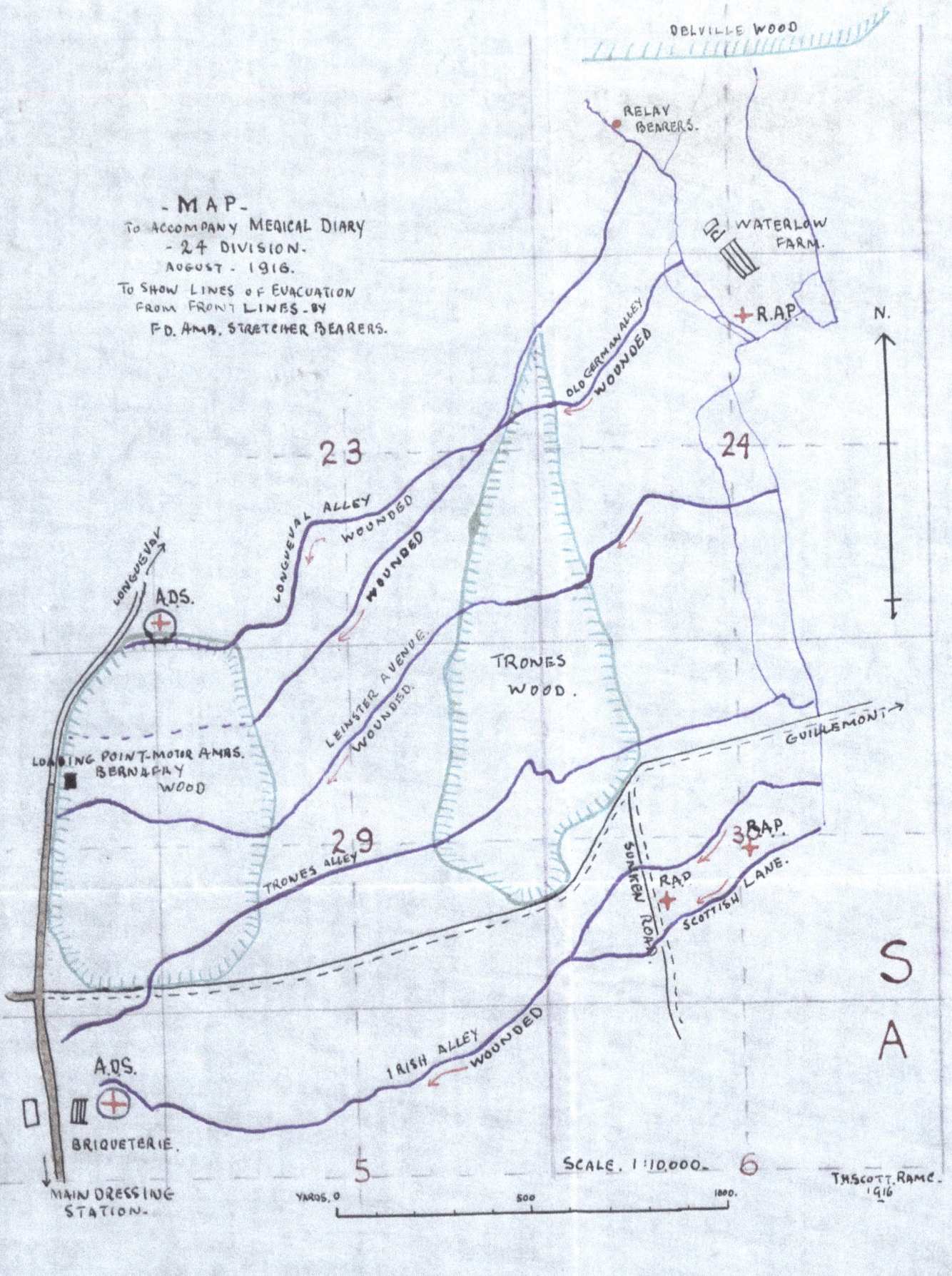

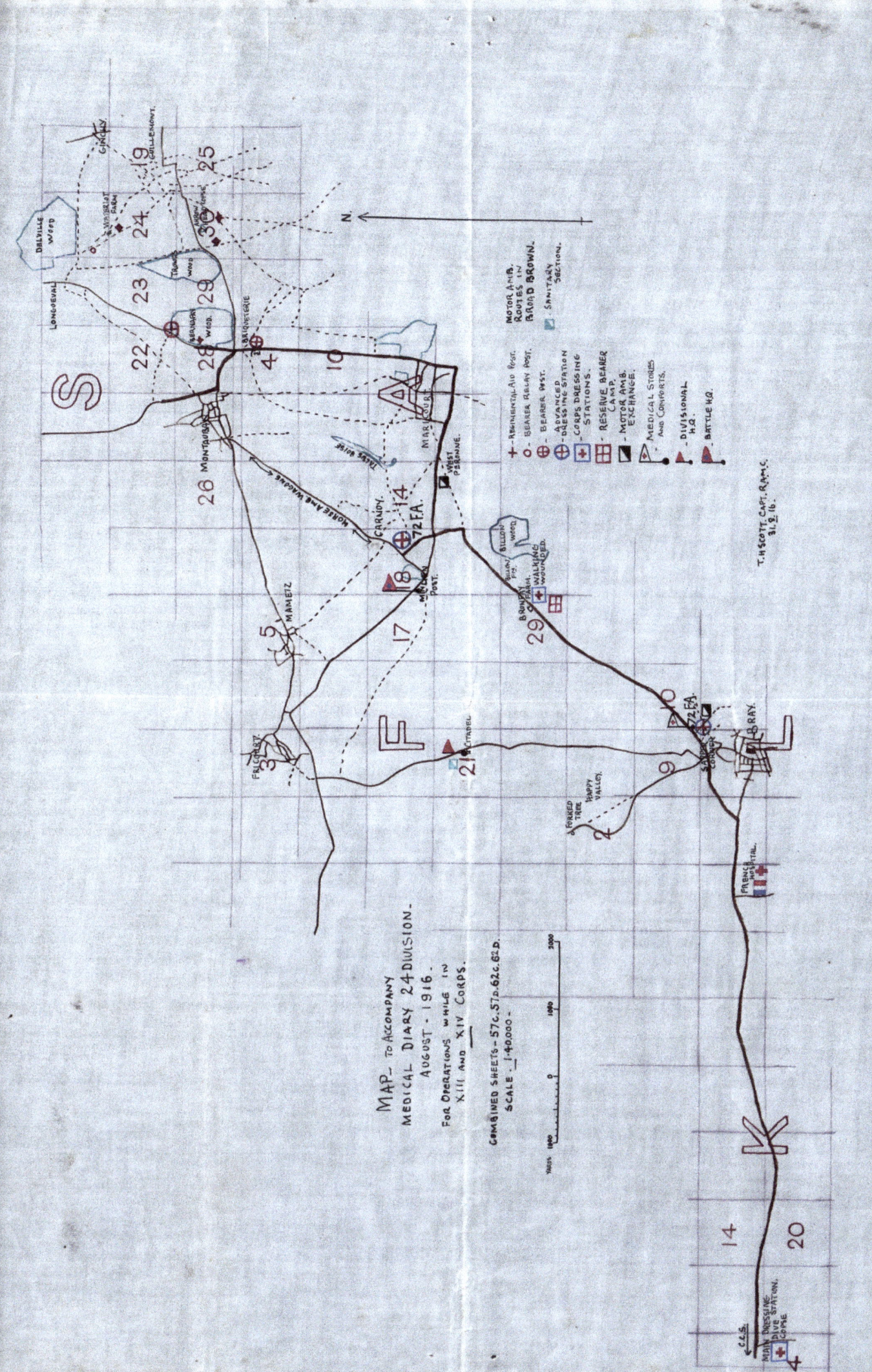

WAR DIARY
or
INTELLIGENCE SUMMARY.

Army Form C. 2118.

24 / 140/1724 Vol 13

A.D.M.S.
24 DIVISION
VOL XIII - SEPTEMBER
- 1916 -

A DMS Sep 13
72 " 13
73 " 13
74 " 12
41 San Sec 13

WITH 3 MAPS

COMMITTEE FOR THE
MEDICAL HISTORY OF THE WAR
Date 30 OCT. 1916

Army Form C. 2118.

WAR DIARY
INTELLIGENCE SUMMARY.
(Erase heading not required.)

A.D.M.S. 24 DIVISION
VOL XIII (SEPTEMBER) (1)

Instructions regarding War Diaries and Intelligence Summaries are contained in F.S. Regs., Part II and the Staff Manual respectively. Title pages will be prepared in manuscript.

Place	Date	Hour	Summary of Events and Information	Remarks and references to Appendices
Sd ALBERT E. 11 Central	September 1918. 1st	7a	To Amiens to the M.Gen. S.T.S., M.O.i.T.H.S., B.M.S. and F.B.&.i.O. The team had made the start from the Gravity S'Liz. C.O.S. The A.D.S. very bad. The motor ambulances on route to back the A.D.E. but the horse ambulances a wait 6 hours. Present very valuable instead worked incessantly during the night. 3 i/i Apps. In total a i+ a few field which has not been shelled lately. 2 a morgue tents with the usual heavy batteries near. The convention up to now today.	
"	2nd		Visited 74th Fd Amb. which has opened at about E.6.6.87. in Bellevue Farm. Into Corle of marquees. Trams to open dump at S.16.D.3.5 with R.E. to see what work is to done there to shelter accommodation to be case of an advance. This have telephone with from a good chimney station. Can walk up to Ivan today. Wm. O.C. OR 168. Sketches from O.13. OR 150. Their firm shelter have been shelt on by the enemy. Affecting this i/t & 12.00 a fusilier who was being exposed bother gas have had to be kept quiet for ½ after effects.	
"	3rd		with FB and Lt. XX Corps. Rest Station and then to Walking Wounded Clearing Station. A gentleman of rich beauty of their division our sin at this station. Compliment to CR.S. that comm. 2 complete Capon. have being sent on by 73rd Fd. Amb. From Lt. 72nd Lt. Amb. £ H.M.M.B.T.S. in opinion of evening examined of wounded going very well. the horse ambulance so clearing the dust of the wounded, have proved of the greatest value when the weather is their cloudily wet.	

WAR DIARY
INTELLIGENCE SUMMARY

Army Form C. 2118.

Place	Date	Hour	Summary of Events and Information	Remarks and references to Appendices
(Attock) E.H. Central	September 1916			
	4th		About 5.15" train in. Talking over from the train in. 61st had told me the Benan way but at Green Swamp, and where the Rest is Grassy. The 72? Fd Amb MAMETZ with stated all well. Making arrangements transport to increase the endowment of accommodation as the situation of those entrained is by no means safe. Very heavy dew showing the nights to very cold. My heavy mills came safe.	
"	5th		Writing faring all round. Train in snow mopped out into districts, where are sanitary inspection who make reports to the Officer i/c of the districts. Sanitation of camps within the area should under the O.C. 41st Sanitary Section. Camps in canvas not as yet occupied by our trained troops or not. In canvas out by the O.C. units. A three days ex. In Italian 122 Camps have been inspected. Incursions erected & larger mounts of train previous on being built. The heavy rain makes them work very difficult but with a great draught & great deal can be done all the train in are out of the line. The 72? Fd Amb came out at M. Mon Colony Infirmary.	
"	6th		The 73 w & 74 Fd Amb in Colony. move by road & rail today with their Brigades to their best- area. Fine today but cool.	MMcS

WAR DIARY
INTELLIGENCE SUMMARY

Army Form C. 2118.

Place	Date	Hour	Summary of Events and Information	Remarks and references to Appendices
(AILLY) E-11 Central 7	September 1916		At 3.4.6: this morning, the enemy dropped four bombs in the vicinity of the Camp. Causing considerable disorganisation & disturbing of the Eye. Arti's intricate, & likely indicating knotty other which lasted about an hour.	
AILLY.			Left Camp at about 9.15. & on AMIENS arrived at AILLY (& have Electric) Blue STH G are situated. Visited villages of no particular merit, saw loss of it on in the centre of the area. Violin & Scarce.	
	8th		With HQ & find & AVLT to visit - the encampment & country opened & off leaside for about 2000 troops. 6.0. & 150 O.R. daily to stay 48 hours. Lt Col. establish 72 at EUCURT with encampment brigade in vicinity. 73 at BOUGNON. and 74 at ERGNIES. He almost total absence of motored for christians which almost invariably happens when a division run back to rest. Staying here in their area, He h. v.t Bundles is buying what won't Carms he can get - to make decent He first latrine invention, france etc & then Woodeners washing appliance.	

Army Form C. 2118.

WAR DIARY
or
INTELLIGENCE SUMMARY.
(Erase heading not required.)

Place	Date	Hour	Summary of Events and Information	Remarks and references to Appendices
AILLY	September 1918			
	9th		With R.A. at Sanitary Section. Visit. has improvement camps at MOUFLERS. also BAVEHON. 73rd Lt Amb. CONG. & Capt. Bird of EVCOURT 72nd Amb. Fine but autumn hits on Roads. The diarrhoea is diminishing.	
"	10th		Fell cold. To 13th Middlesex Regt. at MOUFLENS. 5 to 7 men of a bombing coming behind hut fill & first aid. In the recent operation 3 have been killed & 1 wounded. a somewhat large percentage of casualties. To ENGMES. to 74th Lt Amb. situated in a very fine farm, in the centre of a old ROMAN camp. Quite a good place with plenty hutting.	
"	11th		Summer routine.	
"	12th		" "	
"	13th		Trains to PONT NOYELLES 4th Army gas school to hear Gas Lecture. Then got dir. to visit the 3 Fd Ambulances. Very wet & cold.	
"	14th		Summer routine.	
"	15th		To BOUCHON. 73rd Fd Amb.	

WWS

Army Form C. 2118.

WAR DIARY
or
INTELLIGENCE SUMMARY.
(Erase heading not required.)

Instructions regarding War Diaries and Intelligence Summaries are contained in F.S. Regs., Part II. and the Staff Manual respectively. Title pages will be prepared in manuscript.

Place	Date	Hour	Summary of Events and Information	Remarks and references to Appendices
AILLY	16th		Series of inspections…. Fireline incidence greatly improved.	
"	17th		To L.O.N.C. Hy. x. Corps. All ambulance to Cairo to be taken over by the Division. Holus, Ops returning.	
"	18th		Received. H.Q. to MENERIES, all motors by Corps transport. Preparation for move. Very heavy rain.	
"	19th		All original operations cancelled. H.Q. to BRUAY. Temporary. 72nd Fd Amb to VALHUON. 73rd Fd Amb at MANIFS les MINES & 74th Fd Amb at PERNES. Lieut 36 B France. Capt AILLY at 11.45 am rierourgon for 4 Corps H.Q. at RANCHICOURT, & then on to BRUAY.	
BRUAY	20th		The heavy of the Ambulance ears & motor cycles to our patrol in J thorets & front line hospitals. There are no sick awaiting & my fd amb an hung up for lack of the means of collecting sick. The men have gone hungry for lack of ambulance were. The ORMS 63rd Manit. Tries in vain please text fd Amb at our disposal for the admission of sick but the gods is to get them these.	
	21st		73rd Fd Amb to KEYSTRIKE with 75 L.O.S. Men knowin as to whom the 9th Fd Amb will relieve the 21st Fd amb at & 9nd SERVINS & the 74th Fd Amb into relieve the 12th Fd amb at Grand SERVINS & the South African Fd Amb at ESTRÉE COUCHUS into Fd Amb with releving the South African Fd Amb at ESTRÉE COUCHUS.	MWS

2353 Wt W3.H/1458 700,000 5/15 D.D.&L. A.D.S.S./Forms/C.2118.

Army Form C. 2118.

WAR DIARY
or
INTELLIGENCE SUMMARY.
(Erase heading not required.)

Instructions regarding War Diaries and Intelligence Summaries are contained in F.S. Regs., Part II. and the Staff Manual respectively. Title pages will be prepared in manuscript.

Place	Date	Hour	Summary of Events and Information	Remarks and references to Appendices
BRIGY.	22		Sept. 1916. The motor ambulance lorries from the 50th Div. had met the motor cyclists from 8th IV Corps. traffic. Routes known the new general and motor	Stables
	23		& 9th Kiarin.	
	24		General routines	
	25		" "	
	26		" "	
	27		Left BRIGY. for new area. S.A.y. at CEMARAIM. L'ABBAI. with G.O.C. to visit the 8 Fd Amb. There are distinctive in very good French huts. & there is an Main hospital of eight beds at 7&T for Amb. L.E.4. VE MTS has found up & very comfortable where lifts came are fixed.	
	28		MONT er KAY. when 7&T Fd Amb has an advanced dressing station in a barn with & fine cellars. A very good end grid for Ambulance Cars. The wounded an brought down by light trollery at night.	
	29		To CABARET ROUGE. Advanced dressing station. 7&T Fd Amb clear 130 grid. For Front line but with every long carry by hand trench to hospital corner. up to kilns in Cairo, Low corner. The motor James Stretcher Carriages have	

Army Form C. 2118.

WAR DIARY
or
INTELLIGENCE SUMMARY.
(Erase heading not required.)

Instructions regarding War Diaries and Intelligence
Summaries are contained in F. S. Regs., Part II.
and the Staff Manual respectively. Title pages
will be prepared in manuscript.

Place	Date	Hour	Summary of Events and Information	Remarks and references to Appendices
COMBLAIN L'ABBÉ	September, 1916. 29th		Men adapted to the trench by approximating the tin which what unable, then take part in a harrow chick road when receiving. In day out	
	30th		of the MDS was very front of the waiting shed is be strengthened throughout. Line entire. Visited 73rd Tatrouldwa & TST COL HIN H 14-5 H RE. Very few dug outs & good site accommodation. Improvements can only receive thereinto cover at night.	

J. W. Burner
Lt B Fr
Col.
ADMS

"A" Form
MESSAGES AND SIGNALS.
Army Form C. 2121

SECRET

TO: ~~O.C. 70, 72, 74~~ ~~FIELD AMBS~~ ~~HQ G~~ ~~ARMS~~
~~9 DIVISION~~

Sender's Number	Day of Month	In reply to Number	
O.O. 76	20.9.16		A A A

The following relief will take place at a date to be notified later aaa 72 F.A. will relieve 27 F.A. 9 DIVISION 73 F.A. the 28 F.A. 74 F.A. the SOUTH AFRICAN F.A. of 9 DIVISION aaa O.C. 72 & 73 F.As. will detail advance parties to proceed forthwith to their respective F.As. aaa The officer i/c each party will forward a report as early as possible to this office on the working, personnel etc of the F.A. to which he proceeds aaa The ~~boots~~ advance parties will not return to their units until relief completed aaa 74 F.A. will form the DRS aaa acknowledge aaa

From: Adml. 24 Div
Time: 2.20 pm.

Cx 320

SECRET

Preliminary
Medical Dispositions
The Division
on taking over line – Sept. 20th 1916.

MAP REFERENCE
sheets 36B, 36c
1:40,000.

ADVANCED DRESSING STATIONS.
1. MONT ST ELOY   (F.8. sheet 51c N.E. 1:20,000) – 73 F.A.
2. CABARET ROUGE (S.13. 36c)   – 72 F.A.
3. HOSPITAL CORNER (X.14.b.1. 36B)   – 72 F.A.
4. ABLAIN ST NAZAIRE (X.10. 36B)   – 73 F.A.

DRESSING STATIONS and FIELD AMBULANCES
72 F.A. LES 4 VENTS   (W.9. central)
73 F.A. GRAND SERVINS (Q.34. central)
74 F.A. ESTRÉE-CAUCHIE (W.2)

DIVISIONAL REST STATION
CAUCOURT   (V.5)   74 FIELD AMB.

41st SANITARY SECTION
CAMBLAIN-L'ABBÉ   (W.22)

DIVISIONAL BATHS & LAUNDRY.
1. CAMBLAIN-L'ABBÉ
2. CAUCOURT.
3. GOUY-SERVINS   (Q.35.d)
4. VILLERS-AU-BOIS (X.19)
5. HOUDAIN   (J.33) – LAUNDRY.

20.9.16

Capt. D.A.D.M.S.

740/1814

Oct 1916

24th Division — A.D.M.S.

COMMITTEE FOR THE
MEDICAL HISTORY OF THE WAR
Date -9 DEC. 1915

CONFIDENTIAL

D.A.G. 3rd Echelon.

Please find enclosed herewith War Diary for 24th Divn - Medical Services - for October 1916.

24 D.H.Q.,
1/11/16.

Leslie Capt D.A.D.M.S.
for Colonel,
A.D.M.S.

Army Form C. 2118.

WAR DIARY
INTELLIGENCE SUMMARY.
(Erase heading not required.)

A.D.M.S.
24 DIVISION
VOL. XIV.
OCTOBER 1916.

— WITH MAP —

Place	Date	Hour	Summary of Events and Information	Remarks and references to Appendices
				A D M S Vol #4
				72 3 cards " 14
				73 " " 14
				74 " " 13
				Sanitary " 14

Army Form C. 2118.

WAR DIARY
or
INTELLIGENCE SUMMARY.
(Erase heading not required.)

A.D.M.S. VOL XIV.
2nd DIVISION - (OCTOBER)

Place	Date	Hour	Summary of Events and Information	Remarks and references to Appendices
CAMBLAIN L'ABBÉ	1st		Work at the four battns is in hand. The endeavour has been known by bearers to provide dryness, undressing & dressing rooms, drying rooms, & entertainment of the army nature.	
"	2nd		General routine	
"	3rd		" "	
"	4th		General routine to D.M.S. 1st Army. Very heavy rain. The intention of the C.R.A. is to represent officers from each of the 4 Austr Inftde very diff with do hosp units to do finished artillery the hospitals but at the present time & depending continues the hostpital but at the present upon their supports while the division is in the SOMME area from today. Heavy Lorries or exact collecting Posts. Private cars of the 5th & 6th field Ambulance in in working order. The object is to train a large numbers of men in treatment of wounded.	
"	5th		Read Rep. F. 150/2nd. Proceeded on leave. Ebou E. 74.2 by Amb.	
"	6th		General routine	
"	7th		General routine	

[signature]

WAR DIARY or INTELLIGENCE SUMMARY

Army Form C. 2118.

Place	Date	Hour	Summary of Events and Information	Remarks and references to Appendices
CAMBLAIN L'ABBÉ	October 1916			
	8th		Very wet. Tents & 72nd Spare the improvements, especially connected with drainage.	
	9th		Inspected 2 Hos. of ECOP. There by duck boards from County to Base Hos. in the BETHUNE-ARRAS Road. A distance of three miles. A very long carry for stretcher bearers. The Base Hos. is very good. Ample accommodation for 24 stretchers in deep steel huts dug outs served by a light railway to HEZOP. to evacuate the wounded. Would be connected with FDS during active operation.	
	10th		Rode to STS. EUCOURT. Where huts & drainage scheme are actively progressing. Beds in stretcher uprights ready for patients.	
	11th		Rode to 73rd Fd Amb. Grand SERVICES. Great Improvement & arms inspections taken. Huts erected. Last rails for existing scheme in heart heavy. Went to wire fed. Considered granted which make a great improvement to the Comfort of the sick. The ambulance finds the stores most useful.	
	12th		Cases. Cold & dull. Strong wind.	

WAR DIARY or INTELLIGENCE SUMMARY.

Army Form C. 2118.

A.D.M.S.
24th DIVISION.

Place	Date	Hour	Summary of Events and Information	Remarks and references to Appendices
CAMBLAIN L'ABBE	16/10/16		A.D.M.S. 24th Division went on leave from this date. - Duties taken over by Staff. A.M. Rose R.A.M.C. - Inspection of Baths at VILLERS-AU-BOIS: - Arrangements made in order to prevent depletion of reserve stock of underclothing at Divisional Laundry at HOUDAIN.	An Rose Lieut R.A.M.C. An.R.
CAMBLAIN L'ABBE	17/10/16		Received 24 Divisional Chaplain's Order No 101. - Prices of Battalions & Personnel in works of 72nd, 73rd, 74th Field Ambulances requested from each Ambulance to facilitate housing cases of Area when relieved by incoming Division. Nothing unusual to report. - Weather rather cold. - Some rain. - General health of troops good.	An.R.
CAMBLAIN L'ABBE	18/10/16		Inspection of Divisional Laundry at HOUDAIN. - The erection of new store room and drying Room are proceeding. - Inspection of Baths at CAUCOURT where improvements are also being carried out, the dressing room is	An.R.
CAMBLAIN L'ABBE	19/10/16		completed and the dressing room is in course of completion. - The clothing store is satisfactory. - Weather very wet.	An.R.
CAMBLAIN L'ABBE	20/10/16		By Car to BRAQUEMONT to see A.D.M.S. 1st Division - Question taken over by him and arranged date of taking over. - Weather also rainy. Millicent Sunshine	An.R.

WAR DIARY or INTELLIGENCE SUMMARY

Army Form C. 2118.

Army: 2nd Division

October 1916.

Place	Date	Hour	Summary of Events and Information	Remarks and references to Appendices
CAMBLAIN L'ABBE	21/10/16	—	Visited A Section 1st Corps Rest Station, LABREUVIERE - also 1st Corps Officers Rest Station AIRE.	McRae MacNamara
	22/10/16		Met D.D.M.S. 1st Corps at AIRE. - General health of troops good - nothing unusual to report. - weather dry and very cold - brilliant sunshine. - Nothing unusual to report. - weather cold and dry. - Health of troops good.	McR
CAMBLAIN L'ABBE	23/10/16		Visit from ADMS 1st Canadian Division - regarding taking over of the area - Attends arranges location CCS and dug-	McR
CAMBLAIN L'ABBE	24/10/16		Arranges for transfer of sick remaining in Dressing Stations and Divisional Rest Station to incoming Canadian Field Ambulances - weather cold and wet.	McR
CAMBLAIN L'ABBE	25/10/16		Took by DADMS 2y Division to hand over transport & personnel - Dressing Station etc. - No 2 Canadian Fd Amb. relieved No 72nd Fd. Amb.	McR
"	26		Returned from leave FNB. General routine. Canadian San Section relieved No 41 San Section. No 72nd Fd Amb. relieved No 136th Fd Amb. at Blangmont (40th Div).	FNB
"	27.		S.H.V. left for BAVAY. 9.30 am. No 1 Canadian Fd Amb relieved 73rd Fd Amb.	
"	28		No 3 Canadian Fd Amb relieved No 74th Fd Amb.	FNB

WAR DIARY
INTELLIGENCE SUMMARY

Army Form C. 2118.

Place	Date	Hour	Summary of Events and Information	Remarks and references to Appendices
BRUAY	28		October 1916.	
			5th G. 1st Corps visited office	
	29		No 74 & Field Amb. relieved No 137th Fd Amb. at LABOURIERE.	
"	30th		5th G. home to BRAQUEMONT. at 10 a.m. No 73rd Fd Amb. relieved No. 136	
BRAQUEMONT			Fd Amb. at Very hot + stormy. Southerly gale.	
			Went greater [?] Fd Amb. at their place in School very good buildings.	
			Stay was showing. Inspected 69 F.B. here at NOEUX LES MINES. the morning.	
"	31st		Visited No 73rd Ft Amb. Swimming started in gate School here, my first recommendation	
			Also No 72nd Fd Amb. in the Temp school. accommodation also very good.	
			Made stores arrangements in late area General COMBRAIN L'ABBE	
			attacks.	

Jennings Burner [?] Col.
CDMS in [?]

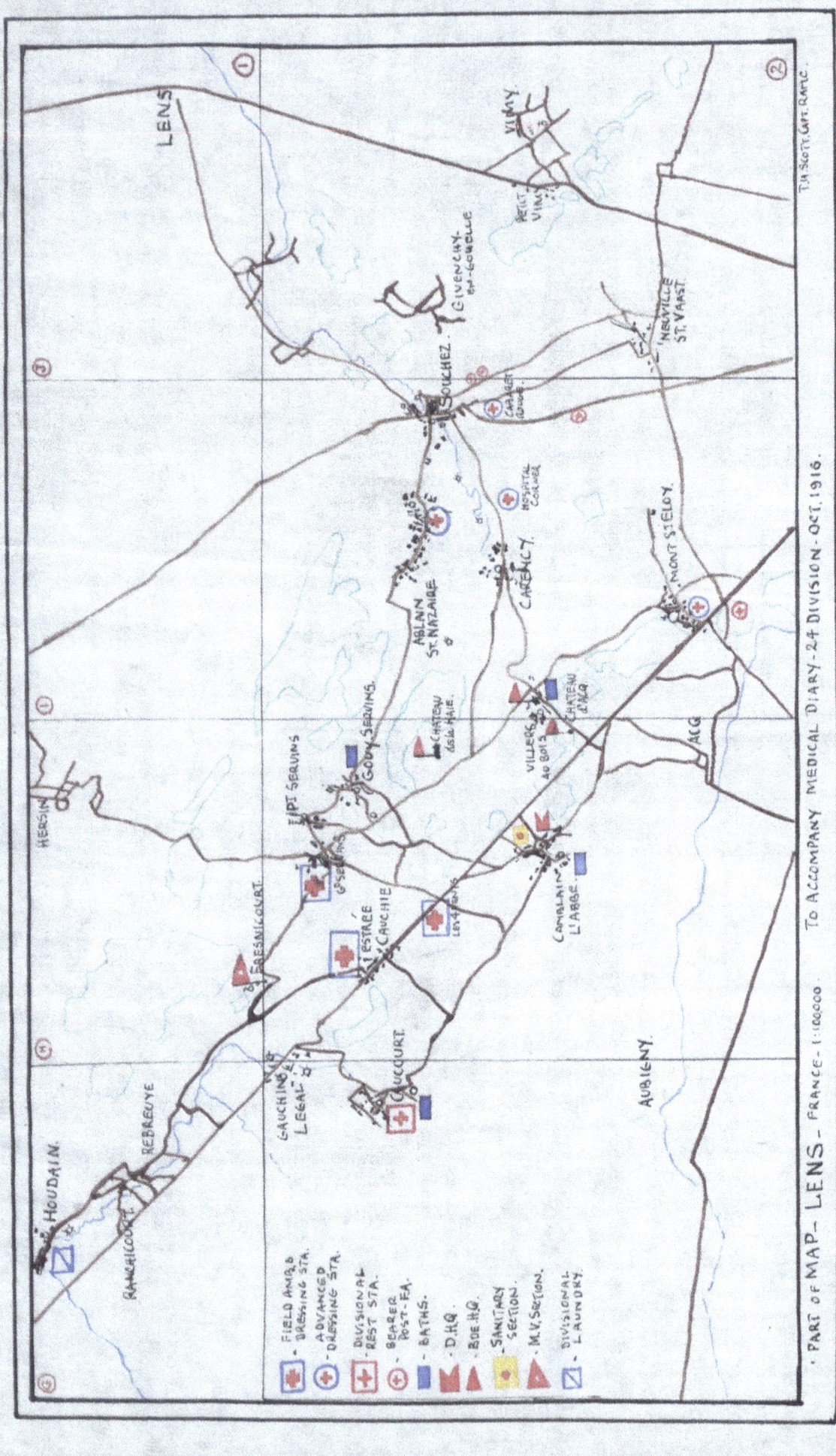

Secret.  R.A.M.C. Operation Order
No 81. by
Colonel F. R. Buswell A.M.S. A.D.M.S. 24 Div

Copy No. 6

22nd October 1916.

Gx123/13
22/10/16

1. The 24th Division (less Artillery) will relieve the 40th Division (less Artillery) in the line.
2. The 72nd Field Ambulance will relieve the 135th Field Ambulance on 27th October.
3. The 74th Field Ambulance will relieve the 137th Field Ambulance on 29th October.
4. The 73rd Field Ambulance will relieve the 136th Field Ambulance on 30th October.
5. Advance parties will proceed under arrangements to be made between Os.C.
6. All details of reliefs will be arranged direct between Os.C. concerned.
7. Reliefs to be completed by noon on respective dates.
8. 41st Sanitary Section will relieve 83rd Sanitary Section on 27th October; an advance party will proceed on 26th October to take over.
9. Completion of all reliefs to be reported to this Office.
10. Os.C. Field Ambulances will arrange for Ambulance transport to accompany their respective Brigades on the march.
11. Acknowledge.

22/10/16

T. Scott
Capt. R.A.M.C.
D.A.D.M.S. 24th Division

Issued at 11 am.

Copy No 1 - Diary   Copy No 9 - 17 Inf Bde
"   2 - 72 Fd Amb   "   10 - 72 "   "
"   3 - 73 Fd Amb   "   11 - 73 "   "
"   4 - 74 Fd Amb   "   12 - C.R.A.
"   5 - 41 San. Sec.   "   13 - C.R.E.
"   6 - H.Q. 24 Div 'G'   "   14 - A.D.M.S. 40 Div
"   7 -   "   'Q'   "   15 - D.D.M.S. I Corps
"   8 - O.C. 24 Div Train "   16 - D.D.M.S. XVII Corps

SECRET   R.A.M.C. OPERATION ORDER No.83
                    by
            Colonel F.R.BUSWELL A.M.S.,
              A.D.M.S. 24th Divn.

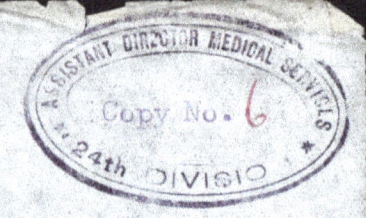

Gx 123/14.
23/10/16

                                                23/10/16.

1. No.2 Canadian Field Ambulance will relieve the 72nd Fld
   Ambce on 25th Octr.

2. No.1 Canadian Fld Ambce will relieve the 73rd Fld Ambce on
   28th Octr.

3. No.3 Canadian Fld Ambce will relieve the 74th Fld Ambce
   on 28th Octr.

4. All trench stores will be handed over to incoming units and
   lists forwarded to this office.

5. All details of reliefs to be arranged direct between
   Officers Commanding concerned.

6. Reliefs to be completed by 12 noon.

7. Canadian Sanitary Section will relieve 41st Sany Section on
   26th Octr.

✓ 8. Acknowledge.

                                          W.F.Scott
     Issued at 12 noon.   Captain R.A.M.C.,
                                       D.A.D.M.S., 24th Divn.

     Copy No. 1 Diary   Copy No. 9 17 I.B.
              2 72 F.A.   10 72 I.B.
              3 73 F.A.   11 73 I.B.
              4 74 F.A.   12 C.R.A.
              5 41 Sany Section   13 C.R.E.
              6 H.Q. "G"   14 A.D.M.S. 1st Cdn Divn
              7 H.Q. "Q"   15 D.D.M.S. Cdn Corps
              8 24th Divl Train   16 File

149/1862

A.D.M.S., 24th Division

Nov. 1916

COMMITTEE FOR THE
MEDICAL HISTORY OF THE WAR
Date −3 JAN. 1917

Vol 15

SECRET.

WAR DIARY.
A.D.M.S.
24 DIVISION
VOL. XV
NOVEMBER
1916.

WITH MAP.

Army Form C. 2118.

WAR DIARY
or
INTELLIGENCE SUMMARY.
(Erase heading not required.)

A.D.M.S.
24 DIVISION
VOL. XV (1)
NOVEMBER

NOVEMBER 1916. Summary of Events and Information

Place	Date	Hour	Summary of Events and Information	Remarks and references to Appendices
BRAQUEMONT	1st		Strong wind & rain. General routine.	
"	2nd		Visited 1st Corps & inspected 72nd & 73rd Fd Ambulances at Braquemont at Bequement commencing at 10.30 a.m. Also visited 72nd & 73rd A.D.S. at Chateau de BREBIS. and debouches of No. 41. Duimbay trench. Also to 71st Fd Amb. A.D.S. at Philosophe front cellar accommodation, his HQrs have entered lines has destroyed. Parts of it in Mackat dump. The Adv Dsg Stn at LA BOUVRIÈRE D.17.A (Sheet 36B) Febulae in or abrentory but accommodation for about 300. & line by the 74th & St Annes. Heavy improvements especially with regard to Latrines an already in hand and the place well ventilated is very good. Return at to H.Q. about 6.30 p.m.	
"	3rd		First case of trench feet received in hand of 9th R. Sussex, who has had too attacks. Previously & inspite of all precautions has again presented itself swelling. troops continues good.	
"	4th		Fine today & warmer.	
"	5th		Routine	
"	6th		Advised 6th Fd. Ambce be taking on the land which is known to MINES that is underlying.	A.N.D.

2353 Wt. W2544/1454 700,000 5/15 D.D.&L. A.D.S.S./Forms/C.2118.

WAR DIARY or INTELLIGENCE SUMMARY

Army Form C. 2118.

NOV. (2)

Place: BARQUEMONT

Date	Hour	Summary of Events and Information	Remarks
	6ᵃ	The 6th Div is standing up large parties to dig in the front, but the weather is not at present taking on any line.	
	7ᵃ	Routine.	
	8ᵃ	Very heavy rain. S/M to Le Buhu, visited A.D.S, Divnl Kitchen & butcher.	
	9ᵃ	M.M. the Duke of Connaught arrived at H.Q. of Grenadier Guards & 3 R.B.	
	10ᵃ	to LE BREUIL, here talked to Adjutant, who reports all very good. Jenny arrangement = foot, also separate dressing & undressing rooms. 2 huts MAROC, visited R.A.P.s of bgds & M.O.s of their front line & fire Ren of what is planned. Very front close to front line & fire Ren of what is planned. From an O.P. in a stable. Blanket arrangements said for 6 in good order.	
	11ᵃ	Routine	
	12ᵃ	Conference at H.Q. Subject of care of Prisoners shall stand of descipline, outlines were adopted. Also the prevention of trench feet. (NB Books on trot prevalent	
13/11/14		General lecture.	MWK

Army Form C. 2118.

WAR DIARY
or
INTELLIGENCE SUMMARY.
(Erase heading not required.)

Nov. (3)

Place	Date	Hour	Summary of Events and Information	Remarks and references to Appendices
Blaringhem	15th		NOVEMBER 1916 Conference by Stand. 1st Corps held at La Bovine. Strin went twenty. Received improvement statement.	
"	16th		Inspection of the 72nd Battand. & 74th Battand. by 1st Corps Commander, who was pleased with the units.	
"	17/18th		General routine	
"	19th		Gen. Browning inspected the 72nd Batt and.	
"	20th		Genl. Browning inspected the 74th Batt and. Good class Ambulance trip long drive, creating plenty of work for the A.D.S. Form to Grouly, stretch bearers by train to 3 R.A.P. Supported Trench to Philosophe A.D.S. then to railway alley, to St Patricks R.D.S. then by Capt Reid King & R.M.O. then by railway alley, creating plenty & happiness, & then still took on a first class A.D.S. Covering the phenomena the first time set up no q.m.s. for the 8th Butts. Visited the three R.M.Ps. of 12th Bremont. 12th Middlesex, & the 8th Butts. The Butts R.A.P. is for employment with the other tw., but to have its bro. selected where then is more accommodation. The c try lord of stopping both took along Mallow top trench & PHILOS & PHIL. Can him at night right up to St Patricks. In case of emergency, to these in Covered & visibility. Also directions in Case of emergency, to these in Covered & visibility, the every Stretch Carr of walking along in the trial task, to be covered.	
	21/22		General routine	

Army Form C. 2118.

Nov (4)

WAR DIARY
or
INTELLIGENCE SUMMARY.

(Erase heading not required.)

Instructions regarding War Diaries and Intelligence Summaries are contained in F.S. Regs., Part II. and the Staff Manual respectively. Title pages will be prepared in manuscript.

Place	Date	Hour	Summary of Events and Information	Remarks and references to Appendices
Bruay	23rd		Visited 72nd & 73rd Sqy Amulatoria. When been noticed that been of the 3rd Australian Pioneer Company infants themselves in very large numbers at the morning sick parade at 73rd but the orders with Chronic Chest Trouble "Silicosis". The average age of the men is 37. They but it they have not yet brought a cases... they will be able to be done. Reported mister to F.A. Corps by letter. Then on examination between 60 + 70 % were out of about 600 men.	
"	24th		To Laundry (Bellune area) (2.3. Central. 36 B. Map.) about the disposal of dirty water. The spot indicated runs from the laundry along a drain to the main road & so on to the stream. Sanitary Officer & R.E. Officer formulated plan for treatment of liquid. 300 gallon of water 2.00 lbs of crystalines. Plan sent to C.R.E. & Adjutant Armentières.	
	25th		General sanitaire.	
	26th		Laundry started. Laundry & Bellune. To 72nd to see P.B. men	
	27th		To La Biache to see P.B. men & A.D.S. 72nd to see	
	28th		To Laundry & touchin to see P.B. men. All lathe & buildings at	
	29th		the latter place been to use by P.B. men. Went to Amettes Hesne to see 70 P.B. men.	

2353 Wt. W2544/1454 700,000 5/15 D.D.& L. A.D.S.S./Forms/C. 2f18.

Army Form C. 2118.

WAR DIARY
or
INTELLIGENCE SUMMARY.

(Erase heading not required.)

Instructions regarding War Diaries and Intelligence Summaries are contained in F. S. Regs., Part II. and the Staff Manual respectively. Title pages will be prepared in manuscript.

N o v. (S)

Place	Date	Hour	Summary of Events and Information	Remarks and references to Appendices
			November 1916	
BRIGNEMONT	30th		Very cold. General intense frost, during location of the raid inserted creates butter to D.S.v. + M.A.P.'s attached.	

Jaulnu M.B. Powell
a/Am S. 24th
Colonel

2353 Wt. W2544/1454 700,000 5/15 D. D. & L.   A.D.S.S./Forms/C. 2118.

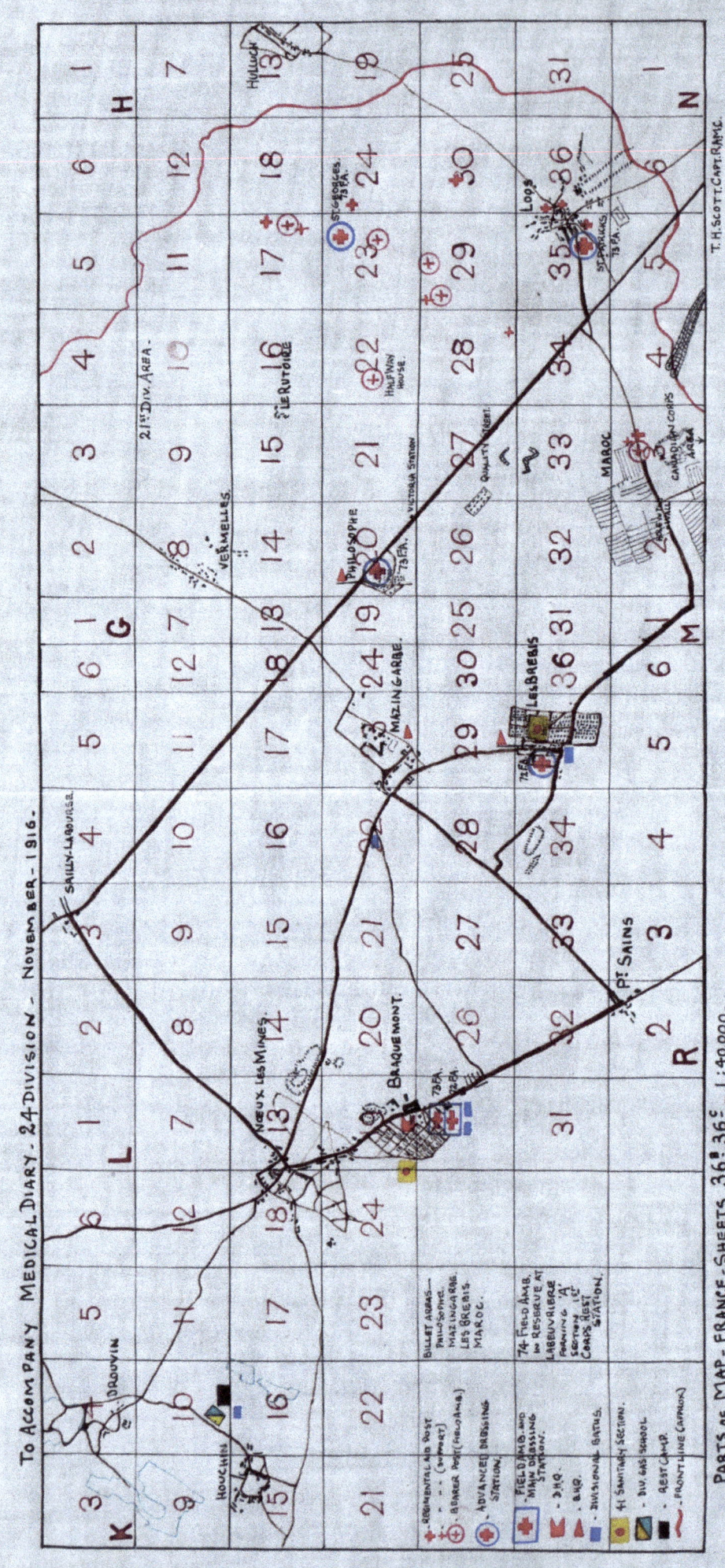

Army Form C. 2118.

DIARY
INTELLIGENCE SUMMARY.
(Erase heading not required.)

A.D.M.S. 24 DIVISION
Vol. XVI.
DECEMBER 1916.

149/90.

A.D.M.S.
24 DIVISION.
VOL. XVI.
DECEMBER 1916.

COMMITTEE FOR THE
MEDICAL HISTORY OF ...
Date 31 JAN. 1917

Army Form C. 2118.

VOL XVI
A.D.M.S.
24 DIVISION
December 1915

WAR DIARY
or
INTELLIGENCE SUMMARY.
(Erase heading not required.)

Place	Date	Hour	Summary of Events and Information	Remarks and references to Appendices
Bruay	1st		General routine.	
"	2nd			
"	3rd		Conference at D.H.Q. A bus of French troops having overrun, all precautions to be vigilantly adopted.	
"	4th		Cases of so called trench feet from inclement weather herewith in sundry. Many orderlies in attendance upon them.	
"	5th		Whilst a day's leave leave from Visited Corps Rest Station at LA BOURSE. Improvements made by the OC, J.C. Stephenson, in to AIRE. By the Cmp. but station very front line in a very front line.	
"	6th		Orders that 1700 the fm 3rd Ambulance etc. extended start of poison fuel for the winter in the town.	
"	7th 8th		Organizing. KMS 1 Corp notted office.	

Lieut Colonel

Army Form C. 2118.

2.

WAR DIARY
or
INTELLIGENCE SUMMARY.
(Erase heading not required.)

Place	Date	Hour	Summary of Events and Information	Remarks and references to Appendices
	December 1916			
Bucquoy	9th	—	All round the bn 41 Sun. Section took up fire tr. and O.P. held 41. S.S. first been in occupation at BR& gVEMONT and run LES BREBIS at present. line has been looked into the communication upon which has hitherto depended at—a Type. C. most standard but increasing by dating with the "Spur". It is estimated that the men of these is capable traced by little & can with necessary work in execution to capture 50 of dealing with 4 G.S. began work of but before a day, then a to Inspection workshop at LE BREBIS. Very heavy return dept. return trade band inspect any sanitary appliance which can be improvised. Than to Forward Condition, Drop Kitchen & A.D.S. also at LE BREBIS for Very pleased with work of the S.S.	
	10th		Conference at S.H.Q. in talk of employing rams a viewing defence work, which I strongly opposed, a forward Violation of Geneva Convention; the men if captured of them work wearing the lot can would I am sure be shot out of hand. & I think lightly too.	MWB

WAR DIARY
INTELLIGENCE SUMMARY

Army Form C. 2118.

Place	Date	Hour	Summary of Events and Information	Remarks and references to Appendices
BRUQUEMONT	11th	—	Some difficulty in the matter of orders for gun latrines. Thanks to an enormous number of men detailed, the gun pits are very distinctive as they help almost of men at the hide. Required to supply 3 Candidates for commissions in the Infantry in re from the 3 Fd. Ambulances.	
"	12th		Candidates 2, for 72nd & 1 from 74th Fd. Amb. Interviewed by G.O.C. hdrs. that the inspection of P.B. men held are at P.B. on 15th instant.	
"	13th		Good hack the evening on the main shaft. Close to find him IV. 14 P.B.2 which still show great carriage of water in limps. Inclement weather. Camp for 7 tent Camp in Torrent buts but sickness amounts limited. 4L supplemented by Curtains of uniforms. General lectures.	
"	14th/15th			
"	16th	—	Camp at ALLOUAGNE. Ole Heavens f. snow falling. & proceed to main late NoCalm.	

Army Form C. 2118.

WAR DIARY
or
INTELLIGENCE SUMMARY.
(Erase heading not required.)

Place	Date	Hour	Summary of Events and Information	Remarks and references to Appendices
BARQUEMONT	16th	—	7. Photographs ADS. and then saw country very heavy going to ADS. served by 73rd Fd Amb. Visited RAP. & Bearer posts in St Amour. Roads and things very HOLLVEH potten, all in poor condition but kept up.	St Georges
"	17th	—	Adjt for Temp left for Allemagne Camp. Conference at SMG.	
"	18th	—	Sanitary arrangements at Allemagne most promising. The three lower lines the 1st Corps R.E. won't allow much cement to done to this & said be going to take the matter in hand.	
"	19th	—	General routine.	
			The frequent inspection of regimental notes calls his troubled in stream bay. Very hard hotter kept in any way. This also by the Sanitary Section.	
"	20th		General routine.	
"	21st			
"	22nd			
"	23rd		7. ALLOUAGNE Sanitary Camp. The new R.E. been taken down little in bettering in the way of sanitation. Latrines work however Kitchen off of the front promise style splended matter to S.M.G. the 41st Div Section with help of the C.E. endues promised to press to this purpose. Conference at SM.G of dresser himden for evacuation of wounded & up J.B. work	
	24th		to be finally settled.	

Army Form C. 2118.

WAR DIARY
or
INTELLIGENCE SUMMARY.
(Erase heading not required.)

Instructions regarding War Diaries and Intelligence Summaries are contained in F. S. Regs., Part II. and the Staff Manual respectively. Title pages will be prepared in manuscript.

December 1916.

Place	Date	Hour	Summary of Events and Information	Remarks and references to Appendices
BRAQUEMONT	25th	—	Xmas day. Excellent dinners and entertainments provided by all the Fie Amb	
	26th	—	to patients & personnel by general nature.	
	27th	—	To LA BOUVRIERE 7th D Fie Amb. everything very satisfactory. Similarly an entertainment by the "Whiz Bangs" in the theatre for the patients in the	
	28th	—	Corps Rest Station. Visited white front & saw trench front. Weather been like this 4 & 5 — seen this month. Rain later. Inspected P.B.s at Vieux le Vienne proposed P.B's. knowing & afternoon of the twenty stricken Braquemont & St Pierre.	
	30th	—		
	31st	—	Came & toured front trenches in spite of all precautions the changes from front to them; with a quick death of listen in the trenches being responsible for of losses during the Smith was 10.	

[signature] M. Burnett Col
A/ADMS

1577 Wt.W10791/1773 500,000 1/15 D.D.&L. A.D.S.S./Forms/C. 2118.

140/1943

COMMITTEE FOR THE
MEDICAL HISTORY OF THE WAR
Date 13 MAR. 1917

A.D.M.S. 24th Division

Jan 1917

24

JC 17 Army Form C. 2118.
VOL. XVII
A.D.M.S.
24 DIVISION.
JANUARY 1917.

WAR DIARY
or
INTELLIGENCE SUMMARY.
(Erase heading not required.)

Army Form C. 2118.

Place	Date	Hour	Summary of Events and Information	Remarks and references to Appendices
BRAQUEMONT	JANUARY 1917.			
	1st		Cold. Care of cubic spaced meningitis 8th R. West Kents notified. 21st Mobile Laboratory. All precaution taking. Immediate contacts isolated and interspersed at by 72nd Fd Amb. & throats taken by O/C the Laboratory. First lecture upon Infectious Inoculation by Capt 7th R.A.M.C. stationed 7/- 3 Plane.	
	2nd		Men & 7 Nights. Offering.	
	3rd		Practical Sanitary demonstration by Capt W.S. Committee Room C. O. & 21st Sanitary Section to all officers.	
	4th		One case of trench foot in 8th Buffs. weather less & cold.	
	5th		No case of trench foot in the 8th Buffs.	
	6th		Case of cubic spinal meningitis notified by 21st Mobile Laboratory in a man of 9th R. Sussex Regt. 4 new drafts arriving under the R.E. Contacts isolated & counts taken by O/C Mobile Laboratory. No connection between the two cases.	
	7th		Conference S.M.O. Corps stated that during the recent cold spell the division was still low in so called "trench fever", there will be no leave typic counterpart.	
	8th		All the counts taken from the C.C.S. meningitis case contacts have been returned as sterile.	

WWB

WAR DIARY
INTELLIGENCE SUMMARY

Place	Date	Hour	Summary of Events and Information	Remarks and references to Appendices
GRAND GUEMONT	January 1917			
	9th		Sunny. Accompanied by SDM of 1st Corps, inspected all the [?] Ambs of the Division & the 4th Sanitary Section & some of the advanced dressing stations. The trench equipment to be standardising.	
	10th		Cold, frost. In new building in the Division — M. Surge Line is at always hung up. The busses to front & regions to return which is but always available. The light Railway on the filled site Railway carrying to be possible throughout the CRE by — the CO's expo.	
	11th		Visits ADP & C80 & C.6 — 2 perry unsatisfactory owing to the decision of the Corry letting his horses & new Rap to leave Constantia which to house in TOSH. Alley. C 36 A 7–8. Pm where can be kept.	
	12th		By front to St Patricks ADS in LOOS. & great saving of labour. Walk & int. trench to 17th Fld Amb. & Medical arrangements for —	
	13th		Cold. Cold & wet. Said slowly copying off the ADS LOOS PMS. Health of Troops good up to 9 am for bicks with a strength of 19,999. Asked told the admissions for centage	
	14th		Snow . 08.	
	15th		Improve ar. SH.Y. general [?]	

NMB

Army Form C. 2118.

WAR DIARY
or
INTELLIGENCE SUMMARY.
(Erase heading not required.)

Instructions regarding War Diaries and Intelligence Summaries are contained in F. S. Regs., Part II. and the Staff Manual respectively. Title pages will be prepared in manuscript.

Place	Date	Hour	Summary of Events and Information	Remarks and references to Appendices
	January, 1917.			
Marquampole	16th		Captain E.V. RUSSELL R.A.M.C. took on the duties of Sanitary Division ft. Captain T.H. Scott M.C. R.A.M.C. proceed to command of 14th Fd Amb - Divisn Municipal has appeared in the 3rd Australian Municipal C. 3 cases up to date.	
"	17th		Sanitary hint. Captain Scott reported has departure. Two cases of Trench foot in 9th E. Surrey Regt	
"	18th		Very cold.	
"	19th		General Situation	
"	20th		Cold. No cases are above the tolerating man Sanitary when the division proceeds to keep area.	
"			Captain F.W.M. Cunningham Ram C. late StFANS 17th Corps, arrived to take Command of the 73rd Fd Amb. Lt. Col. Wade proc. On case of meningitis sent to L. of C. was adm. P stated. 21st Divn to taking over	
"	21st		General untiring.	
"	22nd		Ord. 21st Divn to Batths: Marquample & St Blehun. Very cold.	
"	23rd		Capt StM Pat Ram C. reported general attached 75 Fd Amb. to T.M. & STORE Rooms. TC also Petrached 7 & 8 Fd Ambs.	MB

Army Form C. 2118.

WAR DIARY
or
INTELLIGENCE SUMMARY.
(Erase heading not required.)

Place	Date	Hour	Summary of Events and Information	Remarks and references to Appendices
MAZINGARBE	January, 1917.			
	Jan. 24th		Status visit to Buties MOAVC Soup Kitchen & enquire into the question of hot food to the troops Satisfactory. Front Centenues —	
	25th		General Routine.	
	26th		Relief by XX1 Div. Cancelled, owing to Intelligent prints the inoculations &c. Belgian are stopped orders & hopes promptly hurry activity. All Commands by train cancelled. Leave stopped.	
	27th			
	28th		Captn Rowell. W.M. Pam. C.T.F. Station 66th arrives for instruction.	
	29th		General inspection of hygiene (MAROC) sector. Visit front centenues. Laundry Luther down. Water difficulty continues.	
	30th		Officers ran for water with value. apparently 1 Box explosives issued at 12 gr for Kitchen to prevent freezing 1 valve.	
	31st		Inspected F.A. B.S.s & visited to Parities AS's & the train outposts of fors. also Dismount Truckn. Soup Kitchen	
			Total Trench feet for the month equal 18. —	

Jubw M Brown
Lt
A/Drm 24th Div

A.D.M.S., 24th Division

14/9/1994

Feb. 1917

COMMITTEE FOR THE
MEDICAL HISTORY OF THE WAR
Date 4 APR. 1917

Army Form C. 2118.

WAR DIARY
or
INTELLIGENCE SUMMARY.
(Erase heading not required.)

Vol 18

A.D.M.S
24 Division
Vol 18
February

Army Form C. 2118.

WAR DIARY
or
INTELLIGENCE SUMMARY.
(Erase heading not required.)

Instructions regarding War Diaries and Intelligence Summaries are contained in F.S. Regs., Part II. and the Staff Manual respectively. Title pages will be prepared in manuscript.

February 1917.

Place	Date	Hour	Summary of Events and Information	Remarks and references to Appendices
MARQUEMONT	1st		Strong Westerly breezy buffeting at ALLONCHE, 1 Bombing Scheme	
"	2nd		at LOUVIERES. 2 medical attendance this first. June nature.	
"	3rd		Capt. Wm. Rowell started 66th Fd. Ambce. for England. afts week instruction. Captain M.O. Carruthers from C.Z.F. Fd. 45 for section. evacuated sick to C.C.S. 1 car trench fort.	
"	4th		Capt. Mc. Macpherson Rann C. Took over Command 41st Fan Section. 3 cars trench Point.	
"	5th		meeting of 1st Cdn. Medical Society. 3 cars trench fort.	
"	6th		June antine. 1 car trench fort.	
"	7th		DDMS 1st Corps inspected HQ. & Ram C. port L. O.S. staked inspected ADS. St Georges. fides that the train in transit to return in the heat by Fan 37. train in visiting Allongin, Labeyrinine & O.S. 37 Train	
"	8th		medical arrangement at OHS 37. Train visited Ypres.	

Army Form C. 2118.

WAR DIARY
or
INTELLIGENCE SUMMARY.
(Erase heading not required.)

Instructions regarding War Diaries and Intelligence
Summaries are contained in F. S. Regs., Part II.
and the Staff Manual respectively. Title pages
will be prepared in manuscript.

Place	Date	Hour	Summary of Events and Information	Remarks and references to Appendices
BRAQUEMONT	9th		FEBRUARY 1917. Found operation order to move. 1 Car tents front Cl.s to Ambs exchange rides	
"	10th		Advance party of 50th Fd Amb. arrived, also for 40th Fd Amb	
"	11	a	General routine. Tent entraining.	
"	12		72nd Field Amb. to ALLOUAGNE. Found billets but no accommodation for patients. A.D.M.S. 37th Div. visited office re move	
"	13th		73rd Field Amb. to NOEUX LES MINES. Not open. 24th Divion move into rest area between LILLERS and BETHUNE. Office closed here & opened at LABOUVRIERE at 4 p.m. 41 Fd. Station moved to same place. Visited training battalion at Allouagne & 72nd Fd Amb. also 73rd Fd Amb. at NOEUX-LES-MINES.	
LABEUVRIERE	15th		Show command – nothing unusual to report –	

signatures

Army Form C. 2118.

WAR DIARY
or
INTELLIGENCE SUMMARY.
(Erase heading not required.)

Place	Date	Hour	Summary of Events and Information	Remarks and references to Appendices
LABEUVRIERE	16/2/17		Col. Bruoville - kept in leave this date; duties of ADMS taken over by Lt Col AM Rose - Routine - Inspection of 1st Corps Officers Rest Station, ARE, - Inspecting Sanitation of Pt Corps Bombing and Technical School by San. Officer -	AMRose Lt Col
LABEUVRIERE	17/2/17		General Routine. Nothing unusual to report.	AMR
LABEUVRIERE	18/2/17		Inspection visit - time rain - nothing unusual to report	AMR
LABEUVRIERE	19/2/17		General routine - nothing unusual to report.	
LABEUVRIERE	20/2/17		ADMS. - OC. 41st San. Sec. to ALLOUAGNES to investigate to occurrence of ? cerebro-spring meningitis - Capt. W.M Biden - Raine - reports for duty + proceeds to 73rd Field Ambulance - - Lt J.B. Cook Reine reports for duty and transfers attached 74 field Ambulance. - - Nothing unusual to report - heavy rain -	AMR
LABEUVRIERE	21/2/17		resumed. -	AMR
LABEUVRIERE	22/2/17		Nothing unusual to report -	AMR

Army Form C. 2118.

WAR DIARY
or
INTELLIGENCE SUMMARY.

(Erase heading not required.)

Instructions regarding War Diaries and Intelligence
Summaries are contained in F. S. Regs., Part II.
and the Staff Manual respectively. Title pages
will be prepared in manuscript.

Place	Date	Hour	Summary of Events and Information	Remarks and references to Appendices
LABEUVRIERE	23/2/17		Accompanied ADMS 1st Army, DDMS 1st Corps. DDMS Can. Corps, on inspection of Hospitals & projects. ADS. ABLAIN - ST NAZAIRE. - HQ 3 Can Field Amb. - at FOSSE 10 - near SAINS-EN-GOHELLE. ADS. - AIX-NOULETTE - and 3 bearer posts in tunnels (not formerly used). AIX-SOUCHEZ road - out bearer post - at Reg. aid post in same trenches - Also visited ADS. BULLY GRENAY.	AhiRae DCal
LABEUVRIERE	24/2/17		DADMS. interviewed ADMS 1st Canadian Divison re defence to mine - projects. ADS. a left relief (near mine) - (BULLY-GRENAY, PONT GRENAY). -	AhiR
LABEUVRIERE	25/2/17		DADMS interviewed ADMS 1st Canadian Divison re arrange class of mine - -	AhR
LABEUVRIERE	26/2/17		Ordinary routine - Observation Range No 162 inches to all concerned	AhR
LABEUVRIERE	27/2/17		Nothing unusual to report - Draft to accession of bearer class of works in training -	AhR
LABEUVRIERE	28/2/17		Weather improving however - nothing unusual to report	AhR

AhiRae
DCrineene
for ADMS 1st Divison

SECRET.   Copy No 2

R.A.M.C. Operation Order No 101
by
Colonel F. R. Buswell C.M.G. A.M.S.
A.D.M.S. 24th Divn.

                                                                                                10th Feb. 1917

Map Ref.
Sheet 36B.
(1/40000)
HAZEBROUCK 5A
(1/100.000)

1. The 24th Division will remove to Rest Area on relief by 37th Divn.; relief to be completed by midnight 13/14 Feby.

2. No 72 Field Ambce will be relieved by No 50 Fld Ambce on the 12th, and will then proceed to ALLOUAGNE.

3. No 73 Fld Amb. will be relieved by No 48 Fld Amb. on the 13th and will then proceed to ANNEZIN (School)

4. No 74 Fld Amb. will remain at LABEUVRIERE.

5. The Officer Commanding No 72 Fld Amb. will hand over the baths at MAZINGARBE and LES BREBIS on 11th inst to O.C. No 50 Fld Amb.

6. All trench stores will be handed over to incoming units and lists forwarded to this Office.

7. The 41st Sanitary Section will be relieved by the San. Section 37th Divn. on the 13th inst, and will then proceed to LABEUVRIERE.

8. All details of reliefs to be arranged direct between Officers Commanding concerned.

9. Completion of reliefs to be reported to this Office.

10. Reliefs to be completed by 12 noon.

11. Officers Commanding Fld Ambces will arrange for Ambulance transport to accompany their respective Brigades on the march.

12. Officer Commanding No 72 Fld Ambce will send a billeting party forward with the billeting party of his Brigade

13. Officer Commanding No 73 Fld Ambce will send a billeting party forward with the billeting party of 17th Brigade.

14. Brigade Areas are as follows:-

P.T.O.

17th Inf. Bde.	72nd Inf. Bde.	73rd Inf Bde
NOEUX LES MINES	BUSNETTES	LABEUVRIERE
FOUQUIERES (B.H.Q)	BASRIEUX	LAPUGNOY
ANNEZIN.	CANTRIANNE	FOUQUEREUIL
	ALLOUAGNE (B.H.Q)	GOSNAY.
	LE HAMEL	

12th Battn Sherwood Foresters - ALLOUAGNE.

15. Office of A.D.M.S. will close at BRAQUEMONT at 4 p.m. on Feby 13th and open at the same hour at LABEUVRIERE.

16. Acknowledge.

E. U. Russell
Capt. RAMC
D.A.D.M.S. 24th Divn

Issued at 11 a.m.

Copy No 1 - 3 War Diary & File
4. 72 Fld Amb.
5. 73 Fld Amb.
6. 74 Fld Amb.
7. 41 San. Sec.
8. HQ 24 Div 'G'
9. HQ 24 Div 'A'
10. Divl Train

11. 17 Inf Bde
12. 72 Inf Bde
13. 73 Inf Bde
14. CRA.
15. CRE.
16. ADMS 37th Div
17. DDMS 1 Corps.

Secret   Copy No 1

R.A.M.C. Operation Order No 102.
by Lieut-Col Ambrose O.S.O. R.A.M.C.
for A.D.M.S. 24th Division.

                                                      26th February 1917.

Reference
Map 1/40,000
Sheet 36B.
  and
Trench map
1/10,000
Sheets 36C.S.W.1
36C.S.W.2.
36B.S.E.2.
36B.S.E.4.

1.   The 24th Division will relieve the 1st Canadian Division on the front SOUCHEZ RIVER to DOUBLE CRASSIER. The relief to be completed by March 6th.

2.   On 2nd March No 74 Field Ambulance will take over the Main Dressing Station at FOSSE 10 (R.8.central) from the 3rd Canadian Field Ambce, and the A.D.S. AIX NOULETTE (R.22.a.2.6) together with the advanced posts from the 2nd Canadian Field Ambulance.

3.   On 3rd March No 73 Field Ambulance will take over the Boys School, BRAQUEMONT from the 50th Field Ambulance, 37th Division, as a Main Dressing Station, and the Advanced Dressing Stations BULLY GRENAY (R.11.a.77.) and PONT GRENAY (M.1.a.6.2.) together with their advanced posts from 3rd Canadian Fld Amb.

4.   On 1st March the 72nd Field Ambulance will take over the Officers Rest Station, AIRE from 74th Field Ambulance; and on 4th March the 1st Corps Rest Station ('A' Section) LABEUXRIERE from the same unit.

5.   Field Ambulance reliefs to be completed by 12 noon on their respective dates.

6.   On 5th March the 41st Sanitary Section will relieve the Sanitary Section, 1st Canadian Division at BOYEFFLES (R.13.b.2.3); relief to be completed by 6 p.m.

7.   All details of reliefs to be arranged direct between Officers Commanding concerned.

8.   Completion of reliefs will be wired in B.A.B. Code to this Office.

9. All trench stores will be taken over and a list forwarded to this Office.

10. Officers Commanding Field Ambulances will arrange for Ambulance transport to accompany their respective Brigades on the march.

11. Office of A.D.M.S. will close at LABEUVRIERE and open at RUE ADOLPHE LE GRAND, BARLIN at 12 noon on 6th March.

12. Acknowledge.

C. U. Russell.
Capt D.A.D.M.S.
for Col. A.D.M.S.

Issued at 9 a.m.

Copy No 1-3 War Diary & File   11 . 17 Inf. Bde
         4 . 72 Fld Amb   12 . 72 Inf Bde
         5 . 73 Fld Amb   13 . 73 Inf Bde
         6 . 74 Fld Amb.   14 . C.R.A.
         7 . 41 SanSec.   15 . C.R.E.
         8 . H.Q. 2t Div 'G'   16 . A.D.M.S. 1 Can. Div
         9 . H.Q. 2t Div 'A'   17 . A.D.M.S. 37 Div.
         10. Divl Train   18 . D.D.M.S. 1 Corps.

SECRET.

War Diary.

Para. 11 of Operation Order.102 dated 26/2/17 is cancelled.

Office of A.D.M.S. will close at LAHEUVRIER and open at RUE ADCLIEF LE GRAND, BARLIN, at 4-0 p.m. on 5th March.

24th D.E.Q.

28/2/17.

E.U. Russell
Capt. D.A.D.M.S.
for A.D.M.S.

Copies to :— War Diary and File.
72 Field Ambce.
73 Field Ambce.
74 Field Ambce.
A.D.M.S. 37th Div.
A.D.M.S. 1st Can. Div.
41st Sanitary Sec.
D.D.M.S. 1 Corps.

140/2037.

A.D.M.S, 24th Division.

WAR DIARY
or
INTELLIGENCE SUMMARY.

Army Form C. 2118.

A.D.M.S.
24th Div.
r.t.l.k
March
1917

Original

WAR DIARY
or
INTELLIGENCE SUMMARY.
(Erase heading not required.)

Army Form C. 2118.

Place	Date	Hour	Summary of Events and Information	Remarks and references to Appendices
LABEUVRIÈRE	1/3/17		Invalids still return cold - no rain - four fresh cases of measles -	Mr Rae Cochrane
	2/3/17		Nurses returned from leave. Very cold.	
	3/3/17		Measles incidence on the increase. 73rd Fd Amb. completed move to Bryas School BRUQUEMONT.	
	4/3/17		Opened routine 72nd & 74th Fd Ambs. completed move to LABOURIERS & FOSSE 10. respectively.	
	5/3/17		M.O. moved to BARLIN. No 41. Sanitary Section moved to BOYEFFLES.	
	6/3/17		Slight fall of snow. White sisters. General routine.	
	7/3/17		Visited 74th Fd Amb. at Fosse 10. A.D.S. at AIX NOULETTES & Rear of line held by the 73rd Bde.	
	8/3/17		Funeral routine.	
	9/3/17		To Braquemont 73rd Fd Amb. BULLY GRENAY A.D.S. & Mme RAP & Rear Posts Post Chenny & Colonne Trench & Cité Calonne thence to Maroc Aid Tunnel & 207. Tamarisk trench, Chipilly Alley, Olympia trench. 15 R.A.P. 12 R.P. in Boyan Alley. — to Bully	
	10/3/17		Opening. To Fosse X. 74th Fd Amb. very poor accommodation.	
	11/3/17		Conference at Lt W.	

Army Form C. 2118.

WAR DIARY
or
INTELLIGENCE SUMMARY.
(Erase heading not required.)

March 1917.

Place	Date	Hour	Summary of Events and Information	Remarks and references to Appendices
BARLIN	12th		Force X. inspected men of P.B. also battns.; A.T.S. also Ambulances in good independent accommodation for about 250. by my Cars. Ran to Ambulance Cars.	
"	13th		General Routine.	
"	14th		To some X. 74th Div. Stunt. 6 Regiment to B suppressment Stations to 5 Stunt. also W Wounded MRA.S. Rd byp. also being badly wounded. They went slick to the Line called Jenny Station. also 73rd Fd Amb.	
"	15th			
"	16th		La Bruyment. G.S. Fd Amb. New 12 Cpe. called.	
"	17th		To Fosseux. 74th Fd Amb. great improvement being effected by the O.C. this Unit.	
"	18th		Conference at H.Q. 16 Fd Amb. Noeux les mines of Staff M. Corps H.T.M.S.S. 6th & 24th Div. & Fd Amb. commands subject. Evacuation wounded for the two Divs and areas. To 73rd Fd Amb.	
"	19th		Visited both Batty Passny 1st & 2nd & June 10. also inspected men of T.U. T.P.S also Nations.	
"	20th		Return visited the 3 Ambulances. Officers & Rankmen.	

WAR DIARY or INTELLIGENCE SUMMARY

Army Form C. 2118.

(Erase heading not required.)

Place	Date	Hour	Summary of Events and Information	Remarks and references to Appendices
BERLIN	20th		General routine.	
"	21st		Pte Amb. to evacuation etc.	
"	22"		Snow fell. General routine.	
"	23"		Weather very bad. General routine.	
"	24"		To Pte Amb. at Foss x, a letter for walking wounded attention. Into between the NOULETTE, BUISSEULT & Foss x. To avoid very frequent shelling stokes on the ARRAS, NOEUX LES MINES Rd.	
"	25"		Conference at 17th Fd. Hy. Box reporter to return on Gen. & staff to be performed with the separator a. NOEUX LES MINES shelled. Sentries.	
"	26"		To FDs & 1st Corps. re. impending change. The physique of the new labour Companies is extremely bad. The incoming draft, the same of the Flemd. being very largely present. Many of them men on absolutely useless to hinderer to work & should have been rejected.	

Army Form C. 2118.

WAR DIARY
or
INTELLIGENCE SUMMARY.
(Erase heading not required.)

Instructions regarding War Diaries and Intelligence Summaries are contained in F. S. Regs., Part II. and the Staff Manual respectively. Title pages will be prepared in manuscript.

Place	Date	Hour	Summary of Events and Information	Remarks and references to Appendices
BARLIN	March 1917.			
	26th		Letter to O.C. 1st Corps. When the returns had physical conditions of the Labour Companies Kings Liverpool Regt. L.W.R. S.C. 6th Div & is taking on more men to the Regt. 1 N.C.O. & men O.C. stationed at A.M.C. post N.M.& O.C.	
	27th		Rams J. & Billy Ferry Column when the two A.D.S. can run accommodate 81 by Cars. well protected in cellars. Trenches very bad condition enough to front & stations	
	28th		Fine & sunny. Tent during night. C.R.E. called with whom to see R.A.P. dug out in Hersin Trench, A.R.R.H. Rd. To A.D.S. Ablain St Nazaire with S.M.S. Lt Gibson is taking on the duties by Gustin to 2nd Life Ambulance from the 12th Canadian Field Amb. in the extending of the front of right. Many scattered cellar etc. with possibilities.	
	29th 30th		Heavy snow storms at A.D.S. Ablain St Nazaire with O.C. 72nd Canadian. About 4th Canadian Divn in traffic to improving. Change hands on his A.D.S. at Ablain St Nazaire. Had return A.D.S. at Carencey.	
	30th		To front 74th to Carencey. Transport is excellent condition. Improvements continued.	

MMB

WAR DIARY or INTELLIGENCE SUMMARY

Army Form C. 2118.

Place	Date	Hour	Summary of Events and Information	Remarks and references to Appendices
BERLIN	31st		March 1917. 7o Regiment 70th Bn amb. all ready to CRS. LITHOUVIEZEN. 72nd Fd Amb. many improvements during the month on case of Trench Foot. revealed only 7 cases this month - the incidence has greatly diminished. 68 cases all told + 24 cases of mumps almost entirely contracted with the 3rd Australian Training Company. Captain W.D. Carruthers RAMC S.T.F. at 41st Sanitary Section has been evacuated to England severely ill after influenza. The form of which he has found in this front. The Officer has done consistently excellent work while in command of the unit, which maintains a very high standard of efficiency.	

Lieut. Col ADMS 2nd Div

Secret   Copy No 2

R.A.M.C. Operation Order No 102.
by Lieut-Col Ambrose DSO. RAMC.
for A.D.M.S. 74th Division.

26th February 1917.

Reference
Map 1/40,000
Sheet 36B.
  and
Trench map
1/10,000
Sheets 36C S.W.1
36C S.W.2.
36C S.E.2.
36B. S.E.4.

1. The 74th Division will relieve the 1st Canadian Division on the front SOUCHEZ RIVER to DOUBLE CRASSIER. The relief to be completed by March 6th.

2. On 4th March No 74 Field Ambulance will take over the Main Dressing Station at FOSSE 10 (R.8. central) from the 3rd Canadian Field Ambce, and the A.D.S. AIX NOULETTE (R.22.a.2.6) together with the advanced posts from the 2nd Canadian Field Ambulance.

3. On 3rd March No 73 Field Ambulance will take over the Boys School, BRAQUEMONT from the 50th Field Ambulance, 37th Division, as a Main Dressing Station, and the Advanced Dressing Stations BULLY GRENAY (R.11.a.7.7.) and PONT GRENAY (M.1.d.6.2.) together with their advanced posts from 3rd Canadian Fld Amb.

4. On 1st March the 72nd Field Ambulance will take over the Officers Rest Station, AIRE from 74th Field Ambulance, and on 4th March the 1st Corps Rest Station ('A' Section) LABEUVRIERE from the same unit.

5. Field Ambulance reliefs to be completed by 12 noon on their respective dates.

6. On 5th March the 41st Sanitary Section will relieve the Sanitary Section, 1st Canadian Division at BOYEFFLES (R.13.b.3.3); relief to be completed by 6 p.m.

7. All details of reliefs to be arranged direct between Officers Commanding concerned.

8. Completion of reliefs will be wired in B.A.B. code to this Office.

9. All trench stores will be taken over and a list forwarded to this Office.

10. Officers Commanding Field Ambulances will arrange for Ambulance transport to accompany their respective Brigades on the march.

11. Office of A.D.M.S. will close at LABEUVRIERE and open at "RUE ADOLPHE LE GRAND, BARLIN at 12 noon on 6th March.

12. Acknowledge.

C. U. Russell
Capt D.A.D.M.S.
for Col. A.D.M.S.

Issued at 9 a.m.

Copy No				
1-3	War Diary & File	11	17 Inf Bde
4	72 Fd Amb	12	72 Inf Bde
5	9 Fd Amb	13	73 Inf Bde
6	110 Fd Amb	14	C.R.A.
7	41 Sankee	15	C.R.E.
8	HQ 2 Div G	16	A/Q
9	HQ 2 Div Q	17	ADMS 37 Div
10		18	DDMS 1

Army Form C. 2118.

WAR DIARY
or
INTELLIGENCE SUMMARY.
(Erase heading not required.)

140/1085

Original

AD MS
94th Div
Vol XI
April 1917

COMMITTEE FOR THE
MEDICAL HISTORY OF THE WAR
Date −6 JUN. 1917

Army Form C. 2118.

WAR DIARY
or
INTELLIGENCE SUMMARY.
(Erase heading not required.)

Instructions regarding War Diaries and Intelligence Summaries are contained in F.S. Regs., Part II. and the Staff Manual respectively. Title pages will be prepared in manuscript.

Place	Date	Hour	Summary of Events and Information	Remarks and references to Appendices
BERLIN.	April 1917.			
	1st		Conference at 17th Bn. H.Q. Bouzincourt. Recruit order that H.Q. move to Saras EN GOHELLE. Drive to BRAQUEMONT.	
"	2nd		Met 1st Corps Corps at BRAQUEMONT. 735 for Amd. inspection, then to 74th Bty RMA from S. AIX NOULETTE & BULLY GRENAY Corps Commander expressed himself very pleased with all arrangements.	
"	3rd		Drove officer to BRAQUEMONT at 12 noon. Heavy gale & snow in the morning	
BRAQUEMONT	4th		To 73rd Hank to 74th Hank. Walking wounded entries &c. afternoon along trenches.	
"	5th		To B.H.Q. Barricourt.	
"	6th		Heavy shelling in front of Loos. X. Brass a C.M. prisoner at 74th for Amb. Lt. Col. Ortona Holmes CAMC Rear C. Neurologic Specialist. Seen a Reuardeer from from	
	7th		to be mentally deficient. Fine but cold Matine	
"	8th		Matine	
"	9th		Inspected men of him in for P.B. & T.V. Inspected 74th for Amb. Preparations being made for impending events.	

Army Form C. 2118.

WAR DIARY
or
INTELLIGENCE SUMMARY.
(Erase heading not required.)

Place	Date	Hour	Summary of Events and Information	Remarks and references to Appendices
BARQUEMONT	10th		Preparation for the attack.	
"	11th		Followed by an attack by 24th Div. a Vimy Ridge is successful. In Fonne & A.S.S. the Brigade attacked BOIS EN HACHE there & our D.F. Barrage by Trench to Reper K.D.S. situated in Martin Trench PARADE Road.	
"	12th		Heavy shelling all the morning. Arrangements quite satisfactory. Canadians attacked Vimy Ridge at 6 a.m. Successfully, taking the Pimple. The 24th Divisn taking BOIS EN HACHE. First Reina Lui Vimden. Evacuation worked very well in spite of the unable the harries of the Arras Road. Reconstated Shelter Stretcher in places of cars. Stns & 1st Cdn. with 74th Fd. Ambe.	
"	13th		Up to 9 o'ck the memory on Caswalhes were 12 Officers & 233 O.R. Wounded. Enemy is now retiring from Chief the enemy is now retiring Trenches. Our troops advancing. Brunt Stnin Colony.	
"	14th		Gas Shells fired into 74th & Amb also storms but following up in Carwallies. All patients Hacey in the Cellars & elsewhere evacuated. One trooper –––	

T2134. Wt. W708—770. 5000/0. 4/15. Sir J. C. & S.

WAR DIARY
or
INTELLIGENCE SUMMARY.

Army Form C. 2118.

Place	Date	Hour	Summary of Events and Information	Remarks and references to Appendices
Kragujevac	15	1	Considerable difficulty has been experienced in keeping intact the tt Regiments whose reports in the Rifle Rgts. when the MMR lost men away from the new line of the Coon county but do not exist. Invaders to almost entirely done. Except the advanced observing station at "Gilmore" for all the Regt. which to Emergm. L.E.N.S.	
"	16		With very last RAS opened by 73rd Ft Tank & 74th Ft Line at 4.P.M. More repair are at present & later also & to get to RSS Column & return. Very heavy pros & heavy shelling.	
"	17		Very wet. Left hand allaying operation by preventing the movement of guns.	
"	18		Orders 48th Div. 1st Officer to taking our barrage arrangements & station 2nd Army 1st Army is leaving part of 73rd Ft Tank at Programme & account. No 7 (?) He joined this.	/MMR

Army Form C. 2118.

WAR DIARY
or
INTELLIGENCE SUMMARY.
(Erase heading not required.)

April, 1917.

Place	Date	Hour	Summary of Events and Information	Remarks and references to Appendices
Bapaume	19th		Advanced parties for Ambulances 46th Div to begin lettering over A.D.S.s Cold but fine.	
"	20th		Left Bapaume at 9 am for Morrent Fortes. Office opened. The 74th Ft Amb to Sapignies. The 73rd on return only to LIVOUART. And the 72nd Ft Amb to LA COUTURE in rest area.	
MORRENT FORTES	21st		Very dull but fine. Visited Fortes 2nd Corps & 73rd & 74th Ft Ambs in morning & the 72nd Ft Amb in the afternoon. Examination posts.	
"	22nd		Dull but fine.	
"	23rd		Continue. Visit to min. Division.	
"	24th		Left Morrent Fortes at 9 am arrived B.o.M.K. at 10 am.	
B.o.M.K.	25th		Ft Ambs in the trenches. Orders except that 73rd & 74th Ft Ambulances will relieve with the 73rd & 172nd Fd Ambs. Being sent on into the Bethune & Divent le Vache Area, that in supports to Division in the line & then to being out at rest.! 73rd La Amb & 74th Ft Amb. Meadow today as stated above.	
"	26th		72nd Ft Amb stands fast	MMB

WAR DIARY or INTELLIGENCE SUMMARY

Army Form C. 2118.

Place	Date	Hour	Summary of Events and Information	Remarks and references to Appendices
B.O.M.Y.	27th		74th Lt Amb arrived C & H. Hospital Bethune accommodation of 100.	
	28th		73rd Lt Amb (C section) arrived HOUCHIN	
			To billets 72nd Lt Amb.	
	29th		To & from 11 Corps AIRE. Bethune 74 & L.O. 73° 70 ADS Beuvry	
			C. Let. Houchin return	
	30th		Visited Scottish Hospital, now working at Challenge Farm	
			just accommodation. 4 mile west BUSNES. 1 mile N. of Hinges	
			Being depôt army to engineer of trench & very cold weather	
			thirteen in cases of "trench foot", all slight	
			There were 28 cases of infection again. Greater than guessto	
			orders received for Off Lt Col R.M. ROSE to report to Dive Rouen	
			upon sanitary aux. command of 74th Lt Amb.	
			Captain R.W. Macpherson RAM C. reported H.Q. for duty on leaving	
			ou command of 41 San Sector which has been left the Division	

Leslie W.B. Morrell
O. Fd. Amb
24 Fd Bn

COPY.

B.E.F.

SUMMARY OF MEDICAL WAR DIARIES of

24th DIVISION,

    1st Corps, 1st Army, till 20.4.17.
    2nd Corps, 1st Army, from 20.4.17.-12.5.17.
    2nd Corps, 2nd Army, from 12.5.17.

WESTERN FRONT, APRIL - MAY, 1917.

A.D.M.S. Colonel F. Busnell.
D.A.D.M.S. Capt. E. H. Russell.

SUMMARISED UNDER THE FOLLOWING HEADINGS:-

Phase "B" - Battle of Arras. "April - May, 1917."

1st Period, April 1917. Attack on Vimy Ridge.

2nd Period, May 1917. Capture of Siegfried Line.

24th Division, B.E.F. Western Front.

A.D.M.S. Col. F. Busnell. April 1917.

1st Corps, 1st Army, till 20.4.17. 1.
2nd Corps, from 20.4.17.

Phase "E" - Battle of Arras. April - May, 1917.

1st Period, April 1917. Attack on Vimy Ridge.

April	H.Q. at Barlin.
3rd	Moves. To Braquemont.
6th	Operations Enemy. Heavy shelling on front Fosse 10.
7th	Med. Arr. A 'Super' A.D.S. at S.1.b.9.5. administered by 74th F.A. formed.
	A.D.S. - Aix Noulette.
	M.D.S. - Fosse 10.
12th	Operations Cdns. attacked Vimy Ridge.
	Evacuation Worked well, in spite of weather and state of roads. Wheeled Stretchers used in lieu of Amb. cars.
13th	Casualties 24th Divn. 12 & 233 W.
14th	Operations Enemy. Some large shells in 74th F.A. No casualties.
15th	Operations & Med. Arr. British advanced. Considerable difficulty in keeping touch with Regts. especially in R. Sector where Arras Rd. turned from new line. Cross country roads did not exist. Attached App. 2. (Put back in Diary)
	Evacuation Almost entirely done through A.D.S. Calonne from all of front.
	Military Situation Front line converging on Lens.
	Med. Arr. 73rd and 74th F.A's opened A.D.S. Lievin.
16th	Evacuation, Terrain & Ops. Enemy. About 4 hrs. to A.D.S. Calonne and return owing to very heavy going and much shell fire.
19th-20th	Military Situation & Med. Arr. Attached App. 3. (Put back in Diary)
20th	Moves & Transfer To Norrent Fontes and to 2nd Corps.

24th Division B.E.F.   Western Front.

A.D.M.S. Col. F. Busnell.   April 1917.

2nd Corps, 1st Army.

Phase "B" - Battle of Arras. "April - May, 1917."

1st Period. April 1917. Attack on Vimy Ridge.

April   H.Q. at Norrent Fontes.

20th   Moves & Transfer   To Norrent Fontes and to 2nd Corps.

24th   Moves   To Bomy.

30th   Med. Arr. Div. Scabies Hospital at Mallonoy Farm, one mile N. of St. Hilaire, 4 miles W. of Busnes, O.31.a.5.5. (36A)

Health of Troops   Owing to exigencies of service and very cold weather, there were 14 cases of Trench Foot, all slight.

Infectious diseases = 28 (mostly Rose Measles.)

Appendices   Ops. O. 104   d/7th

    2.   Med. Arr.   d/15th

    3.   Ops. O. 105   d/18th

             Med. Arr.   d/17th

All Apps. attached to 1st copies.

<u>24th Division, B.E.F.</u>　　　　　　　　　<u>Western Front.</u>

A.D.M.S. Col. F. Busnell.　　　　　<u>April 1917.</u>

<u>1st Corps, 1st Army, till 20.4.17.</u>　　1.
<u>2nd Corps, from 20.4.17.</u>

<u>Phase "B"- Battle of Arras. April - May, 1917.</u>

<u>1st Period, April 1917. Attack on Vimy Ridge.</u>

April		H.Q. at Barlin.
3rd	<u>Moves.</u>	To Braquemont.
6th	<u>Operations Enemy.</u>	Heavy shelling on front Fosse 10.
7th	<u>Med. Arr.</u>	A 'Super' A.D.S. at S.1.b.9.5. administered by 74th F.A. formed.

　　　　　　　　A.D.S.　-　Aix Noulette.

　　　　　　　　M.D.S.　-　Fosse 10.

12th　　<u>Operations</u>　Cdns. attacked Vimy Ridge.

　　　　<u>Evacuation</u>　Worked well, in spite of weather and state of roads. Wheeled Stretchers used in lieu of Amb. cars.

13th　　<u>Casualties</u>　24th Divn. 12 & 233 W.

14th　　<u>Operations Enemy.</u> Some large shells in 74th F.A. No casualties.

15th　　<u>Operations & Med. Arr.</u>　British advanced.
　　　　Considerable difficulty in keeping touch with Regts. especially in R. Sector where Arras Rd. turned from new line. Cross country roads did not exist. Attached App. 2.
　　　　<u>Evacuation</u>　Almost entirely done through A.D.S. Calonne from all of front.
　　　　<u>Military Situation</u>　Front line converging on Lens.
　　　　<u>Med. Arr.</u>　73rd and 74th F.A's opened A.D.S. Lievin.

16th　　<u>Evacuation, Terrain & Ops. Enemy.</u> About 4 hrs. to A.D.S. Calonne and return owing to very heavy going and much shell fire.

19th-20th　<u>Military Situation & Med. Arr.</u> Attached App. 3.

20th　　<u>Moves & Transfer</u>　To Norrent Fontes and to 2nd Corps.

24th Division B.E.F. 　　　　　　　　　　Western Front.
A.D.M.S. Col. F. Busnell.　　　　　　　April 1917.
    2nd Corps, 1st Army.　　　　　　　　　2.

Phase "B" - Battle of Arras. "April - May, 1917."
1st Period. April 1917. Attack on Vimy Ridge.

April　　H.Q. at Norrent Fontes.
20th　　Moves & Transfer To Norrent Fontes and to 2nd Corps.
24th　　Moves To Bomy.
30th　　Med. Arr. Div. Scabies Hospital at Mallonoy Farm, one mile N. of
　　　　St. Hilaire, 4 miles W. of Busnes, O.31.a.5.5. (36A)
　　　　Health of Troops Owing to exigencies of service and very cold
　　　　weather, there were 14 cases of Trench Foot, all slight.
　　　　　　Infectious diseases = 28 (mostly Rose Measles.)
　　　　Appendices　Ops. O. 104　　d/7th
　　　　　　2.　　Med. Arr.　　　d/15th
　　　　　　3.　　Ops. O. 105　　d/18th
　　　　　　　　　Med. Arr.　　　d/17th

```
D.D.M.S. I Corps        72 Fld Ambce
24th Divn "G"           73    do
24th Divn "Q"           74    do
H.Q. 17 I.B.            C.R.A.
     72 do              C.R.E.
     73 do              24th Divl Train
```

The disposition of Field Ambulances with regard to Brigades will be as under :-

    72 Fld Ambce to 72 I.B.   A.D.S. at BULLY GRENAY
    73 Fld Ambce to 17 I.B.   A.D.S. at CALONNE
    74 Fld Ambce to 73 I.B.   A.D.S. at AIX NOULETTE

In connection with these A.D.Ss. advanced posts will be established as required.

24 D.H.Q.,
15/4/17.

                                                        C. U. Russell
                                                      Captain D.A.D.M.S.,
                                                      for Colonel A.D.M.S.

SECRET.

R.A.M.C., OPERATION ORDER No. 105.
by
Colonel F.P. Buswell, C.M.G., A.M.S., A.D.M.S. 24 Divn.

Map Ref. Sheet 36B S.E.2. and Sheet 36C S.W.1. 1/10000

1. 24th Division will be relieved by 46th Division. Relief to commence 18th April and the Infantry reliefs are to be completed by the night 19-20th April. On relief 24th Divn will be withdrawn into the Rest Area in the ST HILAIRE Area.

2. No.1 North Midland F. Amb'ce will take over FOSSE 10 (B-8- central), the Advanced Dressing Station, CALONNE (M-14-c-7-8), and Advanced Dressing Station, LIEVIN (M-22-c-7-7).

3. No.2 North Midland F. Amb'ce will take over the Rest Station LABEUVRIERE and the Advanced Dressing Station, BULLY GRENAY (B-11-a-7-7), and the R.A.M.C. Post at Cite St Pierre (M-11-c-1-1).

4. No.3 North Midland F. Amb'ce will take over Advanced Dressing Station, AIX-NOULETTE (B-22-a-2-6) and the Main Dressing Station and the Advanced Dressing Station at LIEVIN-White House, (M-28-b-4-1).

5. No.73 F. Amb'ce -less "C" Section" complete, will remain at the Boys' School, BRACQUEMONT (L-25-b-3-7), to assist No 7 C.C.S. "C". Section will proceed to LIVOSSART in the Rest Area.

6. No.74 F. Amb'ce will proceed on relief to LCOUECELES.

7. No.72 F. Amb'ce will proceed on relief to LA COUTURE.

8. F. Amb'ces will arrange for Motor Amb'ce Cars to accompany their respective Brigades on the march.

9. All Trench Stores will be handed over to in-coming Units.

10. All details of reliefs to be arranged between Officers Commanding concerned.

11. Relief of Advanced Dressing Stations and R.A.M.C. Posts to be completed by mid-night 19-20th April.

12. Relief of Main Dressing Stations to be completed by 12 noon 20th April.

13. Completion of reliefs to be reported to this office.

14. A.D.M.S. Office will close at Bracquemont at 10 am. on the 20th April and will re-open at a place to be notified later.

E V Russell
Capt D.A.D.M.S.
for Col A.D.M.S.

24 D.H.Q.
18-4-17.

Copies to:-
4-3 War Diary & File.
4-6 72-73-74 F.As.
7-8 H'qrs "C" & "A"
9   41st Sany Section.
10   24 Divl Train

11-13 17-72-73 Infy Bdes.
14   C.R.A.
15   C.R.E.
16   A.D.M.S., 46th Div.
17   D.D.M.S. 1 Corps.

1st Corps

72,73,74 Fld Ambces
17,72,73 Inf.Bdes
24 Divn "Q" & "G"
C.R.A.
C.R.E.
Divl Train
D.D.M.S. I Corps

MEDICAL ARRANGEMENTS.

No.73 Fld Ambce have now formed an Advanced Dressing Station at LIEVIN: map reference M-22-c-8-8. The R.A.M.C. Posts in connection with this are situated at M-21-a-central and M-21-c-9-8. Evacuation is by wheeled stretcher, rail and hand carry to CALONNE, thence by car to BRACQUEMONT.

As soon as the road from CALONNE to LIEVIN is open, motor ambulances will be used.

No.74 Fld Ambce have opened an Advanced Dressing Station in the Chapel of the WHITE HOUSE, LIEVIN: cases are evacuated to CALONNE by wheeled stretcher.

24 D.H.Q.,
17/4/17.

Captain D.A.D.M.S.,
for Colonel A.D.M.S.

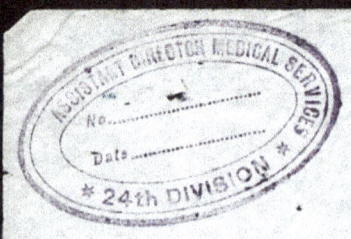

Copy No. 3

R.A.M.C. OPERATION ORDER No. 104
by
Colonel F.R.BUSWELL C.M.G., A.M.S.,
A.D.M.S. 24th Divn.

April 7th, 1917.

Reference Trench Map
1/10,000

Reference 24th Division Operation Order No. 126
dated 4/4/1917.

1. A Super Advanced Dressing Station will be located at S.1.b.9.5, administered by Officer Commanding 74th Field Ambulance, from Advanced Dressing Station AIX NOULETTE and Main Dressing Station FOSSE 10.

2. Medical Officers of Units concerned will get in touch with Officer i/c Super Advanced Dressing Station, to ensure co-operation.

E. H. Russell
Captain R.A.M.C.,
D.A.D.M.S. 24th Division.

Copies. 1 File
2 War Diary
3 do
4 73 Inf.Bde
5 74 Fld Ambce
6 24th Divn "G"

SECRET

Amb. Operation Order No. 103.
by
Colonel F.R. Buswell C.M.G., A.M.S.,
A.D.M.S. 24th Division

Reference   29th March 1917.
1/10,000   I.   No 72 Field Ambulance, 24th Division will take
Secret French   over the Advanced Dressing Station, ABLAIN St NAZAIRE
Map   (X.10.d.9.8) and the Ramb. Post in connection
                 with it, from No 12 Canadian Field Ambulance,
                 4th Canadian Division on 1st April 1917.
           II.   All French Stores will be taken over and
                 lists forwarded to this Office.
           III. All details of relief to be arranged direct
                 between Officers Commanding concerned.
           IV.   Relief to be completed by 12.0 midnight 1st/2nd
                 April.
           V.   Completion of relief to be reported to A.D.M.S.
                 24th Division in B.A.B. code.
           VI.   Sick and wounded will be evacuated in
                 24th Divisional Ambulance cars to No 12 Canadian
                 Field Ambulance, GRAND SERVINS (Q.34.a.3.6).
           VII. Acknowledge. Done

                                        C.U. Russell.
                                        Capt. Ramb.
                                        D.A.D.M.S. 24th Divn.

Copy No 1 – 3   War Diary & File   11.   17th Inf Bde
          4.   72 Field Amb.   12.   72nd "   "
          5.   73   "   "   13.   73rd "   "
          6.   74   "   "   14.   C.R.A
          7.   41 San Section   15.   C.R.E.
          8.   HQ 24 Div 'G'   16.   A.D.M.S. 4th Cdn. Div.
          9.   HQ 24 Div 'A'   17.   D.D.M.S. 1 Corps.
          10.   24 Divl. Train

  G 295/130.
7.4.17.

Copy No. 6

R.A.M.C. OPERATION ORDER No.104
by
Colonel F.R.BUSWELL C.M.G., A.M.S.,
A.D.M.S. 24th Divn.

April 7th, 1917.

Reference Trench Map
1/10,000

Reference 24th Division Operation Order No.126
dated 4/4/1917.

1. A Super Advanced Dressing Station will be located at S.1.b.9.5, administered by Officer Commanding 74th Field Ambulance, from Advanced Dressing Station AIX NOULETTE and Main Dressing Station FOSSE 10.

2. Medical Officers of Units concerned will get in touch with Officer i/c Super Advanced Dressing Station, to ensure co-operation.

Acknowledge
7/4/17.

E.U. Russell
Captain R.A.M.C.,
D.A.D.M.S. 24th Division.

Copies. 1 File
2 War Diary
3 do
4 73 Inf.Bde
5 74 Fld Ambce
6 24th Divn "G"

A.D.M.S, 24th Division

COMMITTEE FOR THE
MEDICAL HISTORY OF THE WAR
Date 10 JUL. 1917

Army Form C. 2118.

WAR DIARY
or
INTELLIGENCE SUMMARY.
(Erase heading not required.)

Vol 21

Original

A.D.M.S
24th Division
XXI
Vol 20
May 1917

WAR DIARY or INTELLIGENCE SUMMARY

MAY 1917

Place	Date	Hour	Summary of Events and Information	Remarks and references to Appendices
B M Y.	1st		Great improvement in the weather. Visited 72nd Fd Amb.	
"	2nd		H & an Am. [personnel] went to Review. Evacuation of P.O.W. units to labor - P.B. men at Esquelbecq. Arlington [Carriageers] Arlingham. Gave a lift. Visited Boxing & welders. Ypres & Chateau	
"	3rd		Fine day.	
"	4th		Routine	
"	5th		Paths by the road opposite Boxing completed	
"	6th		The Fd Amb leave Bethune (where the shelling was a little too heavy at present Hq where all the Battalions of Brigade H.Q. have been moved) & proceeds to Maloney Farm sheet 36 A 0.31. a 5.5. where they will establish the Div. Scabies Hospital & open the Fd Amb. Capt. E.V. Russell R.A.M.C. to-day proceeded on leave. Reinforcements Capt. A.E. Jelbe, Lts. V.T.C. Burton, Lt L. du Vergé & Lt. J. F. Winter R.A.M.C. joined division. Cold wind from the North today.	

Army Form C. 2118.

WAR DIARY
or
INTELLIGENCE SUMMARY.
(Erase heading not required.)

Summary of Events and Information

May. 1917.

Place	Date	Hour	Summary of Events and Information	Remarks and references to Appendices
BOMY	7th	—	Platoon	
"	8th	"	"	
"	9th	"	"	
Norrent Fontes	10th		Left Bomy for Norrent Fontes 2.45.	
"	11th		Captain Houghton to Lillers on leave to join 1st Army, & Sergt Webb now Coy/Sergt Mjr.	
"	12		Left Norrent Fontes for Winnezeele. 6 am. to Abele then Lorries & Cars to where we are.	
Winnezeele	13th		2nd & Capt. Abele Pefinghem Poperinghe Brandhock turning billets interior. A Road 28/4/47	
"	14th		Arrangements for men 7 to 7.30 open Gs, St S. & a Corps for highly recruited [?] Brandhock a Poperinghe, Cavanaghs Rd Against deal of Consolidation work to do done. 13th Ft Amb. Hqs, 1 Section Marches with Bde 2 Section Lorries at Steenvoorde Block at 6. 2. Battalion 17th JB. t Transport Training Battalion J. R.Y.G. to Headquarters of Caswell. 14th Full talk new cement Rue de Brackstaple Poperinghem & STrs. Left Winnezeele. 6 am. 15 Bttg Brandhock in tents. Very cold in night	[signature]
	15th			

Army Form C. 2118.

WAR DIARY
or
INTELLIGENCE SUMMARY.
(Erase heading not required.)

Instructions regarding War Diaries and Intelligence Summaries are contained in F.S. Regs., Part II. and the Staff Manual respectively. Title pages will be prepared in manuscript.

Place	Date	Hour	Summary of Events and Information	Remarks and references to Appendices
BOMBSHOEK	16th	—	Cold dull. Visited front area via Ypres Lille gate to Zillebeke. Found when ADS in Ypres dugout not adjacent Ypres railway along N.Z. Wieltje tunnel. Duckwalk to Com. from A division accommodates about 20 per place. All protected cellar full of water. Pumped out & cleaned. Then on to Zillebeke village to ADS of Wessex battalion 9th East Surreys also for place walking two. Are clear. Showed day since the division in the line. She a few days returned without incident. Ypres look much more battered especially the Asylum which he had to vacate on ADS many to other buildings in the Ypres. Known killing 3 & wounding 4. Penn C. Conference at 2nd Brigade & Capt. of Aus. 23, 24, 41, 47. Division in present Visited 74th Fd Amb at Poperinghe & 72nd at Brandhoek. Capt. Russell Spoke [?] returned from leave. Very hot weather. Heavy Cannonade. Gas alarms. to 72nd Fd Amb. Captain E.V. Russell Penn C. returned from leave.	
"	17th			
"	18th			
"	19th		To 72 Fd Amb. x Cops. h.S.S. for lightly wounded preparing well.	

T.P.134. Wt. W708-776. 50000. 4/15. Sir J.C. & S.

Army Form C. 2118.

WAR DIARY
or
INTELLIGENCE SUMMARY.
(Erase heading not required.)

May 1917.

Place	Date	Hour	Summary of Events and Information	Remarks and references to Appendices
Bandhoek	20th		Returned to forward area Ypres & Zillebeke. Heavy shelling.	
	21st		7/72nd Fd Amb. Inspected P.B. room.	
	22nd		C in C visited 2nd Fd Amb. H.Q. Inspected P.B. at 71st, 73rd Fd Amb.	
	23rd		Got 2nd Army & 5 M.B. Visited M.F.S. & C.C.S. being used as Provisionals.	
			by 72nd Fd Amb.	
	24th		Conference at X Corps KMS. Visited 74th Fd Amb Poperinghe.. at 8 pm	
			the Ambulance is heavily shelled & Lt & Gen Perrigman M.F.C	
			had left by storm. Off Capt seriously injured. His patients injured.	
	25th		7th Fd Amb. moved to L 20 c.5.6. S.E. of Poperinghe	
			Inspected 97 & Empl. unit. Co attached 24th Div. 17 Julsen in spite	
			Looked hopeful for any employment. Got the visited Brandhoek	
			72nd Fd Amb	
	26th		Visited forward area 41st Fd Amb with Hugh Thomson Here & Lt Ang 41st	
			Runyhook. Outside Kulatpest A.D.S. Via Duckwa & Middleton Lane	
			thence Visited the 4 R.A.P.s I walk to Pommergoles, Colostray Post.	
			Very hot day.	

WAR DIARY
or
INTELLIGENCE SUMMARY.

Army Form C. 2118.

Place	Date	Hour	Summary of Events and Information	Remarks and references to Appendices
	May		1917.	
Nieuwkerke	27th		Very hot. Heavy shelling in Kemmel vicinity of camps.	
"	28th		Open shell attacks on night very slight Washington officer.	
"	29th		Staffs toured the front line (74") Bn been O.C. 73 = to teach	
"	30th		Officers moved to Reninghelst. 73 = to teach moved to	
			R 5. a. 5.0. that 27.	
"	31st		Conference of X" Corps. Officers visited 73 = Bde + 73 = of the line	
			moved 73 = to Reninghelst Tunnels.	
			74" Bn took over, 15 - K 15. a 3. 1. that 27. to X Corps	
			training area.	

140/229

A.D.M.S., 24th Div.

June 1917

COMMITTEE FOR THE
MEDICAL HISTORY OF THE WAR
Date -7 AUG. 1917

WAR DIARY
or
INTELLIGENCE SUMMARY.

Army Form C. 2118.

Original

A D M S
94th Div
Vol 22
June 1917

Army Form C. 2118.

WAR DIARY
or
INTELLIGENCE SUMMARY.
(Erase heading not required.)

Instructions regarding War Diaries and Intelligence
Summaries are contained in F. S. Regs., Part II.
and the Staff Manual respectively. Title pages
will be prepared in manuscript.

June 1917.

Place	Date	Hour	Summary of Events and Information	Remarks and references to Appendices
RENINGHELST	1st		The 73rd Flank moved to Reninghelst Hut & Camp Area throughout. 464 Shelter 1580 Hundred to hold enemy operations.	
"	2nd		Continued Preparation. Routine.	
"	3rd		Very heavy shelling of enemy.	
"	4th		H.Q. Camp shelled by naval arms, piercing shells, some wounded. 73rd A. Anks. Attk over building from 138th St. Auck. Open to level risk of which there are great numbers from Army Corps Area. Salvon returns to movements.	
"	5th		Based on Employment company & T.O men. Below operation took all day.	
"	6th		Very heavy bombardment of enemy. Lieut. B.R. to 74 & Anks. Captain S. Nhut Eng. has been avoided the building line & very well observed. Very hot. Intense operations now in force. Capt. F.L Peart same & arrived from base. Lieut. (P. Ryan Ram 2. 10 O.R. reported temporary duty 131 "F.A. (Ran. C. defence of the line. tir amounts to 5.O. & 45 O.R.) 5.O.R. 134 F.A. also reported.	
"	7th		Day. Attack commenced at 3.10 am. 24th Bn. hot at feast engaged. at. 3.15. 24th Bn attacked & with very few casualties attained its objective. (G.O. 2560.R. hrm 7. 10 hrm 8th June. Shelter lawn of reports. 32 Shelter 16... Sir in Road... 30. I Shir Complete. Been Rive in 4. 72 and 73rd F.A. 4MB	

T2134. Wt. W708-770. 500000. 4/15. Sir J.C. & S.

WAR DIARY
or
INTELLIGENCE SUMMARY.

(Erase heading not required.)

Army Form C. 2118.

Place	Date	Hour	Summary of Events and Information	Remarks and references to Appendices
REINGHELST	8th		June 1917. Heavy shelling of huts area. Casualties O.9. OR. 2.18.	
			Captain to Red King M.C. S.R. and 74th Fd Amb. killed late yesterday evening by shell & Captain E.A. WHITTINGHAM R.A.M.C. S.R. also killed tonight. Attached to 12th Royal Fusiliers. Both excellent officers.	
"	9th		Capt. J.R.P. KLEIN R.A.M.C. and Lieut. H.F. BELLMORE R.A.M.C. temporarily assumed 7th instant. Weather very hot.	
"	10th		Lieut Major L. 25 O.R. wounded to their units. Casualties of known has expired 29 O. 6 oo O R.	
	11th		Active operations went to wound at 3 am.	
	12th			
"	13th		General intime - Heavy Thundery storm. 60ty. moved to MICMAC Camp M.31.d. but dusty incomplete plan	
MICMAC Camp	14		17th & 73rd 1.B. attacked enemy at 7.30 pm obtaining their objective recently. Casualties slight in assault by 72nd & 74th to the Clyde Road - Broodhoek (O.4. OR. 68.) main dump station	
"	15		WARDay & Capt to Country of discharged to West 67 M.D.S. for 2nd Field Amb. Located in Ypres-men Avenue Entrance.	

WAR DIARY
or
INTELLIGENCE SUMMARY

Army Form C. 2118.

Place	Date	Hour	Summary of Events and Information	Remarks and references to Appendices
	June 1917			
MICMAC Camp	16"		Lieut P.A. MITCHELL R.A.M.C. arrived & posted to 73rd Ottawa Batt.	
"	17"		72nd Lt.Stand. at Reymants Avenue good site: Indian Tuller, stores i.e. good sheet of iron & dugouts of sorts in great numbers. I stood at Collecting Post Euridant. Killed 6, & wounded 13. O.R. of 73rd Ottawa. Return to subsequently died. Lieut. V.C. Boot-Room &. T.M. Kipford wounded returned duty. Canadian Corps Shelling of long range hy heavy firme entire.	
"	18"			
"	19"			
"	20"		With Col. Fair. to visit 72 & 73rd Ottawa. O.P.s. at R.2.a.9.8. Shell 27. The latter's post situation of great possibilities. The present firing well seen & credited with very nasty stay burst of the shrine of the firing well sanitary section is very much felt. Our firing men Steak explicit that the talking away the Mint efficient Secretary to return but well has been our event	

Army Form C. 2118.

WAR DIARY
or
INTELLIGENCE SUMMARY.
(Erase heading not required.)

Instructions regarding War Diaries and Intelligence Summaries are contained in F.S. Regs., Part II. and the Staff Manual respectively. Title pages will be prepared in manuscript.

Place	Date	Hour	Summary of Events and Information	Remarks and references to Appendices
	June		1919.	
MICMAC Camp.	20th		Upon whom the expenses lets Sits had been. Met Gen. who had seen Gen. Currie of a dinner last expressed the great wish to well trained parties. Section could been provisionally allowed to rehearse a slip of this in the rehearsal opinion of all ranks. Divisim., was on the spot & knew this subject and must familiarise in nothing in the way of efficiency to which I now refer the change.	
"	21st		Lieut. Stone RnmC 12 A.T. gassed & evacuated. Army M.O's very heavy ADMS xxx tin hoffice & Wounded from ADS. Review Control to Paal.	Canadian
"	22d		Heavy rain. Heavy long range fire from troops all night.	
"	23d		Temp. Cpl. Lieut. A.M.Crawford Manl.C. joined as reinforcement yesterday.	
"	24th		Rabies x Conf. & Wounded from HQrs. the dual control. in 30th & 24th Div.	
"	25th		Rescue for the the forward area Conference with H.Q. 72nd & 74th Fd. Amb, a new line of evacuation for the Brigades.	

T2134. Wt. W708-776. 500090. 4/15. Sir J. C. & S.

WAR DIARY or INTELLIGENCE SUMMARY

Army Form C. 2118.

June. 1917.

Place	Date	Hour	Summary of Events and Information	Remarks and references to Appendices
MICMAC Camp	26th		Stand to Enter called to Evacuation of A diff cullen. Zillebeck Bund. Obliged also Racing dugouts by intense shelling.	
"	27th		Capt W Bryn Ram C. found as reinforcement attached to 72nd Fd Amb.	
"	28th		Bombed the Ramming Camp. Shelled. Capt L.H. Stein Ram C. also to Ranc off / Wellesse	
			Gorson returned to duty. Capt Cunningham Ram C off 22nd Bn. returned holt. 72nd / 174th Fd Amb. relieved by Fd Amb 22nd Div. to M.A.C. dich-out unit.	
	29th		Adms 28th Div called in followers over	
	30th		Stay moved to Lumber at 9 am. my let during the present time in the line including this attack, the hour occurring in the Ram C. line. Killed 2 O, wounded 4 O. to 6 OR to 37 OR. Sick & wounds 5	
			72nd Fd Amb to LUMBRES. 74th Fd Amb. Christian Francy H.M.C. ETTON Col To [signature]

B.E.F.

SUMMARY OF MEDICAL WAR DIARIES OF 24th Div. 10th Corps, 2nd ARMY.

Western Front Operations - June 1917.

A.D.M.S.

SUMMARISED UNDER THE FOLLOWING HEADINGS:-

Phase "D" - Battle of Messines - June 1917.

B.E.F.

1.

24th Div. 10th Corps. 2nd ARMY. Western Front.
A.D.M.S.   June 1917.

PHASE "D" - Battle of Messines - June 1917.

Headquarters at Reninghelst.

June 3rd.	Operations.	Heavy shelling.
4th.	Ops. Enemy.	D.H.Q. camp shelled by Naval armour piercing shells.
	Casualties.	"Some wounded."
5th.	Operations.	Very heavy bombardment of enemy.
6th.	Decorations.	Capt. D. Reid King awarded M.C. (74th F.A)
	Operations.	"Active operations now in force."
7th.	Operations.	"Der Tag". Attack at 5.10 a.m. 24th Div. attacked at 3.15 (?p.m.) with very few casualties and attained objective.
	Casualties.	Total noon 7th - noon 8th = 9 & 256 W.
	Medical Arrangements.	Stretcher bearers of Regts. 32. Div. Band 30. & 3 complete Br. Div's of 72nd, 73rd, and 74th F.A.
8th.	Operations Enemy.	Heavy shelling of new area.
	Casualties.	9 & 218 wounded.
	Casualties, R.A.M.C.	7.6.17. Capt. D. Reid King M.C. killed, 74th F.A.
		Capt. C.A. Whittingham M.O. i/c 12th/R.Fusiliers killed.
10th.	Casualties.	Total 29 & 600 wounded.
13th.	Moves.	To Mic Mac Camp H.31.b.

B.E.F.

2.

24th Div. 10th Corps. 2nd ARMY.   Western Front.
A.D.M.S.   June 1917.

PHASE "D" - Battle of Messines - June 1917.

Headquarters at Mic Mac Camp H.31.b.

June 14th. Operations. 17 & 73 I.B. attacked at 7.30 p.m. and
            gained objectives.
            Casualties.)   "Slight" - 4 & 68 wounded.
            Evacuation.)   Evacuated by 72nd and 74th F.A. to
            La Clytte Rd and Brandhoek M.D.S.

17th.   Operations, Enemy.) Shell struck Coll.P. Kruisstraat.
            Casualties, R.A.M.C)

                                 0 & 6 killed.   ) 72nd
                                 0 & 13 wounded (4 D.of W)) F.A.
            Lt. V.T.C. Bent M.O. i/c 1st N. Stafford wounded.

18th.   Operations Enemy.) Shelling by long range gun.
            Casualties.   ) "Very heavy"

20th.   Sanitation. Divisional area crowded.
                        Absence of San. Sec. very much felt.

21st.   Casualties Gas, R.A.M.C. Lt. Skene M.O. 12th R.F. wounded,
            gas.

22nd.   Operations Enemy. Long range guns active all night.
26th.   Zillebeke Bund destroyed also Rly.
            dugouts by intense shelling.

28th.   Camp bombed and shelled.

30th.   Moves. To Lumbres.
            Casualties, R.A.M.C. Total while Division in line.

                      2 & 6 K. 4 & 37 W. D.of W. 0 & 5.

            Appendices. Nil.

B.E.F.

SUMMARY OF MEDICAL WAR DIARIES OF 24th Div. 10th Corps, 2nd ARMY.

Western Front Operations - June 1917.

A.D.M.S.

SUMMARISED UNDER THE FOLLOWING HEADINGS:-

Phase "D" - Battle of Messines - June 1917.

B.E.F.

1.

24th Div. 10th Corps. 2nd ARMY.   Western Front.
A.D.M.S.   June 1917.

PHASE "D" - Battle of Messines - June 1917.

Headquarters at Reninghelst.

June 3rd.   Operations. Heavy shelling.

4th.   Ops. Enemy.   D.H.Q. camp shelled by Naval armour piercing shells.

Casualties. "Some wounded."

5th.   Operations. Very heavy bombardment of enemy.

6th.   Decorations. Capt. D. Reid King awarded M.C. (74th F.

Operations. "Active operations now in force."

7th.   Operations. "Der Tag". Attack at 5.10 a.m.
24th Div. attacked at 3.15 (?p.m.) with very few casualties and attained objective.

Casualties. Total noon 7th - noon 8th = 9 & 256 W.

Medical Arrangements. Stretcher bearers of Regts 32

Div. Band   30

& 3 complete Br. Div's of 72nd
73rd, and 74th F.A.

8th.   Operations Enemy. Heavy shelling of new area.

Casualties.   9 & 218 wounded.

Casualties, R.A.M.C. 7.6.17. Capt. D. Reid King M.C. killed, 74th F.A.

Capt. C.A. Whittingham M.O.
R.
i/p 12th/Fusiliers killed.

10th.   Casualties. Total 29 & 600 wounded.

13th,   Moves. To Mic Mac Camp H.31.b.

B.E.F.

24th Div. 10th Corps. 2nd ARMY.   Western Front.
A.D.M.S.   June 1917.

PHASE "D" - Battle of Messines - June 1917.

Headquarters at Mic Mac Camp H.31.b.

June 14th. Operations. 17 & 73 I.B. attacked at 7.30 p.m. and gained objectives.

Casualties.)   "Slight" - 4 & 68 wounded.
Evacuation.)   Evacuated by 72nd and 74th F.A. to La Clytte Rd and Brandhoek M.D.S.

17th.   Operations, Enemy.) Shell struck Coll.P. Kruistraat.
Casualties, R.A.M.C)

                               0 & 6 killed.   ) 72nd
)
                               0 & 13 wounded (4 D.of W)) F.A.

Lt. V.T.C. Bent M.O. i/c 1st N. Stafford wounded.

18th.   Operations Enemy.) Shelling by long range gun.
        Casualties.   ) "Very heavy"

20th.   Sanitation. Divisional area crowded.
                     Absence of San. Sec. very much felt.

21st.   Casualties Gas, R.A.M.C. Lt. Skene M.O. 12th R.F. wounded gas.

22nd.   Operations Enemy. Long range guns active all night.

26th.   Zillebeke Bund destroyed also Rly. dugouts by intense shelling.

28th.   Camp bombed and shelled.

30th.   Moves. To Lumbres.

Casualties, R.A.M.C. Total while Division in line.

                           2 & 6 K. 4 & 37 W. D.of W. O & 5.

Appendices. Nil.

24th
A.D.M.S. Division

COMMITTEE FOR THE
MEDICAL HISTORY OF THE WAR
Date   10 SEP. 1917

WAR DIARY
or
INTELLIGENCE SUMMARY.

Army Form C. 2118.

Original
ADMS
94th Div
Vol 23
July 1917

Army Form C. 2118.

WAR DIARY
or
INTELLIGENCE SUMMARY.
(Erase heading not required.)

Place	Date	Hour	Summary of Events and Information	Remarks and references to Appendices
	JULY 1917			
LUMBRES	1/7/17	9 a.m.	General Routine. O.C. 72 Field Amb. visited Office. D.A.D.M.S visited 74 F.A at ALINCTHUN	
"	2/7/17	"	M.O ½ R.? returned from leave. M.O ½ 12th Notts & D. enty proceeded on leave. A D M S visited 74 Field Amb.	
"	3/7/17	"	General Routine. A D M S to J.C O hen re dental treatment for Troops in present area.	
"	4/7/17	"	A D M S proceeded on leave. Officer Comdg 72 F A acting for him while on leave. Inventory P.13 forward held at 72 F.A. 24th Div Transferred from 10th to 22nd Corps. 5th Army from this date	
"	5/7/17	"	General Routine	
"	6/7/17	"	Visited D.M.S 22nd Div	
"	7/7/17	"	All medical returns to to now sent to II Corps	
"	8/7/17	"	Lieut O.M. Crawford to 53 C.C.S authority M.S 5th Army. General Routine	
"	9/7/17	"	Lieut Blyth to 5 C D in for Duty General Routine. Visited 27 D W	
"	10/7/17	"	Went Round Line	

WAR DIARY or INTELLIGENCE SUMMARY

Army Form C. 2118.

JULY 1917

Place	Date	Hour	Summary of Events and Information	Remarks and references to Appendices
LUMBRES	11/12	9 a.m.	General routine.	
"	12/13		General Routine. O.C. 92 Fld. Amb. Proceeded on leave.	
"	14		O.R.s returned from leave.	
"	15/16		General routine.	
"	17		Visited 11 Corps at Arques for conference to Impending operations. Route to Lunghem to inspect new chests tried title of Inferior Quality on the 1st N. Stafford Regt. The 1st/7th Bn. moved to DE VES COAS, tried 5th & 6th to LUMBRES.	
"	18		By ret & typically.	
"	19		Left LUMBRES at 8.40 arrived STEENVOORDE about 11 am.	
STEENVOORDE	20		Visited Amb. 23. 2nd at ZEVECOTEN. Run down at the billets & visited him FOS & LOCK on Ypres Canal. 3 govt. Cupola army rate to M. Canal huts. Also tried to get to Da Belle Stay Post at LOMAS Wood, but the shelling around Stray Farm 9 in. to leaving that he had to return.	
"	21/22		General routine & preparation for a Chlor operation pending shortly.	
"	23		Left STEENVOORDE at 9am arriving ZEVECOTEN took over fm Hut amb 23 7.15	

WAR DIARY
or
INTELLIGENCE SUMMARY.
(Erase heading not required.)

Army Form C. 2118.

Place	Date	Hour	Summary of Events and Information	Remarks and references to Appendices
ZEVECOTEN	24		Left ST PROL at 3.30 a.m. to try to get to LINDENHOEK HQrs after journey. Remainder got mixed up in a fog. Shell burst apprehs the eye & hurting our very ill of the 4th. Went an hour or two to return the whole of the Canal bank in the vicinity of LOCRE by flat road with dumps. Epr. shell. The Jn. mining & shell him along the Grand Rhubay life really nervous must down using shrapnel when at the same time. Looking mainly up with shrapnel. He Epo. made on feet very tired in the weakened of wounded. Capt G.S. ROSE R.A.M.C. attached 9th East Surreys a very excellent officer Killed by shell out side his R.A.P. at Compton Ernus.	
"	25		Other difficulty about reinforcements 6 other third of 8 officers have been commandeered for the 11 Corps show during station. Leaving one very short to deal in the front line & the relief brigade casualties, I have represented the matter but am told to delay orders. Lieut G.W. Stephen Name e. fm The Philippines sent as a reinforcement practically useless.	JWMB

Army Form C. 2118.

WAR DIARY
or
INTELLIGENCE SUMMARY.
(Erase heading not required.)

Place	Date	Hour	Summary of Events and Information	Remarks and references to Appendices
ZIVECOTEN.	July 1917			
	26th		Left HQ 72nd Inf. Bmt. with Lt. Col. G.R. Edwards & proceeded to ROARMERSEN & front out new sort of bulletly wounded landing post. Remainder with Lt. Hilton & Lt. Cope them S.S. in field driven by petrol engine. 10 a.m. for trestle sealed on steel tops filled with steam then & A.R.T. Lee B. at Place my front next. We then drew by Captain W.J. Webster. Route 72nd Lt. Bmt. in preparation of the offensive, steering room, kitchen & Latrine Bmte thro following the tram line thro the BroadView Collecting post to trenches accommodates Co. lying down. Engine & Latrines by electricity. When steering has to from through enemy lines barrage but without her help, although shells were very thru. Remained exceedingly land word that B. & C. H.Q. churches today & first lines knocked off. Enemy Aeroplane bombed Rumpelest at 10:45. the evening into casualties to men of hers.	
	27th		Their lies blown here the date of commencement of offensive. Lost a first offered could 31st Inst. Visitor 7th & Lt. Bmt. at Rumpelast where they were very busy with last-tropic training casualties. To 73rd Lt. Bmt. at R Steam Luke. the H.Q.S. made the trays Complete sports front.	
	29th		Preparations for offensive continued. The seen line of the enemies work well although the trying the lines. MKS.	

Army Form C. 2118.

WAR DIARY
or
INTELLIGENCE SUMMARY.
(Erase heading not required.)

Instructions regarding War Diaries and Intelligence Summaries are contained in F.S. Regs., Part II. and the Staff Manual respectively. Title pages will be prepared in manuscript.

Place	Date	Hour	Summary of Events and Information	Remarks and references to Appendices
ZEREGATEM	30th	—	Everything is ready for 2 days' immersion. 1000 lb. line 40 lb. tea. 500 lb. jams, 20 lb. bacon, cigarettes & toilet items for transmission. So at bathing parade men will receive their sandwich, tea & cigarettes at H.Q. Lock 8. & after being dismissed will walk to W.W. landing post at Varengeville. Evacuation learned very smoothly & must but opened by 12th Pluviôse very rapidly. At 3.50. The officers began, with troupe landings. The final loading boarded them arrived at Lock 8. H.Q.S. on Ypres Canal at about 4..45 & stretcher cases were followed Cavalier to him to 24 hrs.	
"	31st	12.0. 16.5. M.	Evacuation broken very well. Captain RV Pleasote Run C. Rodent me at Sir Liberty Post LMCH WTD at the commencement of attack & broken Service Service in connection with evacuation. I visited Lock 8 & at him & found work progressing very satisfactorily, a constant supply of rain being maintained.	

[Signature]
Lieut RWB Howell
Adjut. 24
Col. rfu

B.E.F.

SUMMARY OF MEDICAL WAR DIARIES OF 24th Div. 10th Corps
2nd ARMY.

To   2nd Corps, 5th Army from July 5th.

Western Front - July 1917.

A.D.M.S. -

SUMMARISED UNDER THE FOLLOWING HEADINGS:-
Phase "D" 1. - Passchendaele Operations "July-Nov.1917
                                          1st
(a) - Operations commencing July/1917.

B.E.F.

1.

24th Div. 10th Corps. 2nd ARMY.   Western Front.
A.D.M.S.   July 1917.

2nd Corps, 5th ARMY from July 5th.

PHASE "D" 1. - Passchendaele Operations, "July-Nov.1917."
          (a) - Operations commencing July 1st 1917.

Headquarters at Lumbres.

July 5th.   Transfer.   To 2nd Corps, 5th ARMY.

B.E.F.

SUMMARY OF MEDICAL WAR DIARIES OF

24th DIVISION,

    2nd Corps, 5th Army, till 28.8.17.
    10th Corps, from 28.8.17.
    2nd Army,   "

WESTERN FRONT, JULY - AUGUST 1917.

A.D.M.S. Col. F.R. Buswell.
D.A.D.M.S. Capt. E.V. Russell.

Summarised under the following headings:-

PHASE "D"1. Passchendaele Operations, "July - November, 1917."

    (a). Operations commencing 1/7/17.

B.E.F.

24th Div. 2nd Corps, 5th Army.   WESTERN FRONT.
A.D.M.S. Col. F.R. Buswell.   July 1917.
D.A.D.M.S. Capt. E.V. Russell.   August 1917.

PHASE "D" 1. Passchendaele Operations, "July - Nov. 1917."

(A). Operations commencing 1/7/17.

H.Q. at LUMERES.

July

5th	Transfer. 24th Divn. transferred from 10th Corps, 2nd Army, to 2nd Corps, 5th Army.
17th	Moves F.A.s. No. 72 F.A. to RENESCURE
	No. 74 F.A. to LUMERES.
18th	Weather Very wet and squally.
19th	Moves. To STEENVOORDE.
23rd	Moves. To ZEVECOTEN, and took over from 23rd Division.
24th	Operations Enemy, Gas. Gas shell barrage along Canal Bank with heavy shrapnel at same time.
	Casualties R.A.M.C. Capt. G.S. Pirie attached 9th E. Surreys, killed.
27th	Operations Enemy, Reninghelst bombed by aeroplane at 10.45 Casualties. p.m. with casualties to men and horses.
30th	Operations Enemy. Tram line used for evacuation badly damaged. Repaired by 12th Sherwoods very rapidly.
31st	Operations. Offensive commenced at 3.50 with terrific bombardment.
	Casualties & Evacuation. First wounded arrived at Lock 8 A.D.S. on Ypres Canal at 4.45 a.m. Evacuation very satisfactory. Constant supply of cars clearing cases from A.D.S. Lock 8. 12 & 165 W. admitted

B.E.F.

SUMMARY OF MEDICAL WAR DIARIES OF 24th Div. 10th Corps
2nd ARMY.

T/o 2nd Corps, 5th Army from July 5th.

Western Front - July 1917.

A.D.M.S. -

SUMMARISED UNDER THE FOLLOWING HEADINGS:-

Phase "D" 1. - Passchendaele Operations "July-Nov.1917

(a) - Operations commencing July 1st 1917.

B.E.F.

1.

<u>24th Div. 10th Corps. 2nd ARMY.</u>   Western Front.
<u>A.D.M.S.</u>   July 1917.

<u>2nd Corps, 5th ARMY from July 5th.</u>

<u>PHASE "D" 1. - Passchendaele Operations,"July-Nov.1917</u>
     (a) - <u>Operations commencing 1st July 1917.</u>

<u>Headquarters at Lumbres.</u>

July 5th.   <u>Transfer.</u> To 2nd Corps, 5th ARMY.

B.E.F.

1.

24th Div. 2nd Corps, 5th Army.　　　　WESTERN FRONT.

A.D.M.S. Col. F.R. Buswell.　　　　July 1917.
D.A.D.M.S. Capt. E.V. Russell.　　　August 1917.

PHASE "D" 1. Passchendaele Operations, "July - Nov. 1917."

(A). Operations commencing 1/7/17.

H.Q. at LUMBRES.

July

5th — Transfer. 24th Divn. transferred from 10th Corps, 2nd Army, to 2nd Corps, 5th Army.

17th — Moves F.A.s. No. 72 F.A. to RENESCURE
　　　　　　　　　　No. 74 F.A. to LUMBRES.

18th — Weather Very wet and squally.

19th — Moves. To STEENVOORDE.

23rd — Moves. To ZEVECOTEN, and took over from 23rd Division.

24th — Operations Enemy, Gas. Gas shell barrage along Canal Bank with heavy shrapnel at same time.

Casualties R.A.M.C. Capt. G.S. Pirie attached 9th E. Surreys, killed.

27th — Operations Enemy, Reninghelst bombed by aeroplane at 10.45 p.m. with casualties to men and horses.
Casualties.

30th — Operations Enemy. Tram line used for evacuation badly damaged. Repaired by 12th Sherwoods very rapidly.

31st — Operations. Offensive commenced at 3.50 with terrific bombardment.

Casualties & Evacuation. First wounded arrived at Lock 8 A.D.S. on Ypres Canal at 4.45 a.m.

Evacuation very satisfactory. Constant supply of cars clearing cases from A.D.S. Lock 8.

12 & 165 W. admitted

August.

A.D.M.S. 24th Division.

140/262

Aug 1917

COMMITTEE FOR THE
MEDICAL HISTORY OF THE WAR
Date -1 OCT. 1917

Army Form C. 2118.

WAR DIARY
or
INTELLIGENCE SUMMARY.
(Erase heading not required.)

J 5 24

A.D.M.S.
24th Division

VOL. XXIV

August 1917

Army Form C. 2118.

WAR DIARY
or
INTELLIGENCE SUMMARY.
(Erase heading not required.)

Instructions regarding War Diaries and Intelligence Summaries are contained in F.S. Regs., Part II. and the Staff Manual respectively. Title pages will be prepared in manuscript.

Place	Date	Hour	Summary of Events and Information	Remarks and references to Appendices
ZEVECOTEN	1st		Heavy rain has completely stopped the offensive. The expansion of wounded to serve at had great difficulty. But are worked by companies jus of Rank & leave. pm 7°, 7°, 74 °Splinters. Officer B. O.R. 292. attached. T.M.SS. 2. Officers 12. 6. O.R. The trench road to Canal being abt 40. O.R. On the tramline track from LEACH bend to HQ. LOCR 8 & a considerable distance beside are employed in trenches. No. of wounded 15 – 12 noon since 12 noon 31st July. Officer 41. O.R. 971.	
"	2nd		Weather still very bad. Cold & miserable. Casualties much less. Total wounded for Noon 31st July at Noon today – Officers 53. O.R. 1267. Certain Lewis Gun Tactics given.	
"	3rd		Weather continues wet and the ground is very deep, at least 6 leave. to a stretcher & the Canal front test [Ypres] at HQ B. Efforts are being made to get Guy Dutts up to the Troops who are to work through & up better thighs in water & mud. Rum Ration issued daily with marked effect.	

MWB

Army Form C. 2118.

WAR DIARY or INTELLIGENCE SUMMARY.

(Erase heading not required.)

August 1917

Place	Date	Hour	Summary of Events and Information	Remarks and references to Appendices
ZEVECOTEN	4th		Weather slightly improved. To 74th Squad. 11 Coys my. 75 Ft Amb 2OR. Total evacuated for hour July 31st from Belg: Officers 58 OR. 1537. Evacuation proceeding well, Lot. trying to deflt of mud at best 6 hours to stretcher.	
"	5th		Fine & warm. Personnel staying well. Counter attack by enemy repulsed. Evacuated for hour 31st July Officers 68 OR. 1651.	
"	6th		Weather slight rain. Evacuated for hour 31st July Officers 68 OR 1709.	
"	7th		Captain J. Van der Gripen R.A.M.C. reported arrived for duty. Weather dull.	
"	8th		Heavy thunderstorm. First release of Base officers and evacuation 12 hours. Evacuated up to date from 31st July. Officers 74. OR. 1785. BaDm J. to Lt. Col. B. & R.E.P.L.M.E.N.T work.	
"	9th		Complement of 8th Bn Bps to be hon. arriving evolution of Canada Tunnels Company work & started in this them & repairs Stationary to the lectures shelling of meran and buried the tunnels as a latrine & thus any to the presence of some mules in the tunnels has led to the stating Officers Complement of great deminution & evacuation separating sich & wounded. The transfer of old infantry for 1st to 8th Aug 1917. Ten 10 Officers 795. OR. an improvement. Transfer the Bangoy of 7 men have been hard put very pusher than to best temperatures.	

Army Form C. 2118.

WAR DIARY
or
INTELLIGENCE SUMMARY.
(Erase heading not required.)

Summary of Events and Information

August 1917

Place	Date	Hour	Summary of Events and Information	Remarks and references to Appendices
Zeroster	10th		Fell cloudy. At 4.35 am the two chairmen butts of 24th attempts begun some heft & ground. The front of a big crawl formed operators by the divison and keep indifferent.	
"	11th		To MICMAC Camp, ball lasted at 11pm to Captain Schrotz, g of E Surrey Regt. Was ordered upon to take his company into the trenches, stating that he was sick. The MO battalion, Capt R H FELTON kind stated that the officer is not sick. After examination when Capt Schrotz he was sent to the [?] the Doctor for observation	
			nothing specially wrong being detected. Heavy thunderstorm	
"	12th		Fine day. Preptime. Great falling off in number of sick, owing to improved circumstances	
"	13th		ball cloudy. Preptime inspected the trenches of [?] at [?]	
	14/15 16th		Leave Zeroster. Quarters of Mason Company in absence of the Divisional Sunday Section Gone to get clear of trenches. MS has been true the humour on to MICMAC Camp, which is a more miserables Gradated has been[?] Sunts of manner train upgrades[?] trodden down much cleaning, also [?] be undertaken	
	17th		Bombing by E Aeroplane, very bright-	

2/HLG

WAR DIARY
or
INTELLIGENCE SUMMARY

Army Form C. 2118.

(Erase heading not required.)

Place	Date	Hour	Summary of Events and Information	Remarks and references to Appendices
ZEGGERS CAPPEL	August 1917			
	18th		Fine. Daytime.	
	19/20		Meeting. Nr of wounded during scarce. Phase of active operations much less.	
	21st		Up to 12 noon today ½ 12 noon 9th instant wounded Officers 6. O.R. 419.	
	22nd		Conference Staff and 11 Corps.	
			Fine. Came attack by 14th Div. a. m. left. Heavy bombardment at 4.45. At same time small operation by 1st N.Z. of this division. Result about 40 prisoners. Casualties.	
	23/24		Rain. Front quiet. 11 Corps movement from C. to 72 to route. Sanitation of M.G.C.R. Camp proceeding. Let the ground is very wet & winter tent.	
	26			
	27		To Te Q. to walk to Clancy P.B. seen and to Poperinghe on P.B. visit.	
	28		At noon today this div. in 6th army handed to x 2 Corps to P. ? Called at offices — arranged direction .... Capts Harford and Croston	

Major C... Signed

Army Form C. 2118.

WAR DIARY
or
INTELLIGENCE SUMMARY.
(Erase heading not required.)

Place	Date	Hour	Summary of Events and Information	Remarks and references to Appendices
			August 1917.	
ZEEVECOTEN	29th		Visited 13th Lgt Amb- many improvements an especially ingenious steam bath for scabies cases. Gale of wind destroyed many marquees. Returned to Canter. Hostility of Huns most Rest Station ludytrule out.	
"	30th		Weather very cold, wet and equally tedious. General Routine.	
"	31st		General Routine. Enemy bombing every night. Total Casualties for the month of August- Wounded Officers 77. Other ranks 2245.	

Lieut Col MBurnett Brows ADMS

B.E.F.

SUMMARY OF MEDICAL WAR DIARIES OF

24th DIVISION,

    2nd Corps, 5th Army, till 28.8.17.
    10th Corps, from 28.8.17.
    2nd Army,

WESTERN FRONT, JULY + AUGUST 1917.

A.D.M.S. Col. F.R. Buswell.

D.A.D.M.S. Capt. E.V. Russell.

Summarised under the following headings:-

PHASE "D"1. Passchendaele Operations, "July - November, 1917."

(a). Operations commencing 1/7/17.

August.
1st   Weather, & Evacuation.   Incessant heavy rain completely
        stopped offensive and evacuation carried out under great
        difficulty.
        Evacuation/

B.E.F.

24th Div. 2nd Corps, 5th Army. WESTERN FRONT.
2nd Army, 10th Corps, from 28.8.17.
A.D.M.S. Col. F.R. Buswell. August 1917.

PHASE "D"1 - contd.

(a). Operations commencing 1/7/17.

August   H.Q. at ZEVECOTEN.

1st   Evacuation (contd.) Evacuation carried out by Br. Divns.
(contd.)   of 72nd, 73rd and 74th F.A's - 2 & 126 attached from
            T.M.B's and 40 Divnl. Band and Concert Party.
            Mules employed as tractors on tram line from Larch Wood
            to A.D.S. Lock 8.
            Casualties. Noon 31st - noon 1st   41 & 971 W.

2nd   "   Noon 1st - noon 2nd   12 & 296 W.

3rd   Weather & Evacuation. Weather very bad. 6 Brs. required
            on each stretcher to carry through very deep mud.
            Trench Feet. 12 cases at D.R.S.

4th   Weather. Slightly improved.
            Casualties. Noon 2nd - noon 4th   5 & 270 W.

5th   Weather. Fine and warm.
            Casualties. Noon 4th - noon 5th   10 & 114 W.

6th   5th - noon 6th   0 & 58 W.

8th   Weather. Heavy thunderstorm.
            Casualties. 31/7 - 8/8   74 & 1785 W.

9th   Casualties Sk. & Trench Feet. 10 & 795 reported Sk. 1st-
            8th. Majority mild cases of trench feet due to wet and
            exposure.

10th   Operations. Attempt to gain some high ground at 4.35 a.m.
            partly successful.

12th   Weather Fine.

21st   Casualties. 9th-21st   8 & 419 W.

22nd   Operations. Attack by 14th Divn. on left with 1st R.F!S.
            of 24th Divn. - 40 prisoners.

23rd   Weather. Rain.

28th   Transfer To 10th Corps, 2nd Army.

1st Weather, & Evacuation. Incessant heavy rain completely stopped offensive and evacuation carried out under great difficulty.

Evacuation/

B.E.F.

24th Div. 2nd Corps, 5th Army.   WESTERN FRONT.
2nd Army, 10th Corps, from 28.8.17.
A.D.M.S. Col. F.R. Buswell.   August 1917.

PHASE "D"1 - contd.

(a). Operations commencing 1/7/17.

August	H.Q. at ZEVECOTEN.
1st (contd.)	Evacuation (contd.) Evacuation carried out by Br. Divns. of 72nd, 73rd and 74th F.A's - 2 & 126 attached from T.M.B's and 40 Divnl. Band and Concert Party. Mules employed as tractors on tram line from Larch Wood to A.D.S. Lock 8. Casualties. Noon 31st - noon 1st 41 & 971 W.
2nd	" Noon 1st - noon 2nd 12 & 296 W.
3rd	Weather & Evacuation. Weather very bad. 6 Brs. required on each stretcher to carry through very deep mud. Trench Feet. 12 cases at D.R.S.
4th	Weather. Slightly improved. Casualties. Noon 2nd - noon 4th 5 & 270 W.
5th	Weather. Fine and warm. Casualties. Noon 4th - noon 5th 10 & 114 W.
6th	5th - noon 6th 0 & 58 W.
8th	Weather. Heavy thunderstorm. Casualties. 31/7 - 8/8 74 & 1785 W.
9th	Casualties Sk. & Trench Feet. 10 & 795 reported Sk. 1st-8th. Majority mild cases of trench feet due to wet and exposure.
10th	Operations. Attempt to gain some high ground at 4.35 a.m. Partly successful.
12th	Weather Fine.
21st	Casualties. 9th-21st 8 & 419 W.
22nd	Operations. Attack by 14th Divn. on left with 1st R.F!S. of 24th Divn. - 40 prisoners.
23rd	Weather. Rain.
28th	Transfer To 10th Corps, 2nd Army.

140/2426

A.D.M.S. 24th Division

COMMITTEE FOR THE
MEDICAL HISTORY OF THE WAR
Date — 5 NOV. 1917

B.E.F.

SUMMARY OF MEDICAL WAR DIARIES OF 24th Div. 10th Corps.

2nd ARMY.

4th Corps Area 3rd ARMY from 20th Sept.

Western Front Operations - Sept. 1917.

A.D.M.S. - Col. F.R. Burnell.

D.A.D.M.S.-

SUMMARISED UNDER THE FOLLOWING HEADINGS:-

Phase "D" 1. - Passchendaele Operations," July-Nov. 1917.

(a) - Operations commencing 1st July 1917.

B.E.F. 1.

<u>24th Div. 10th Corps 2nd ARMY.</u>   Western Front.
<u>A.D.M.S. Col. F.R. Burnell.</u>   Sept. 1917.

<u>4th Corps Area 3rd ARMY from 20th Sept.</u>

<u>PHASE "D" 1- Passchendaele Operations,"July-Nov. 1917."</u>
    (a) - <u>Operations commencing July 1st 1917.</u>

<u>Headquarters at Zevecoten from 5th Army.</u>

Sept. 1st. - 12th.	<u>Operations R.A.M.C.</u>	Routine.
13th.	<u>Military Situation.</u>	G.O.C. 23rd Div. took over command of line.
14th.	<u>Moves F.A.</u>	72nd F.A. to Rouge Croix.
15th.	<u>Moves.</u>	To Merris.
	<u>Moves F.A.</u>	73rd F.A. to Doulieu.
		74th F.A. to Merris.
20th.	<u>Moves and Transfer.</u>	To 1.34.c.(57c) between Beugny and Hoplincourt in 4th Corps area 3rd ARMY.

B.E.F.

SUMMARY OF MEDICAL WAR DIARIES OF 24th Div. 10th Corps.

2nd ARMY.
4th Corps Area 3rd ARMY from 20th Sept.
Western Front Operations - Sept. 1917.

A.D.M.S. - Col. P.R. Burnell.

D.A.D.M.S.-

SUMMARISED UNDER THE FOLLOWING HEADINGS:-

Phase "D" 1. - Passchendaele Operations,"July-Nov. 1917.

(a) - Operations commencing 1st July 1917.

B.E.F. 1.

24th Div. 10th Corps 2nd ARMY.   Western Front.
A.D.M.S. Col. F.R. Burnell.   Sept. 1917.

4th Corps Area 3rd ARMY from 20th Sept.

PHASE "D" 1- Passchendaele Operations, "July-Nov. 1917."
    (a) - Operations commencing July 1st 1917.

Headquarters at Zevecoten from 5th Army.

Sept. 1st. - 12th.	Operations R.A.M.C.	Routine.
13th.	Military Situation.	G.O.C. 23rd Div. took over command of line.
14th.	Moves F.A.	72nd F.A. to Rouge Croix.
15th.	Moves.	To Merris.
	Moves F.A.	73rd F.A. to Doulieu
		74th F.A. to Merris.
20th.	Moves and Transfer.	To 1.34.c.(57c) between Beugny and Hoplincourt in 4th Corps area 3rd ARMY.

Army Form C. 2118.

WAR DIARY
or
INTELLIGENCE SUMMARY.
(Erase heading not required.)

Vol 25

A.D.M.S.
74th Division
Vol XXV
September 1917

Army Form C. 2118.

WAR DIARY
or
INTELLIGENCE SUMMARY.
(Erase heading not required.)

Instructions regarding War Diaries and Intelligence Summaries are contained in F.S. Regs., Part II. and the Staff Manual respectively. Title pages will be prepared in manuscript.

Place	Date	Hour	Summary of Events and Information	Remarks and references to Appendices
			September 1917.	
LEVE COTEM.	1st		General routine.	
	2nd		To see O.Ret. 26th Division about taking on new line extending from Menin road (Clapham Junction) to S. end of Bodmin Copse. O.R.'s. Menin road and Wood eat. house.	
"	3		Visited O.R.'s. Inverness house, & very good place indeed. Menin Road. The kurve of the two Trenches Ypres / Roulers good.	
"	4		R.S.M. J— up the line. looking for site to shelter wounded. O.R. of P	
"	5		Routine. In forth coming operations	
"	6		Selected site for holding wounded in Westhoeck Ridge. 3 Elephant shells to be erected and then line connected by duck to walk up to dressing R.A.P. to For. Life.	
	7		In Conference at H.Qu. 5 x P Corps. O.Re 23rd Division defeated to site selected for holding wounded and walk it at Valley cottages. Lt. Vatta place, for Champion according to capture.	*[signature]*

T2134. Wt. W708—776. 500000. 4/15. Sir J.C. & S.

Army Form C. 2118.

WAR DIARY
or
INTELLIGENCE SUMMARY.
(Erase heading not required.)

Instructions regarding War Diaries and Intelligence Summaries are contained in F.S. Regs., Part II. and the Staff Manual respectively. Title pages will be prepared in manuscript.

Place	Date	Hour	Summary of Events and Information	Remarks and references to Appendices
ZEUR CAMP	7th	7.	To see Lt. Plinio & Shumanti about the Mullah Turned Post & the relief by still kept at selected spot. To 72nd Pt Amblance and DHQ 25th Divin	
"	8.		All seven Esvad up between Kod: Imbay & site. RAPS. 1st Combs Opolunan and Lew Bray. USA joined for duty	
	9th		At Aug. 28th Sir ajun to the site selected on Verlandan Rd. for T.G.R. which is just as well as it is the only site available not under observation & comprising two from still line and two of the three elephant shelters are already completed. Working party of 60 O.R. from the 72, 73, 74 Pt Amb: at work at site & R.C.S. for Valley wounded & RAPS. Captain Forrow & Billing Reme: deputed for duty in Indian + Mesopotamia	
	10th		Passed up the limited Capt. Marston on 25th Div. Welus a Story & from officer. Sr outr in friend when. Ealend, Capt. L & Russell Punile to 57PS	
	11th			
	12th		Inspected 74th Pt Amb: Actioned pachew Reme C. 23rd Div: arrived with seventy ephemeral received. JPNB

Army Form C. 2118.

WAR DIARY
or
INTELLIGENCE SUMMARY.

(Erase heading not required.)

Instructions regarding War Diaries and Intelligence Summaries are contained in F. S. Regs., Part II. and the Staff Manual respectively. Title pages will be prepared in manuscript.

Place	Date	Hour	Summary of Events and Information	Remarks and references to Appendices
Zevecoten			September 1917.	
	13th		Opr 23 = Rn took on command of Brie. at 6 P.m. Gnl Pethy. to England. Enquiry of contest. Wrote to RnPn handed on to 69th to Brnt.	
	14		7th Bullent' moved to Range Crois. Philip J. 7th = H Ant by Cut. of 23rd Rn.	
	15		RHQ moved to MORRIS. 10.30 am 8ths. 78th to Brnt. show down	
	16		Voted 7th = Retn. to 92 = Return to trenches	
	17		73 = T.O. at trenches 7th = Fortnrt. take for now to Mereur.,	
	18		Capt L.H. Ste Ronie Buyhow a coy's y contest	
	19		Voted 72 = T.O.	
	20		RHQ. moved to 1.34.c. Shill S.T.E. about 81 rnds. a m.. leken	
			Bearson and hosp. in cart to IV Cat. aim.	
	21		72 = RHQ Boisseure 73.76. Boisseure 7 a 70 LEEHOUR.	
	22		Rn em. to IV Corps HQ. 7111 Cmp. HQ. and HQ 34th Rn. at	
	23		Conference of these Bust. Command en on the new line & relief arrangements.	

[signature]

WAR DIARY
INTELLIGENCE SUMMARY
(Erase heading not required.)

September 1917.

Army Form C. 2118.

Place	Date	Hour	Summary of Events and Information	Remarks and references to Appendices
Bruay	24th		Admst troops drew cars visiting stns & Q Scalos taken at DOUAI HQS of Arml & Renfloss & present. MG 342 stn. at NOTRE DAME from Bruay to M.D.S. BERNES. & Hts. JEAN Conit.; Bruay to Hq St Aord Pouilly & Hts VadenConit.. 73rd Fd Amb to Most ALL H N.G. 74th F.A. took over Pouilly	
	25th 26		3 General nature	
PERNOIS	27		typh. fr. Staincourt detail of Personn Café Wallers fm. Q5 k 72nd ft Ank. Coytfield. WRE fm 5tc. Nt to RMY VSA to 5tc. Infacts 5ns & ESSy en Tringue backing Ethure by 72nd ft Ank	
	28th		Rtng to Notencourt Farm	
	29th		rived spell in an orchard. Uncle from any when Capt JPP ALLEN move to England. T.E. Cpton Pearon to 107 Pole RtrA	
	30		74th Ft Amb. took on Hts. at JEAN Conit fm 73rd Ft Amb	

J W Burnett Sir
A Amh 2nd

1402+96

A.D.M.S. 24th Division

COMMITTEE FOR THE
MEDICAL HISTORY OF THE WAR
Date -5 JAN 1918

WAR DIARY
or
INTELLIGENCE SUMMARY.

Army Form C. 2118.

Vol 26

Original

1 D M 8
XXII Division
Oct 1919

Vol. 26

WAR DIARY
INTELLIGENCE SUMMARY
(Erase heading not required.)

Place	Date	Hour	Summary of Events and Information	Remarks and references to Appendices
Malanjaat Farm	October 1917			
	1st		Visited 7th & 8th Cmdr. Yesterday M.O. & 2nd T Cmdr. Refitted Progr.	
	2nd		being made in improvements.	
	3rd		Genl. Ramel England on W.O. letters.	
			Forwd. A P.B. Board of Revd. hostile 7/8 Simpson Reps. of	
			Maj Carroll & Two others about 7/8 Pde by.	
	4th		Routine.	
	5th		Captain Sir Russell Tufnel in lieu Capt C.J. Rettay & Lieut Lewis	
			to 7th & Capt J.M. Topham. H/Q. Rade crest & Ralls & 3rd Pdn	
			& 8th Buffs— the Batty & along in yard in front of the Front line	
			transon although there an great in advance of Ft. Very cold &	
			bright Heavy rain.	
	6th		Cols. Houston & Roning Bgs. Captain Archer & Ryft. Ren & Grint &c.	
			Capel 46 & 43 Infantry. The coy of 8th in Innipregnate to our Mundally	
			by Genl Lilly. The quality unwish Cannot stand apparently spread	
			at Amsterdam, birth & great any storm.	
	7th		Captain T.O. Williams Relvs C. at 2nd Remonts, place on arrival of "Huntington"	

MWB

WAR DIARY
or
INTELLIGENCE SUMMARY.
(Erase heading not required.)

Army Form C. 2118.

Place	Date	Hour	Summary of Events and Information	Remarks and references to Appendices
Métérèn			October - 1917.	
	8"			
	9"		1st Lieut Goodman. O.M. U.S.A. & Lt. Quarles U.S. Capt Williams.	
	10"		First Case of Trench Foot Received in 6th Queens. Increasingly cold & wet.	
	11"		2nd Case of T.F. in 2nd Queens. Weather still very bad.	
	11"		3 more cases T.F. in Queens. 1 & 2 in 2nd Leinsters. No ground sheets available.	
	12"		To R.A.S. Road to examine area for P.B. & O.R. permanent. P.B. for R.P.s Huts etc.	
			Very bad. The ground heavy.	
	13"		Lieut General Parker U.S.A. to inspect. M.Os, 73rd Lt Amb. at Borre	
			1 am T.F. 1st Wilts but O.F.O.R. Yes Andersen. Wounded by ground lyre.	
	14		Q.M. & Capt T.D. Williams Perm. C. Charge with Ambulance. 1 am T.F. 7th Welsh Fus.	
	15		Evening Drove for the 3 Brigade Statest to inc T.F. Pneumonia.	
			Very frequent though taken very time clear	
	16		to M.D.S. Borre. to See P.B. area. Tree Hay. Capt P.L.O'Connell travel returned.	
			From Leave. 2 T.F. cases. 1st N Staffs	
	17		Feature	
	18		To R.A.S. project. 73rd Lt. Amb.	
	19		1st Lieut Quarles U.S.A. joined detached 73rd Lt Amb. K Stens 5th Cav. Field Amb. 9/Xic.	

WAR DIARY
or
INTELLIGENCE SUMMARY.

Army Form C. 2118.

(Erase heading not required.)

Place	Date	Hour	Summary of Events and Information	Remarks and references to Appendices
Notre Croix	October 1917			
	19th	—	Capt Hughes came to 3rd R.B. vice Lt Nag Kellog V.S.R.	
	20th		Visited 4 Batn in Cps. & 7.3.T pat Cmdt. Strong. The T.T. Lt Alexander	
	21st		7o 73.T pat Cmdt Bernier.	
	22		Rontine	
	23rd		With 73rd T.T. Cps. to Ost. Amer, Templeur June came & Mrs Bernier	
			Weather all wet	
	24		K.R.T.M. Lt Poetto is here	
	25		Rontine	
	26th		73rd T.T. to Vadencourt, visit men digging bivvy from pits etc.	
			Saw T.T. 2nd & Sainte Eng	
	27		Section of C.C.M. to Cpt T.O. William. ThuC attached to Neny F.	
			Amalgamated. Examined the majesty Blanca Marie 70	
			to A.P.M. list known.	
	28th		Very Cold. bath.	
	29th		Ch. station running to T. Cps. here no inevention or success	
	30th		October. strong T. Cps. U. came bang. prevented in vain.	

WAR DIARY
or
INTELLIGENCE SUMMARY.

Army Form C. 2118.

Place	Date	Hour	Summary of Events and Information	Remarks and references to Appendices
Ytterseat	October 1917			
	30th	—	1st Lieuts Copeland Danes, NEEDWELL, HUNTER, & KERR, U.S.A. M.C. joined the Division & are attached to the 3 Ambs.	

Edwd M Brown Col
ADMS 23rd Div

Originals 9/61 27

No. 1a

WO/579

War Diary of A.D.M.S 24th Divn
for Nov 1917

Vol XXVII

COMMITTEE FOR THE
MEDICAL HISTORY OF THE WAR
Date 17 JAN. 1918

WAR DIARY / INTELLIGENCE SUMMARY

November 1917

Place	Date	Hour	Summary of Events and Information	Remarks and references to Appendices
NOBESCOURT	1st		Lt Edwards. Num. C. on one month leave to England.	
"	2		Routine	
"	3		Routine Offr in to Indian Army Reserve. to a 2nd Lt Farmer R.W.K's R.T.O Route, however here on deferring from furnished prison. the loaded shirt of shell shock (elevated in prison Brook on serious endeavour). Working party. 40 Men O.R. to construct long A.T.S keys and Rent when heat and lodged in case of absence on Bell court Rd.	
"	5th		Routine	
"	6th		Lt Col C.R.E. + R. 73rd. Stout to see the site for new H.T. also received from Shelling. 1st Lieut Graham USA attached 2nd Lieuts to Kellog, with the Off. + Clerk 12 O.R. to attend the Rifts theorem.	
"	7th		1st Lieut Capehane USA. attached 12 O.R. theorem.	
"	8th		Capt. Ronalds USA. M.C. to 2nd Lieut thumb.	
"	9th		To M. Fr. Bemm. J. 2nd Lieut thumb. 1st Lieut Kellog USA. had exp. to 8th R W Kents to duty. vice Capt In Laity, Englans T.E. Rug leave. Capt In Woenlyn Ameer from 55th trim in to 26th A.A Georges	

Army Form C. 2118.

WAR DIARY
or
INTELLIGENCE SUMMARY.
(Erase heading not required.)

Place	Date	Hour	Summary of Events and Information	Remarks and references to Appendices
NOEUX LES MINES	10th		Routine	
"	11		Capt E.U. Reynolds Trench Fever evacuated. Field Ambulance Practice	
"	12		A Wrist (sceptic) & smaller injuries to 73rd Fd Amb evacuation. P.B. Beard	
"	13		Routine	
"	14		To Poperinghe 74th Fd Amb ADS Vlamertinghe Wieltjie & C types	
"	15/16		Quiet. 72 h.s. Very poor huts at ADS by Fd Amb Hanover	
"	17th		USA Med corps.	
"			Routine. Infantry for evening operation	
"			All arch. evacuated. FMDS 7 std	
"			stretcher party on Bellevue Rent locality	
"			S.O. 3. M.G. 24. O.R. to No 3 C.C.S. & Trinity clearing	
"	18th		Conference. O.C. 73rd 74th Fd Amb	
"			Routine	
"	19th		Ground attack. Ins cavil by 26th Div. to oppose attack	
"	20th		Enemy shelling. Cannelleur, S.O. & 26 O.R.	MUD

WAR DIARY
or
INTELLIGENCE SUMMARY.

Army Form C. 2118.

Place	Date	Hour	Summary of Events and Information	Remarks and references to Appendices
MOSES CAMP	Sept 21st		Many land, no word when an attack. Patrol	
"	22nd		2 73rd I.B. patrol to examine approach to P.B.	
"	23rd		to transpt trenspect 3 M.G. noted. 2nd 5th Corps.	
"	24th		Status Quo. Open fire from & mercury post. Kingani	
"	25th		Patrols	
"	26th			
"	27th		Lt. M.J. Lecture Name taken a strength of 74th I Res Bottennews	
"			at F.A. Corps Convalescent dept	
"	28th		Captain Sir Russell Reun of base. Europe Machine G	
"			73rd I.B. and fires in la Elevento in Turni by 3rd, 4th & 6th Cav Sq	
"	29th		2nd Cav Corps called a Kakinyan clear ARms 4 @ Cav. Div.	
"	30th		Opened German attack on 12th & 5-6th Sie Punts at 6.20 am	
"			Fire in F Khan Kinin were moved to staff sectors on Rt flank	
"			3 section it counter with two it unnubiate	
"			All they have carefully to advance patrols of 3rd & 4th Cav. Sq	
"			but tack in view of possible attack on our Front. Personnel	
"			A.D.S.S. Reemporced	MM8

WAR DIARY
or
INTELLIGENCE SUMMARY.

Army Form C. 2118.

Month and Year: November 1917

Place	Date	Hour	Summary of Events and Information	Remarks and references to Appendices
Morbecque	30th		Considerably shelling in vicinity of A.D.S. Morbecque. A new feature. Cases of Trench feet during the month 19, in all, 3 cases of dysentery, + 4 of measles. Total admissions to division 1107. Nontransferable 128.	

Lieut Col
A.D.M.S. 24th Division

ASSISTANT DIRECTOR MEDICAL SERVICES ★ 24th DIVISION ★

VOL. XXVIII

War Diary
ADMS 24th Divn
Decr 1917

COMMITTEE FOR ...
MEDICAL HISTORY OF THE WAR
Date -4 MAR. 1918

Army Form C. 2118.

WAR DIARY
or
INTELLIGENCE SUMMARY.
(Erase heading not required.)

Place	Date	Hour	Summary of Events and Information	Remarks and references to Appendices
Nibrewelt	1st		Night quiet. German attack withdrawn. 4 M.O. 16 O.R. 3rd Cav Bde Fd Amb reported at M.D.S. Barre 3rd 1st Amb transit with casualties in Cavalry who have arrived in support.	
"	2nd		4th Amb 3rd Cav Bde reported arrival at Loow on enf — 5th's front.	
"	3rd		To attack on our front. Very Cold.	
"	4th		Sharp frost two mornings. To 73rd Fd Amb BERVES. Held P.B. examinations.	6
"	5th		Routine.	
"	6th		74th Cavalry Bde Intelnce Pt letter of Instructions on subject of 7/8th Divs Car Corps to Offrs. 74th F.A. Agent to be relieved in the line by	7/8
	7		H.Q. Pouilly by 3rd & 7th Cavalry Fd Ambulances. Visited the Amb this a.m. also at Road from 73rd Stations into M.D.S. at Buresnit. Let Dr truck Can Queen BERVES. Transport at Buresnit. Not working up on account of thaw. Corps from 10 a.m.	

WAR DIARY or INTELLIGENCE SUMMARY

Army Form C. 2118.

Place	Date	Hour	Summary of Events and Information	Remarks and references to Appendices
	December 1917			
Metelcourt	9th		Handing over of ADS: Jenicourt & Vadencourt completed.	
"	10th		12. 97th Reinforcement joined. 1st Lieut Copeland USA & 12th Lieut Thurmond to Captn Quelle USA att 2nd Reinforcement DCS with orders to evacuate to Base.	
"	11th		All evacuations by Motor Amb Cars M. A.C. not available	
"	12th		Captain E. V. Russell RAMC posted to 12th Div exchange with Capt Faulkner, the latter to join Division unit.	
"	13th		Two Orderly input. In 13th Inf Fd Amb Regimental orders for description to 55 CCS or 72 to Havre — MAB	
"	14th		Routine	
"	15th		1st Lieut. Bluer Thym & Peck & Sherman U.S.A. joined Thym & Peck attached to Field Amb others evacuating	
"	16th			
"	17th		50 73rd Reinforcement Men to Declanations reporting No. 4 or 1st Amn Very cold all day — Snow	Injuries No 1, 55 CCS

WAR DIARY
INTELLIGENCE SUMMARY

Place	Date	Hour	Summary of Events and Information	Remarks and references to Appendices
November	18th		December	
"	19th		Cards came into 5th Army.	
"	20/21		Ministries, MAC Cars been available for evacuating K.S.	
"	22		Motors. Very cold. Loud Frost.	
			In detail 3 m.o.f. hi closing of 55 CCS. The function of taking MO's from the front to CCS was not good.	
"	23rd		Heavy shelling on ADS Templeux. First list on Enekhern wired to concentrate spoiled. ADS being strengthened by elephant shelter & iron girders.	
"	24th		Captain E.V. Ansell Mann C. left Wipers to KGHs 38th Div. Heavy rain during day. Very cold.	
"	25th		Heavy followed by snow. Motors.	
"	26th		1st ambulance.	
"	27th		Captain F.I.H. Elliot Hunt joined 72nd FAmb. pog of the reported off Duco.	
"	28th		72nd FA aut to" clear upstation of 74th FAmb.	
"	29th		Nature	
"	30th		Capt E.D. Faulkner Hume. repined 74th Fd Amb.	

WAR DIARY
or
INTELLIGENCE SUMMARY.

Army Form C. 2118.

December 1914 Summary of Events and Information

Place	Date	Hour	Summary of Events and Information	Remarks and references to Appendices
NOBESCOURT	31st		Man E. posts in view. R.A.P. at Leave train started. Visited A.F.S. Templeux to see the new strengthening work being put in. Very satisfactory.	
			18 cases of trench foot during this month.	

J. [signature] Howell Evans
ADMS 24th Division

A.D.M.S. 24th Div.

140/2/82

Jan 1918

COMMITTEE FOR THE
MEDICAL HISTORY OF THE WAR
Date -8 APR. 1918

WAR DIARY or INTELLIGENCE SUMMARY

Army Form C. 2118.

ADMS 24th DW

ASSISTANT DIRECTOR MEDICAL SERVICES · 24th DIVISION

Place	Date	Hour	Summary of Events and Information	Remarks and references to Appendices
MOESCROIX	January 1918 1st		Arrived to assume station. BATCHES to new DDMS Cavalry Corps. Inspected MDS	
	2nd		ADMS proceeded on leave. W/Sd Edwards to Cmdg 72nd Field Ambulance took over duties during his absence.	
	3rd		Went to Conference at DDMS Cav Corps Bureau of accommodation for Cavalry troops at 36 DRS discussed. Arrangements made for increased accommodation at DRS from 200 to 245 beds. 15 GR reinforcements arrived. Noted to Field Ambulances.	
	4th		Rode in afternoon to examine 30 B. new and up to Sherwood Foresters to replace A new. R 20e.6t – Service. Hos hospital treatment.	
	5th		Arrived accompanied DDMS Cav Corps on inspection of 1st DRS. 72 beds allotted to units of Cavalry Divisions. Ordinances to 1st Jt-Black Watch to proceed fortnight to England. Report to American Reinforcement Camp WINCHESTER. M Black.	

WAR DIARY
or
INTELLIGENCE SUMMARY

Army Form C. 2118.

Place	Date	Hour	Summary of Events and Information	Remarks and references to Appendices
MOBECOURT	January 5th 1918		Reported from No 55 CCS and provided fortnight	
	(6th)		Capt PARSONS RAMC attd 107 Brigade RFA left to report to A.D.M.S. 16th Div – who has applied for him	
			Capt ARCHER LT DUTHIE reported from In Corps. Capt ARCHER remains for the present with 2nd Dm Depot Battn LT DUTHIE to 74th Field Ambulance	
	7th		Posted to 73rd Field Ambulance to examine men for reclassification	
			Routine	
	8th		Routine Orders issued to protect all buildings at E.A.s Foulcourt Splinter etc	
	9th		Attended conference by A.D.M.s Ca Corps Formation of Corps Res Centre at 73 Field Ambulance discussed & report asked for	
	10th		Routine Capt Rice attd ? Mother at present on leave	
	11th		Routine Heavy Shelling of TEMPLEUX Nr EA at A.D.S was	

WAR DIARY
INTELLIGENCE SUMMARY

Army Form C. 2118.

Place	Date	Hour	Summary of Events and Information	Remarks and references to Appendices
NOBESCOURT Farm	January 1918		hot and burnt. Complaints from Sau Section about Camps at HANCOURT & RAINES. Asked them to put it out these. There is but equipment accommodation for men and horses, providing as rapidly as possible.	
	12th		Captain & men of Brit San Squad to work in Camps at HANCOURT & RAINES. Asked to see RE re improved accommodation at the ADS TEMPLEUX.	
	13th 14th		Routine. CRE reports that it is not advisable to increase accommodation at ADS Templeux, as it would mean hutting thousands - whereas huts hereon. Arrive the hutting for men ADS two yet down TEMPLEUX - ROISEL Road. whether or suitable hut. Consulting Surgeon Fifth Army lectures to RC Field Ambulances and Medical Officers at 73rd Field Ambulance	

WAR DIARY
or
INTELLIGENCE SUMMARY

Army Form C. 2118.

Place	Date	Hour	Summary of Events and Information	Remarks and references to Appendices
ROBESCOURT	15th		Routine	
	16th		Attended conference at Divnl Cavly HQrs Discussion on possible reduction in Equipment in Field Ambulance. Decided that no reduction to personnel to proceeds. Lt Col Cummings SS and 3 of 73rd Field Ambulance proceeded on 30 days leave.	
	17th		Routine. 3 ORanks MC RSC Received instructions alls St Queens England on special leave	
	18th		Routine Capt Clough Piets alls St Queens England on special leave	
	19th		Ambulance train lines Guyligh for CCS Rivers Mon Put slight cases today forward Rny's Town when known that the next train	
	20th		H.E. Carnel G Offr morning Ambne waiting rest all sick over to Evac to 11th CCS Capt Rigby Rame S/O to 3 Rifle Brigade when to proceed to 12th Fdambne Co	

WAR DIARY
INTELLIGENCE SUMMARY
(Erase heading not required.)

Army Form C. 2118.

Place	Date	Hour	Summary of Events and Information	Remarks and references to Appendices
No BESCOURT	Saturday 21st		Routine	
"	22		Capt FAULKNER Return from 74th Field Ambulance vice Capt RIGBY to 180 Tunnelling Coy.	
			ASDS works on new A.D.S Templeux and new R.A.P. etc at Leave Train which is nearly complete	
"	23rd		Examined 2 men for reclassification. To Conference at Divell Corps in afternoon	
"	24th		Examined men Employed under Area Commandants - Still one missing. Issued to R.A.P, at Hargicourt and Templeux Queen in afternoon.	
"	25th		Routine	
"	26th		Inspected DRS and Scabies Station Capt PRICE (17 M/Kent) fitted to No 3 Motor Lahore General Hospital	
"	27th		Routine 74th Field Ambulance Head quarters moved from BERNES to new quarters at ADS POISEL	
"	28th		To see proposed site for new ADS at TEMPLEUX H POILFE L Road	

Army Form C. 2118.

WAR DIARY
or
INTELLIGENCE SUMMARY.
(Erase heading not required.)

Place	Date	Hour	Summary of Events and Information	Remarks and references to Appendices
MOBECOURT 28 Cats.	January 1918			
"	29th		Morning ADMS Divisional Ambulances. Left ADMS Car Corps in afternoon to see ADS TEMPLE OX and new quarters of 74th F.A. at BOISEL.	
"	30th		General Routine. To ADMS Our Corps. Conference mostly Cavalry Concerns.	
"	31st		Visit to Verge Name attached 1st RT. to 2nd Corps 254 Tunnelling Cos. Captain S.J. Silley Name stated procedure have very cold night.	
			15 Cases of Trench feet during this month. Some into rate improving during latter part of month.	

J. Howard M.R.C.S.
Lieut Col.
ADMS 24th Div.

War Diaries (original)
ADMS 3rd Division
140/2844.

February 1918
Vol. XXX

Feb. 1918

ASSISTANT DIRECTOR MEDICAL SERVICES
24th DIVISION
No. 3 Div
Date 8.3.18

COMMITTEE FOR THE
MEDICAL HISTORY OF THE WAR.
Date 12 MAY 1918

WAR DIARY
INTELLIGENCE SUMMARY

February 1918

Place	Date	Hour	Summary of Events and Information	Remarks
Nœux-les-Mines	1st		Reorganization of Divisional Artillery. Busy today. Battery C.O's in conference with them. 3 Mun C. O.R. relieved & attached 7's field Art. Batteries are to be broken up. 8 to Buff's & 12. Royal Fusiliers the C.O.'s little interest, but as I am already C. Officer Perm C. their there is still a deficiency of 4. Very well meeting of them.	2nd Division left as last R.A. Quartes, I.S.A.
	2nd		Routine. Fine sunny.	
	3rd		With Gen. Division inspected 5th & Brigade to 72nd Art Brigade the 64th Art Brigade at Noual Both units very busy as employed at entertaining work. Cpl. stationed to Cav Corps in Support Re-taken from the duties of	
	4th		K and that he is to have full harness inclined to burn.	
	5th		K and Cav Corps being present on leave. Seem going to town to Hg. V Army. Conference at Staff office very long decide visits VII Corps cavalry test camp, very fine country with	

WAR DIARY or INTELLIGENCE SUMMARY

Place	Date	Hour	Summary of Events and Information	Remarks and references to Appendices
Nolognet Farm	5th		February 1918. Plots of ground under cultivation by the various units.	
"	6th	—	Routine.	
"	7th	—	Brig. v. th. Army visited 73rd & 74th Brans. & found several items to compliment about, mostly trifling.	
"	8th	—	Visited 73rd & 74th Bns. trying a new tractor. complaints.	
"	9th	—	Cold west but fine.	
"	10th		Routine.	
"	11th		Conference at Cav. Corps. Hd Quarters upon the "defence scheme" in view of critics from the events.	
"	12th		To 5nd V th Army Conference.	
"	13th		To Cav. Corps Hd Quarters. 73rd & 74th Bns. great improvement in latrine buildings going on.	1/18

WAR DIARY
or
INTELLIGENCE SUMMARY

Army Form C. 2118.

February 1918

Place	Date	Hour	Summary of Events and Information	Remarks and references to Appendices
Malincourt	14th		To 73rd Falling trumpets been of declaration.	
"	15th		Gen. centre being quite improved. SO exists programme into MO state.	
"	16th		By Grippier asked for. Captain Colby hand in his resignation from hour. He has intention later up Res. too MO. when an Infan O.S.	
"	17		Sick visit tent Front at night. Not sufficient troupes on the Gr. hollow but attention. Orderline Drille in French bun by the Germans apparently. To here Star very likely to jump on in the expense branches to hand.	Ats
"	18th		To 72nd Infantry. To see own Leanards Hospital train at Montigny concerted. 3 trucks. Carried 2 to hall stated Can. 12. and. 4 me to talking wounded. It rating Enno drum by Petrol engine. Remits buy him 73rd to Frimeter. Captain, bater & off. Musheles Nom C. to No 32 CCS Tracumfrued.	
"	19th		To 73rd Infantry. Declaration of extension of num. & Lt. Studers, 74th to bunk on 30 days leave.	
"	20th			MA

WAR DIARY
or
INTELLIGENCE SUMMARY.
(Erase heading not required.)

Army Form C.

Place	Date	Hour	Summary of Events and Information	Remarks and references to Appendices
Moislains			February 1918	
	21.		Getting AFRs 66th Div. & impending relief in 5 days time. Drive in Troops at 15 'min' for 1 month. Reinforcements Offrs: Revd. C. Jones Capts Dowling, #Tren, J F Wood,—	
"	22	15 M.Men.	C O from issue.	
"	23		1st Lieuts. Kremer & Ginsberg more USA joined from 14th SUS	
"	24		Captain B.W. Kennedy Rev.E joined from HQ 74th Inf. Bde.	
"	25		Capt G.N. Cook McKennie joined from 4 72nd F. Amb.	
"	26		Capt Sweeny Wm R.C. USA joined attached 74 F.Amb. Transport 72 F. Amb & Bgde. Amm	
"	27		72nd F.Amb. handed in SH's & C.S.S. to 2/1 E. LANCs F.Amb & Entrained to rest area (Aubigny)	
"	28		Lt. J & D Buxton Rev.d joined attached 73rd F. Amb. Transport 74th F. Amb. left to rest area (Fort-Mahon) Chiton. More all Candlyn 72nd Pte Beutell and transport then was a strong wind.	
	2 pm		74th Bde turned back on the road.	

Julius M B Worrall Col
Offs. L & E.

96/31

40/2645.

Original War Diary
A.D.M.S. 24th Divn
March 1918
Vol. XXX

March 1918

WAR DIARY
INTELLIGENCE SUMMARY

Army Form C. 2118

Place	Date	Hour	Summary of Events and Information	Remarks and references to Appendices
Notre eglise Farm	March 1918			
	1st		72o F Amb returned from rest at Autryve to duties in a hurry & hurried flight.	
	2nd		Stg. left Notre eglise to MERRIS cont. in a blizzard chapter of cold & sleet, in comparative recent pillage and a brief above of any sunday arrangements. Handed in to ADMS 86th Div in Jh. 73o F Amb been duriced out of their quarters remain at the Sucerie Bermi in the Director of Westerner as all in the open in tents	
MERRIS cont.	3rd		From rain & ? to exhibit A D S at Vernensen (Sunday) at Morriving & returned very cold	
	4th		To visit 3 FA Camps. Very bad conditions. No cover, above & sanitary & stabling decomundation for the men, no plenty & no cattle Statting (Canning) To 72o F Amb at ERISE. Improved accommodation by personnel, very fine stating, (Sunday) we could all obviously be accomondata. The ECS MKB	

WAR DIARY
or
INTELLIGENCE SUMMARY.

Army Form C. 2118.

(Erase heading not required.)

Place	Date	Hour	Summary of Events and Information	Remarks and references to Appendices
Moeuvres	7/3/18		March. 1918.	
	8th		Trying to improve accommodation, which is very bad. Weather execrable. Improved a bit. Rode to Testry & Tupen. Looking for better accommodation.	
			Rode to St Chan, where there is ample accommodation for 5MS, but the Cavalry appear to haunt it.	
	9th		Heavy bombing with 4.6 casualties amongst the cavalry, all wounded removed to Cambrai.	
			Plant of July. & xx cops.	
	10th		Very fine day.	
	11th		To Bourmont. Saw ADMS 8th — Saw site allot him.	
	12th		Rode to Tupen.	
	13th		Left Moeuvres for Bourmont & Vadencourt.	
BOURMONT	14th		To Roisel, Vermand & Vadencourt.	
	15th		To Vermand to meet Pryor RE to arr. accommodation. A great deal of water exits in his already done by Cav. for Amb., who have got it away the trenches wanted for R.A.F. This presents something into it. To Vadencourt Chateau & interview Dr. obviously improper. Cavalry no being in a queer house — sort of daphnoid.	
	16th		To Vermand. Manning & walked to heaquet wood, Rocs, & looking Ricbesire from here of trench lines in front of Bellingtise.	
	17th		Testing 70th to Frank and Joycon 73rd to Bank. This letters & fine place.	
	18th		To Jeancourt. ADS (as stat) & to Le Verguier. VM Little hunts & R&Ps.	

WAR DIARY or INTELLIGENCE SUMMARY

Army Form C. 2118.

Place	Date	Hour	Summary of Events and Information	Remarks and references to Appendices
Bouzincourt	19		To Preuilly 72nd to attack.	
"	20		Nature.	
"	21		German attack begun with tremendous bombardment at 4.30 a.m. in a cold wet + heavy mist. Many HE shells on B.H.Q. Bouzencourt, with heavy casualties. 72nd & Cameleons holding their line very well.	
"	22		B.H.Q. left Bouzincourt to Brie. Germans advancing steadily, great resistance by 24th Bri, who however had heavy losses had to retire. Field took to St Ouen.	
			Trenches spent the whole of last night retiring. 32-34 OCs wounded. Left Bri early to Mandolph. Also at Mr Christo. Wet. Germans shelling west bank of R. Somme. Left Mandolph + "Huille" & attack on bridge of Pargny not many casualties. 8 to Riwoin.	
"	23		At Huille Germans reported on the river opposite Chandro. 5th Army numbers said to being him up all round. B.H.Q. left for Riwoin. 2.47 OCs stated shaken. h.5.+55 also there.	
"	24		Fine cold. 74th to attack at Libermon. 73rd at CHILLY 72nd at Riwoin in reserve. Left Riwoin at 5-30 arrived St MOUIV. All three attacks. By Cay exp. 72nd in Chateau 73rd in Field CCS. 74th pushed onto Linons. (74)	
Riwoin	25		both advance posts in VREILY(?) MENVIELERS(?)V.	

Place	Date	Hour	Summary of Events and Information	Remarks and references to Appendices
DEMUIN	26th		Holding the German infantry Division. Battalion in walking way not being Counter attacked. Held 75°/1 of Cavalern Bdy to other Rive in Chocolates. Last night two German spies came in disguised through strange pickets. which he with different papers. The 24th Div did not Relieve us.	
"	27th		Very heavy Shelling. Outposts & APs at MEZIEL & bivouacs resulted by LEARGIST HAE proving weak being shell. Very cold today, all intermediate time. Also Germans in being shelled.	
"	28th		Germans broke through in the light North & am advancing towards Moreuil via Cair, also E in being shelled. APS. 72nd & General attacked shelled & Cavalry Ambulance had to leave Cayeux the platoon to Berneuil. Machinist formed on the Ridge round of them brought to Berneuil places in Chateau there about 100. All wounded taken on to THENNES & placed in huts Grove for side of village. We can not do very little comforts a number were Shelling German when the wounded were being transport to village. Lot with & is dinner any wounds repairing it. Hurts cleared impossible with little help to it on led till 3 am 29th. Not all the wounded were got away in the lorries to NOUVREL via 'Castel bridges. by the 72nd Field WRe	

WAR DIARY or INTELLIGENCE SUMMARY

(Erase heading not required.)

Army Form C. 2118.

Instructions regarding War Diaries and Intelligence Summaries are contained in F. S. Regs., Part II. and the Staff Manual respectively. Title pages will be prepared in manuscript.

Place	Date	Hour	Summary of Events and Information	Remarks and references to Appendices
Cas.Cl.	29th		March 1918. St. G. Mine. 3 Field ambulances at Rouvrel. All wounded evacuated to CCS at Namps.	
Cottenchy	30th		The German advance held up sjue event but the side of Cayeux line & 608. a lull in affairs. Many French troops about. 72" 73" 74" At Anvils at St Fuscien, & to 74" to H.Q. at Sains en Amiens & worked front with Dts. at Cottenchy, & Cai fork at Dommartin & Thezy. - N Welsh Yeod Reserve Divis in of 70" 7 ant tank of 74" also functioning in reserve. German attack on Moreuil stopped by the French.	
"	31st			

Vol 32

16 0/2906.

Original War Diary
ADMS 24th Divn
April 1918
Vol. XXXII

COMMITTEE FOR
MEDICAL HISTORY
Date -6 JUN.1918

April/18

WAR DIARY
or
INTELLIGENCE SUMMARY.

Army Form C. 2118.

April 1918

Place	Date	Hour	Summary of Events and Information	Remarks and references to Appendices
COTTENCHY	1st		Considerable gun fire during the night. 8th Div. sent up to & counter attacked this morning. Firing line in ... opposite. 9.15 Lt. Aupher also 78th & 74th of same at ...... & ...... in American & ...... with A.D.S. at Cottenchy & rest part of Formation & Thery-Guinard.	
"	2nd		8th Divn in line you not of line but to remain in opposite.	
"	3rd		Evening ..... up Formation 24th Divn in Cottenchy & Lt Quenn line.	
"	4th		Very heavy gun fire all last night. Fairly close morning. Left at 11am for BOVES. Very .... Whether ...... is in ...... the line. ...... order to ...... Bn. & men to Le Pontillous. What a ... my ...... had two packed & last 40 mins cancelled. Went rather ...... Lett Boves this morning. Stayed there & ... an .... an Officer & ...... of 9, 3rd ...... & 5th Aust. Left Bn at Le Pontillous. Divn in ...... & coming on.	
"	5th			

Army Form 2118.

WAR DIARY
or
INTELLIGENCE SUMMARY.
(Erase heading not required.)

Instructions regarding War Diaries and Intelligence Summaries are contained in F. S. Regs., Part II. and the Staff Manual respectively. Title pages will be prepared in manuscript.

Place	Date	Hour	Summary of Events and Information	Remarks and references to Appendices
La Bouteillerie	6		Left Bouteillerie for St Valery, when the 73rd & 74th Fd Amb to Brent.	
St Valery	7		Arrived St Valery. 1 am. 73rd Fd Amb at St Valery - 74th at Valerie. & 74th Fd Amb at Mollière, & rest & refit.	
	8/9.		Requipment. Routine	
	10/11		Refitting	
	12.		Parade to see dispt of 8th Queens. Regt. & 74th Fd Amb.	
	13ᵗʰ		Kaisers XVIIIᵗʰ Corps. hoisted office.	
	14ᵗʰ		To 73rd Fd Amb at Valerie	
	15ᵃ		Order that I am to be relieved by Lt Col. Mackenzie ADMS 1st Cav Division & proceed to England & report to Sec. W.O. Routine	
	16ᵗʰ		Returned from Valerie. 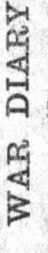	MMS

Army Form C. 2118.

WAR DIARY
or
INTELLIGENCE SUMMARY.
(Erase heading not required.)

Instructions regarding War Diaries and Intelligence Summaries are contained in F.S. Regs., Part II. and the Staff Manual respectively. Title pages will be prepared in manuscript.

Place	Date	Hour	Summary of Events and Information	Remarks and references to Appendices
ST. VALERY LA THIELOYE	1918 Apl 16th		Orders for move of Division to PERNES Area.	
	17th		Divl H.Q. opened at LA THIELOYE 5 p.m., in First Army Area. Capt. Wallace 73 F.Ambce posted to 9th R.Sussex vice Capt. Harris R.A.M.C. to England on expiry of contract.	
	18th		1st Lieut Ginsberg M.O.R.C.,U.S.A. rejoined 74 F.Ambce from duty with No.5 C.C.S. 72nd Fld Ambce at VALHUON 73rd " at BEUGIN 74th " at ORLENCOURT	
	19th		A.D.M.S. 1st Cavalry Division called re taking over. Col. F.R.BUSWELL handed over to Col.T.C.MACKENZIE and left for England. 1st Lieut Shannon M.O.R.C.,U.S.A. rejoined 73 Fld Ambce from duty with No.5 C.C.S. 37 O.R. reinforcements joined, posted as under:- 72 Fld Ambce 17 73 " 6 74 " 14	
	20th		A.D.M.S. to see D.D.M.S. Corps in morning and to conference M.Os. 73 Inf.Bde afternoon, discussing lessons of recent fighting. 72 Fld Ambce moved from Valhuon to DIVION.	
	21st		Conference of Ambulance Commanders in afternoon - lessons of recent fighting. D.A.D.M.S. to O.C. 63 Sanitary Section AUBIGNY in evening.	
	22nd		A.D.M.S. to visit D.M.S. First Army. Case of Rose Measles 8th Queen's admitted 16th, now reported scarlet fever.	
	23rd		A.D.M.S. to 74th Fld Ambce and 17th Inf.Bde.	
	24th		A.D.M.S. with G.O.C. to inspect Fld Ambces. A.D.M.S. and D.A.D.M.S. to Corps in evening.	
	25th		D.D.M.S. Office moved to BRYAS. A.D.M.S. went to 73rd Inf.Bde in morning. Orders received for Capt. W.Graham C.A.M.C. attd 8th R.W.Kents, to proceed to Base.	
	26th		A.D.M.S. to visit D.D.M.S. Corps in morning. Arranged for huts near BRYAS Station to be taken over by 74 Fld Ambce as a Rest Station.	
	27th		A.D.M.S. to Divisional Artillery in morning. Capt. Graham left 8th R.W.Kents for Base in accordance with D.G.M.S. instructions. Capt. H.Tren R.A.M.C., T.C., 74 Fld Ambce, in relief. O.C. 74 Fld Ambce reports that he has been evcted from huts at BRYAS, which belong to the French Railway Authorities.	
	28th		D.D.M.S. called in afternoon. Case of Rose Measles 8th Queen's admitted 22nd instant, now reported Scarlet Fever.	
	29th		Orders for move received. 73rd Inf.Bde Group started, but were recalled en route. Orders cancelled. A.D.M.S. to 8th Queen's in afternoon to investigate cases of infectious disease.	

Army Form C. 2118.

WAR DIARY
or
INTELLIGENCE SUMMARY.
(Erase heading not required.)

Instructions regarding War Diaries and Intelligence Summaries are contained in F. S. Regs., Part II. and the Staff Manual respectively. Title pages will be prepared in manuscript.

Place	Date 1918	Hour	Summary of Events and Information	Remarks and references to Appendices
LA THIEULOYE	April 30th.		Orders received for 24th Division to relieve 3rd Canadian Division. 73rd Inf.Bde Group to move at 11.30 a.m. A.D.M.S. to new area re taking over. 73 Fld Ambce moved to FOSSE 10 and are to run A.D.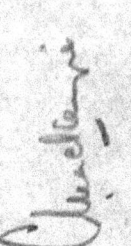 evacuating, taking over from No.10 Canadian Fld Ambce. 1st Lieut H.A.Peck M.O.R.C., U.S.A., M.O. 7th North'n Regt, posted to XVIII Corps reinforcement Camp and struck off strength of Division. Capt. D.A.D.Kennedy R.A.M.C., T.C., M.O. 3rd Rifle Bde, posted to 7th North'n Regt. Capt. G.S.McConkey R.A.M.C., S.R. posted from 72 Fld Ambce to 3rd Rifle Bde.	

24th Divl H.Q.,
30-4-18.

Colonel A.M.S.,
A.D.M.S. 24th Divn.

Vol 33

140/2973

Original War Diary
ADMS 24th Division
for May 1918

Vol. $\frac{I}{XXIII}$

COMMITTEE FOR THE
MEDICAL HISTORY OF THE WAR
Date 9 JUL 1918

Army Form C. 2118.

WAR DIARY
or
INTELLIGENCE SUMMARY.
(Erase heading not required.)

Instructions regarding War Diaries and Intelligence Summaries are contained in F.S. Regs., Part II. and the Staff Manual respectively. Title pages will be prepared in manuscript.

Place	Date	Hour	Summary of Events and Information	Remarks and references to Appendices
LA THIBULOYE.	1918 May 1st		72nd Inf.Bde Group moved to BULLY GRENAY, LES BREBIS, SAINS. 72nd Fld Ambce and take over from No.9 Canadian Fld Ambce. 73rd Inf.Bde go in line tonight - 2 Battalions in line and one in support. No site settled for 74 Fld Ambce yet. Coupigny Chateau suggested by D.D.M.S. XVIII Corps. A.D.M.S. to FOSSE 10, Cité St.Pierre A.D.S., and AIX NOULETTE.	
	2nd		74th Fld Ambce report Coupigny Chateau occupied. A.D.M.S. to see D.D.M.S. and General ABBOTT XVIII Corps. They say 74 Fld Ambce may have GRAND SERVINS for Divisional Rest Station. A.D.M.S. and D.A.D.M.S. to see site at GRAND SERVINS, with O.C. 74 Fld Ambce at 12 noon. A good place but very dirty.	
		6 p.m.	74 Fld Ambce completed move to GRAND SERVINS.	
SAINS-EN-GOHELLE.	3rd		Headquarters 24th Division arrived at SAINS-EN-GOHELLE and A.D.M.S. took over from A.D.M.S. 3rd Canadian Division.	
	4th		A.D.M.S. to FOSSE 10, FOSSE 11, and Sick Collecting Stations at BULLY GRENAY and MAROC.	
	5th	a.m. p.m.	G.O.C. Divn inspected the Fld Ambces with A.D.M.S. in morning. A.D.M.S. to MAROC to see 12th Sherwoods, who have had excessive sick admissions lately.	
	6th		A.D.M.S. to A.D.S. FORT GLATZ, R.A.P. at ST.PATRICK, TOSH KEEP, and 73rd Inf.Bde Headquarters.	
	7th		Accompanied by D.D.M.S. XVIII Corps, the A.D.M.S. visited Divl Main Dressing Station, the A.D.S. Cité St.PIERRE, and the R.A.Ps. of right Brigade.	
	8th		Routine.	
	9th	a.m. p.m.	Conference of A.Ds.M.S. at XVIII Corps re expected German attack tonight. Walking wounded collecting post formed at Fosse 11. Conference of ambulance commanders at 2 p.m. Arrangements made in view of expected operations. A central records office to be at Divl Rest Station, and books kept there. All cars to be under orders of O.C. 73 Fld Ambce. Heavy transport packed and sent back to GRAND SERVINS. D.R.S. partially cleared of worst cases (39 lying). Rear Divl H.Q. established at GOUY SERVINS.	

Army Form C. 2118.

WAR DIARY
or
INTELLIGENCE SUMMARY.
(Erase heading not required.)

Instructions regarding War Diaries and Intelligence Summaries are contained in F.S. Regs., Part II. and the Staff Manual respectively. Title pages will be prepared in manuscript.

Place	Date	Hour	Summary of Events and Information	Remarks and references to Appendices
SAINS-EN-GOHELLE.	1918. May 9th	10-30 p.m.	All quiet. 12 midnight, nothing has developed.	
	May 10th		A quiet night. A gas centre to be formed at Fosse 10: to be run by 73 Fld Ambce. C.R.E. visited Fosse 10 with A.D.M.S. to arrange about the necessary alterations.	
	11th		A.D.M.S. with C.R.E. to see new Walking Wounded Collecting Post at Fosse 11 re improvements. In afternoon A.D.M.S. with O.C. 73 Fld Ambce to A.D.S. ST.PIERRE. D.D.M.S. XVIII Corps called in evening with reference to defence scheme for 'BULLY SWITCH', and went up to see W.W.C.P. Fosse 11.	
		p.m.	Capt. W.C.F.Harland R.A.M.C., T.F., 72 Fld Ambce, to DIEPPE for duty, under orders from First Army. Some gas shelling on 72 Inf.Bde front about 4 a.m.	
	12th		17th Inf.Bde go in line tonight, which is to be changed to a 3-brigade front. About 46 cases of mustard gas poisoning; 20 very slight, result of shelling on 11th: many delayed cases.	
	13th	p.m.	A.D.M.S. to see D.R.S. in afternoon.	
	14th	a.m.	A.D.M.S. to 17th Inf.Bde in morning.	
		p.m.	In afternoon with G.S.O.1. to see the Bde H.Q. of the 17th Inf.Bde in the line.	
	15th	O.C.	73 Fld Ambce called in morning re the new re-adjustment of the line.	
	16th	p.m.	In afternoon, A.D.M.S. to Walking Wounded Collecting Post to see progress in work there. 74 Fld Ambce took over ambulance site at ESTREE CAUCHIE, with a complete tent sub-division, to be run as a Corps Skin Centre.	
	17th		A.D.M.S. to W.W.C.P., D.R.S., and the new Corps Skin Centre ESTREE CAUCHIE, which has possibilities; at present very dirty. New bath house, latrines, etc. required.	
	18th		A.D.M.S. to A.D.S. ST.PIERRE: met M.O. 1st Royal Fusiliers, went with him to JUNCTION R.A.P. and Relay posts. Capt. J.W.GRAY R.A.M.C., S.R. joined and was posted to 72 Fld Ambce.	
	19th		A.D.M.S. to Corps H.Q. to see D.D.M.S. D.A.D.M.S. to HERSIN to see No.9 L.R.O.Coy re service for walking wounded. Capt. LICKLEY J.D., R.A.M.C., T.F. and Lieut M.AIKMAN R.A.M.C., T.C. joined; posted to 72 and 73 Fld Ambces respectively.	

Army Form C. 2118.

WAR DIARY
or
INTELLIGENCE SUMMARY.
(Erase heading not required.)

Instructions regarding War Diaries and Intelligence Summaries are contained in F. S. Regs., Part II. and the Staff Manual respectively. Title pages will be prepared in manuscript.

Place	Date 1918.	Hour	Summary of Events and Information	Remarks and references to Appendices
SAINS-EN-GOHELLE.	May 20th		Visit of D.M.S. First Army, who inspected 73 Fld Ambce - Main Dressing Station and Gas Centre, FOSSE 10.	
	21st	p.m.	A.D.M.S. to conference at D.D.M.S. XVIII Corps. In afternoon to D.R.S., which is only to have 100 cases (by order of D.D.M.S.). 55 evacuations from the Division in consequence.	
	22nd		Capt. J.CULLEN R.A.M.C., T.C. joined from Base; posted to 73 Fld Ambce.	
	24th		Wet and stormy: A.D.M.S. to inspect billets of 73 Inf.Bde in LES BREBIS, billets of 72nd Inf. Bde in BULLY GRENAY, and scabies treatment at 72 Fld Ambce. Gas beam attack on our right.	
	25th		A.D.M.S. to Corps Skin Centre to see improvements. ST.PATRICK'S, LOOS, Post given up: it is no use as there is no direct trench down from front line.	
	26th		Routine.	
	27th		To see new apparatus for hot air disinfection at Canadian Corps Rest Station FRESNICOURT.	
	28th		Shells from 5.9 gun fell in SAINS-EN-GOHELLE about 11.15 a.m.: 12 casualties, 6 serious.	
	29th		Further shelling at noon: no casualties.	
	30th		Shelling of village (SAINS-E-G.) about 4 a.m. 1 O.R./A.M.C. attached D.H.Q. killed: no other casualties.	
	31st		A.D.M.S. and D.A.D.M.S. to A.D.S. ST.PIERRE - many improvements in hand.	

24th D.H.Q.

Lieut-Col. R.A.M.C.,
A/A.D.M.S. 24th Divn.

Confidential

Original War Diary
A.D.M.S. 24th Divn.
June 1918
Vol. XXXIV

Army Form C. 2118.

WAR DIARY
or
INTELLIGENCE SUMMARY.
(Erase heading not required.)

Instructions regarding War Diaries and Intelligence Summaries are contained in F. S. Regs, Part II and the Staff Manual respectively. Title pages will be prepared in manuscript.

Place	Date	Hour	Summary of Events and Information	Remarks and references to Appendices
SAINS-EN-GOHELLE	1918. June 1st		Projector attack on 73rd Inf. Bde. front about midnight: 20 casualties roughly.	
	2nd		Several deaths in field ambulances from delayed gas poisoning (phosgene)	
	3rd		A.D.M.S. to England 14 days' leave: Lieut-Col.F.W.M.CUNNINGHAM, O.C. 73rd Field Ambce. to act for him.	
	4th		The following postings and moves took place:— Captain P.W.L.ANDREW R.A.M.C. from 74th Field Ambce. to 1st Royal Fusiliers. Captain C.N.COAD M.C., R.A.M.C., " 72nd " " 1st North Staffs. Captain H.TREN R.A.M.C., " 74th " " 8th Royal West Kents 1/Lt.J.ROTHMAN M.O.R.C., " 24th D.A.Column " 13th Middlesex Captain R.A.H.FULTON R.A.M.C. " 13th Middlesex " 73rd Field Ambulance. 1/Lt.A.C.SHANNON M.O.R.C. " 73rd Field Ambulance to 13th Middlesex.	
	5th		Actg A.D.M.S. and D.A.D.M.S. to FORT GLATZ A.D.S., 73rd Bde. H.Q., and Post at MAROC.	
	6th		Routine.	
	7th		1/Lt.H.A.PECK M.O.R.C., reported for duty; attached to 72nd Field Ambulance.	
	8th		A/A.D.M.S. to Conference of D.Ds.M.S., Os.C. Stationary Hospitals, and C.C.Ss., First Army, to meet the new D.G.M.S. and consult on the louse problem, delousing, etc., Dental Arrangements.	
	10th		Gas beam attack by us on our front 1-10 a.m. About 20 casualties from leaky cylinder or blow back of gas. 4 deaths in Field Ambulances. A/A.D.M.S. and D.A.D.M.S. to A.D.S. St.PIERRE, R.A.P. JUNCTION POST, and the new R.A.P.'MARTYR RELAY'.	
	11th		Captain C.E.DOLLING R.A.M.C. to England – Contract expired. Ex Lieut. M.AIKMAN R.A.M.C. from 73rd Field Ambulance to 12th Bn. Sherwood Foresters. Admissions from N.Y.D. Pyrexia rather high. 1 Officer and 2 N.C.Os. sent to First Army R.A.M.C. School of Instruction.	

Army Form C. 2118.

WAR DIARY
or
INTELLIGENCE SUMMARY.
(Erase heading not required.)

Instructions regarding War Diaries and Intelligence Summaries are contained in F. S. Regs., Part II. and the Staff Manual respectively. Title pages will be prepared in manuscript.

Place	Date	Hour	Summary of Events and Information	Remarks and references to Appendices
SAINS-EN-GOHELLE	1918 June 12th		Large number of admissions N.Y.D. Pyrexia. Apparently of influenzal type, characterised by frontal headache, pains in back & limbs. Dry cough with no expectoration. Temp. 102 - 103. Pulse 120 - 130. Conjunctival injection. 20 cases from 12th Sherwood Foresters - other cases mostly from 72nd Inf. Bde. Corps and Army informed. Circular sent to all medical officers, "G", "Q", Brigades etc. on the subject.	
	13th		58 cases up to 9 a.m. mostly from 12th Sherwood Foresters and 8th Royal West Kents - several in 72nd Field Ambulance. A/A.D.M.S. to 17th and 73rd Brigades to consult re precautions. Decided to spray all dug-outs daily. O.C., Sanitary Section to 72nd Brigade with same object. 1 Sgt. 10 nursing orderlies sent to No. 1 C.C.S. for duty.	
	14th		54 cases from Division, in addition to about 40 among Corps Troops. All Medical Officers circulated recommending gargles and mouth washes for contacts and suspicious cases. D.D.M.S. XVIII Corps called in afternoon and had no further suggestions as to treatment. A few cases in 73rd Field Ambulance. The epidemic is not confined by any means to the Divisional area.	
	15th		72 cases from Division and 50 from Corps Troops. The epidemic has spread to 1st North Staffs, who relieved 8th Royal West Kents in the line. Extra tentage is being put up at 74th Field Ambulance to deal with the lighter cases.	
	16th		128 cases from Division today. 8th Queens and Machine Gun Battalion now affected. A N.C.O. of the Sanitary Section is to be attached to each Brigade Headquarters to supervise the spraying of dug-outs etc. A supply of cresol and formalin is held at each A.D.S.	
	17th		138 cases from the Division and 40 Corps Troops this morning. Cases coming in rapidly all day. Over 200 by 6 p.m. Two lorries borrowed from Division for evacuating the lighter cases. No. 1 C.C.S. say that Pyrexia lasts about 3 days, convalescence is rapid, and men should be returned within 7-8 days. A.D.M.S. returned from leave. Heavy thunderstorm and rain most of the night. Captain G.S. McConkey R.A.M.C. sick.	
	18th		303 cases - rapid spread of epidemic among units. C.C.S. at WAVRANS full. Capt McConkey RAMC. attached 3rd Rifle Brigade evacuated sick. 2nd circular on precautions issued.	

Army Form C. 2118.

WAR DIARY
or
INTELLIGENCE SUMMARY.
(Erase heading not required.)

Instructions regarding War Diaries and Intelligence Summaries are contained in F.S. Regs, Part II. and the Staff Manual respectively. Title pages will be prepared in manuscript.

Place	Date	Hour	Summary of Events and Information	Remarks and references to Appendices
SAINS - EN - GOHELLE.	1918 June 19th		377 cases yesterday. Captain P.W.L.ANDREWS R.A.M.C. attached 1st Royal Fusiliers sick. 110 cases accommodated at FOSSE 10.	
	20th		361 cases - slight decrease. Captain T.B.WALKER MORC. and 1/Lt. J.ROTHMAN MORC. sick,-getting very short of medical officers. Cases still pouring in this evening. Wet and stormy. 72 Fld. Ambulance have accommodated about 160 cases today. D.R.S. now over 400.	
	21st		486 cases. 1/Lt. H.A.PECK MORC. sick. Disease now general throughout Divisional area. 72 Fld. Ambulance are now accommodating about 270 cases, and 50 are accommodated in SAINS in huts fitted up temporarily as a hospital. Auxiliary hospital at CAMBLAIN L'ABBE has been formed. 200 cases there. Arrangements made for cases to be discharged from Field Ambulances to 24th Divisional Reception Camp.	
	22nd		457 cases - disease now most virulent in 73rd Brigade. Figures :- 17 Inf. Bde. - 86. 72 Inf. Bde. - 60. 73 Inf. Bde. - 165. Total cases accommodated in Divisional Area 743 (P.U.O).	
	23rd		433 cases. Orders received that all cases are now to be evacuated to C.C.S. for transfer to special Base Hospital at ETAPLES.	
	24th		329 cases - a marked decrease. Field Ambulances are gradually clearing their cases.	
	25th		264 cases - further decrease. Vacancies for 4 Officers and 50 other ranks at No. 1 C.C.S. allotted to N.C.Os, gunners and specially valuable men.	
	26th		290 cases. Now raging in 106 Brigade R.F.A.	
	27th		177 cases.	
	28th		141 cases. A.D.M.S. and A.A.& Q.M.G. made a sanitary inspection of forward area (73rd Inf.Bde.)	
	29th		102 cases.	

Army Form C. 2118.

WAR DIARY
or
INTELLIGENCE SUMMARY.
(Erase heading not required.)

Instructions regarding War Diaries and Intelligence Summaries are contained in F. S. Regs., Part II. and the Staff Manual respectively. Title pages will be prepared in manuscript.

Place	Date	Hour	Summary of Events and Information	Remarks and references to Appendices
SAINS-EN-GOHELLE	1918 June 30th		70 cases. Steady decrease. A.D.M.S. to Battalion in line 72 Inf. Bde. to inspect sanitation.	

H.Q., 24th Division.
1st July 1918.

Chalmers
A.D.M.S., 24th Division.
Colonel, A.M.S.

Vol 35
140/3123.

Confidential

War Diary
A.D.M.S. 24th Division
July 1918
VOL. XXXV

July 1918

Army Form C. 2118.

WAR DIARY
INTELLIGENCE SUMMARY.
(Erase heading not required.)

Instructions regarding War Diaries and Intelligence Summaries are contained in F. S. Regs., Part II. and the Staff Manual respectively. Title pages will be prepared in manuscript.

Place	Date	Hour	Summary of Events and Information	Remarks and references to Appendices
SAINS-EN-GOHELLE.	1918 July 1		Only 26 Cases today. The hospital accommodation at the Base is not sufficient for these cases, and it is now proposed to retain a certain number in the Divisional Area again.	
	2nd		42 cases. A.D.M.S. on sanitary inspection of 8th Queens in the line. XVIII Corps has now become VIII Corps.	
	3rd		88 cases. The epidemic has now affected the 107th Brigade R.F.A. - in the 20th Divisional Area. A.D.M.S. to 3rd Rifle Brigade, sanitary inspection of the line. Accommodation in the Divisional area to be increased to 400 cases.	
	4th		A.D.M.S. to Conference at D.D.M.S. VIIIth Corps office re. discussion on Sanitation and supervision of Medical Officers of Corps Troops.	
	5th		A.D.M.S. and O.C. 73rd Field Ambulance to FOSSE 11 to consider possibilities of using this as an Advanced Dressing Station in view of amended Defence Scheme. Decided to construct a road to enable ambulance cars to run direct to Walking Wounded Collecting Post.	
	6th		A.D.M.S. visited A.D.S., CITE ST. PIERRE, and R.A.P. at JUNCTION POST with Divl. Gas Officer.	
	7th		D.D.M.S. proceeded on leave to England. Captain R.A.H.FULTON RAMC., 73rd Field Ambulance to act as D.A.D.M.S. Epidemic quietening - 11 cases today.	
	8th		Two new American officers, Captain H.RUBIN MORC. (USA) and Lieut. W.L.BOTKIN MORC. (USA) joined the Division to Relieve Captain T.E.WALKER MORC. (USA) and Lieut. H.M.GINSBERG MORC (USA) - to American Expeditionary Force.	
	9th		Routine.	
	10th		A.D.M.S. to 72nd Infantry Brigade Headquarters.	
	11th		A.D.M.S. to No. 1 Cas. Clearing Station, No. 1 Canadian C.C.S. and No. 4 Canadian C.C.S. to enquire re cases of epidemic pyrexia.	
	12th		A.D.M.S. to Corps Skin Centre ESTREE CAUCHIE. Ready to open in a few days. Experiments with	

Army Form C. 2118.

WAR DIARY
of
INTELLIGENCE SUMMARY.
(Erase heading not required.)

Instructions regarding War Diaries and Intelligence Summaries are contained in F. S. Regs., Part II. and the Staff Manual respectively. Title pages will be prepared in manuscript.

Place	Date	Hour	Summary of Events and Information	Remarks and references to Appendices
SAINS-EN-GOHELLE.	1918 July 12th		Continued. ORR'S delouser. Visited Divisional Rest Station.	
	13th		Routine.	
	14th		A.D.M.S. to CITE ST. PIERRE.	
	15th		A.D.M.S. to A.D.S. LOOS.	
	16th		D.A.& Q.M.G. VIII Corps and D.D.D.M.S. VIII Corps visited Divisional A.D.Ss. and made remarks.	
	17th		107 Brigade R.F.A. inspected	
	18th		A.D.M.S. to visit FOSSE 11 with C.R.E. and O.C. 73rd Field Ambulance.	
	19th		Inspection of 72nd Field Ambulance AIX NOULETTE with C.R.E.. It was decided to move the 4 Nissen huts and erect them at the Divl. Rest Station. Probably only 3 complete huts could be xxxx constructed from the 4 now in use at AIX NOULETTE.	
	20th		Visit to 7 C.C.S., LIGNY.	
	21st		Sanitary inspection of Divl. H.Q. by D.A.D.M.S.	
	23nd		D.A.D.M.S. returned from leave.	
	24th		Two officers and two other ranks to First Army RAMC. School.	
	25th		A.D.M.S. to opening day of First Army RAMC. School.	
	26th		Capt. A.J.IRELAND RAMC.(TC) and Capt. A.S.HOPPER RAMC.(TF) joined Divn. and attached to 72nd Field Ambce. Lieut. P.A.MANSFIELD RAMC.(TC) joined and attached to 74 Field Ambce. One officer over strength.	
	27th		Routine.	

(Appx: Wt. W4899/M1293. 75m,000. 4/17. D.D. & L, Ltd. Forms/C.2118/4.

Army Form C. 2118.

WAR DIARY
or
INTELLIGENCE SUMMARY.
(Erase heading not required.)

Instructions regarding War Diaries and Intelligence Summaries are contained in F. S. Regs., Part II. and the Staff Manual respectively. Title pages will be prepared in manuscript.

Place	Date	Hour	Summary of Events and Information	Remarks and references to Appendices
SAINS-EN-GOHELLE.	1918. July 28th		Routine.	
	29th		A.D.M.S. to R.A.P. and A.D.S. of Right Sector.	
	30th		Routine.	
	31st		A.D.M.S. to inspect 74 Field Ambulance - also sanitation in GOUY SERVINS area. An officer ordered to be posted to 20th Division.	
24th D.H.Q.				

Colonel, A.M.S.
A.D.M.S., 24th Division.

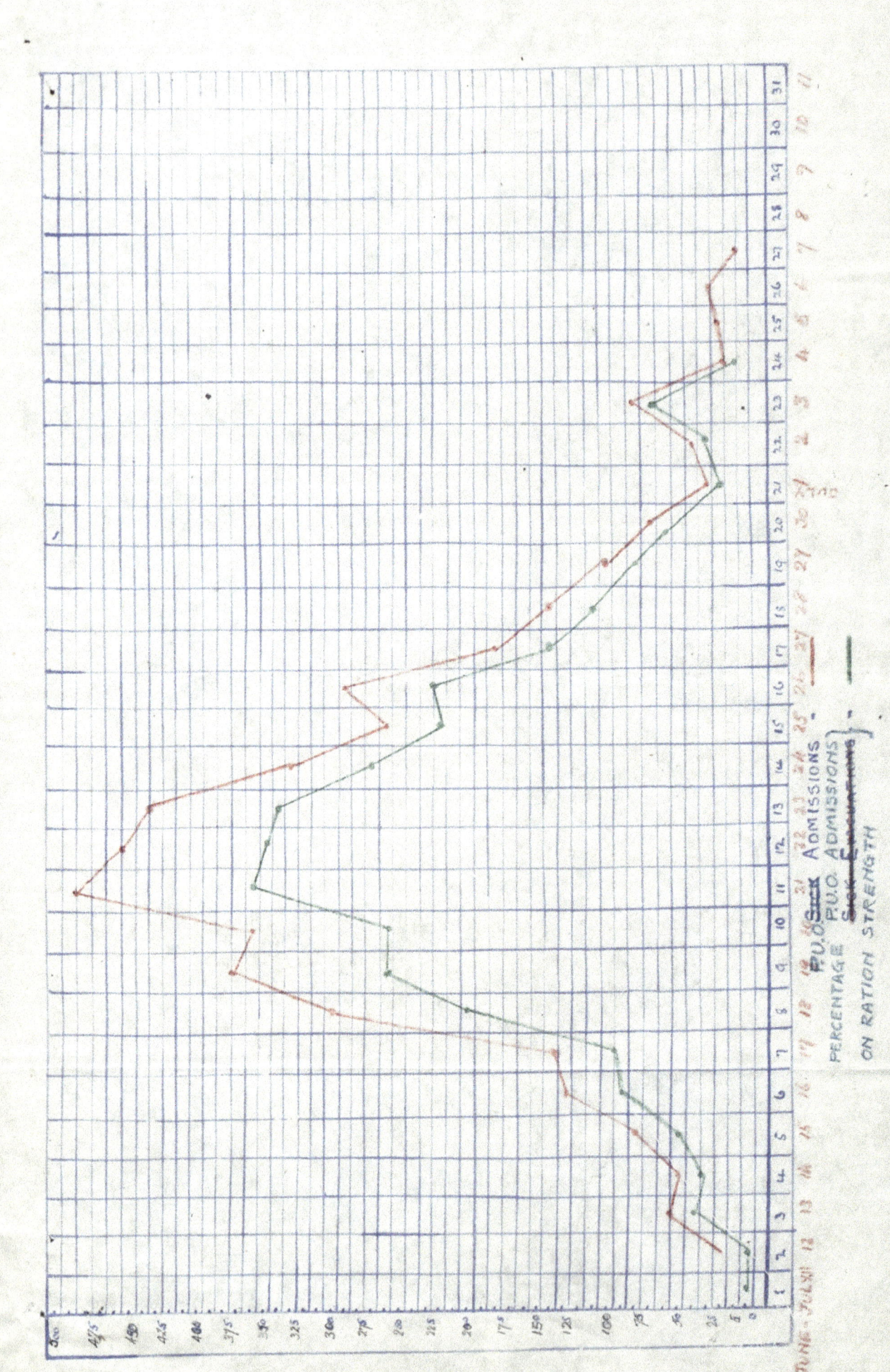

Confidential/9

149/3301
WO 95 36

Original War Diary
A.D.M.S. 24th Divn
August 1918.
Vol. XXXVI

Army Form C. 2118.

WAR DIARY
or
INTELLIGENCE SUMMARY.
(Erase heading not required.)

Instructions regarding War Diaries and Intelligence Summaries are contained in F. S. Regs., Part II. and the Staff Manual respectively. Title pages will be prepared in manuscript.

Place	Date	Hour	Summary of Events and Information	Remarks and references to Appendices
Sains-en-Gohelle.	1918. Augt 1st		30 C.C.S. opened as a Corps Rest Station. Postings. Capt. G.J.L.Patch M.C., R.A.M.C., to 20th Division.	
	2		Routine.	
	3		A.D.M.S. to inspect 106 Bde R.F.A. Wagon lines.	
	4		Routine.	
	5		Routine.	
	6		Routine.	
	7		A.D.M.S. to new R.A.P. Martyr, A.D.S. St.Pierre, Junction. Notice boards very bad in forward area; need renewing.	
	8		30 C.C.S. no longer available; all cases to go to ordinary C.C.S.	
	9		Routine.	
	10		Routine.	
	11		A.D.M.S. round A.D.S. LOOS, ST.PIERRE, and FOSSE 11 with C.R.E., to discuss construction of 'Gas-looks'.	
	12		Much bombing last night; 7 killed, 28 wounded, at Fosse 10. A.D.M.S. and D.A.D.M.S. to First Army School.	
	13		A.D.M.S. to First Army School.	
	14		30 C.C.S. open again for cases for the Divn.	
	15		A.D.M.S. and D.A.D.M.S. to First Army School.	

Army Form C. 2118.

WAR DIARY
or
INTELLIGENCE SUMMARY.
(Erase heading not required.)

Instructions regarding War Diaries and Intelligence Summaries are contained in F. S. Regs., Part II. and the Staff Manual respectively. Title pages will be prepared in manuscript.

Place	Date 1918	Hour	Summary of Events and Information	Remarks and references to Appendices
Sains-en-Gohelle	Aug 16		Inspection by D.M.S. First Army of the Field Ambulances, Battle A.D.S., Walking Wounded Collecting Post Fosse 11, A.D.S. ST.PIERRE, R.A.P. JUNCTION.	
	17		Routine.	
	18		Routine.	
	19		D.A.D.M.S. and O.C. 73 Fld Ambce to see new R.A.P. on right to be taken over tomorrow.	
	20		Division taking over battalion front on right.	
	21		A.D.M.S. and D.A.D.M.S. to visit new Battn H.Q. and R.A.P. 73 Fld Ambce relieved in the line by 74 Fld Ambce. 73 F.A. took over Divl Rest Station.	
	22		Enemy shelled Fosse 10 this evening, xxxxxxxxxxxxxx, a few shells in Sains-en-Gohelle.	
	23		Further shelling of Fosse 10 this evening, but no casualties.	
	24		Question of finding alternative site for M.D.S.: decided to strengthen cellars there and remain. at Fosse 10.	
	25		No more shelling. Major Faulkner 74 F.A. and Capt. Allaman, 12th Sherwood Foresters, evacuated sick.	
	26		A.D.M.S. to conference at D.D.M.S. VIII Corps: in afternoon to inspect sanitation of back areas.	
	27		A.D.M.S. accompanied Corps Commander on his tour of Medical Units of the VIIIth Corps. The Corps is side-slipping tonight on a Brigade front.	
	28		74 F.A. handed over medical posts on left brigade front to F.A. of 15th Divn. 72 F.A. took over medical posts in left brigade area handed over by 20th Divn. Handing over and taking over completed midnight 27/28 Augt.	

Army Form C. 2118.

WAR DIARY
or
INTELLIGENCE SUMMARY.

(Erase heading not required.)

Instructions regarding War Diaries and Intelligence Summaries are contained in F. S. Regs., Part II and the Staff Manual respectively. Title pages will be prepared in manuscript.

Place	Date	Hour	Summary of Events and Information	Remarks and references to Appendices
Sains-en-Gohelle.	1918 Aug. 29th		A.D.M.S. and D.A.D.M.S. visited all new posts held by 72 Fld Ambce: ANGRES and WHITE CHATEAU, also R.A.Ps. CROCUS and QUARRY.	
		30	Routine. Chart showing incidence of Dysentery cases attached.	

Chatene
Colonel, A.M.S.,
A.D.M.S. 24th Divn.

DYSENTERY CHART.
AUG. 1918.

UNITS.	1	2	3	4	5	6	7	8	9	10	11	12	13	14	15	16	17	18	19	20	21	22	23	24	25	26	27	28	29	30	31	TOTAL
1st Royal Scots.																																
3rd Rifle Bde.																	1								1					1		3
8th Queens																	1															1
1st N. Staffs	3/7AB																1															1
8th R.W. Kents																			2	1												3
9th E. Surreys												1														act.RE 1						3
7th Northants																				1	1											1
9th Royal Sussex															1																	1
13th Middlesex																		1														
12th Notts & Derbys.																													act.R+D 1		1	2
106th Bde. R.F.A.																									1							1
107th Bde. R.F.A.								1																								1
24th D.A.C.																																
24th Divl. R.E.																																
24th Bn. M.G.C.																														1		1
	1							1				1			1	2	1	2	2	1				2	2				1	2		17

Confidential

War Diary
A.D.M.S. 24th Divn
September 1918

Vol XXXVII

WR 37
140/382

September 1918

Army Form C. 2118.

WAR DIARY
or
INTELLIGENCE SUMMARY.
(Erase heading not required.)

Instructions regarding War Diaries and Intelligence Summaries are contained in F. S. Regs., Part II. and the Staff Manual respectively. Title pages will be prepared in manuscript.

Place	Date	Hour	Summary of Events and Information	Remarks and references to Appendices
SAINS-EN-GOHELLE	1918. Sep. 1		Routine.	
	" 2		74th Field Ambulance took over Car Loading Post FOSSE 11 from 72nd Field Ambulance. 72 Fld.Amb. now run Right Brigade Area, 74 Fld. Ambce. Left and Centre Brigade Areas.	
	" 3		Routine.	
	" 4		Routine.	
	" 5		Routine.	
	" 6		Much gas shelling of Right Battalion area 73rd Brigade - about 50 casualties - Yellow Cross.	
	" 7		A further 28 casualties - delayed - also some gas shelling with H.V. gun FOSSE 11.	
	" 8		Routine.	
	" 9		Routine.	
	" 10.		A.D.M.S. to Conference of G.O.C., B.Gs.C., C.R.E., and A.A.&.Q.M.G. Division to take part in an attack on present front at an early date. Proposals to be submitted by 12th September.	
	" 11.		Conference at D.D.M.S. VIII Corps - re Medical Arrangements. Proposals re attack how to be submitted by 15th; work to go on.	
	" 12		Conference of Ambulance Commanders A.D.M.S. office. 17th and 72nd Brigades are to attack, 73rd Brigade in reserve. 74th Field Ambulance will run line with 72nd bearers working with their Brigade. 73rd Field Ambulance in reserve.	
	" 13		A.D.M.S., 20th Division called to discuss taking over Right Brigade area. A.D.M.S. to Corps re extra stretchers etc.	
	" 14		Stretcher and blanket dumps being formed at FOSSE 11 and A.D.S., St. PIERRE. The 20th Division will probably take over AIX NOULETTE for a Main Dressing Station, also A.D.S. 'Colonels Post' and medical posts forward of it.	
	" 15		Forward R.A.Ps. to be constructed on the 17th and 72nd Brigade fronts (proposed front of attack) under arrangements between C.R.E. and A.D.M.S. A.D.M.S. to Conference D.D.M.S., VIII Corps.	
	" 16		A.D.M.S., B.A.D.M.S. up the line to select sites for R.A.Ps. Sites chosen well forward for Right and Left Battalion of the Right Brigade. and Right battalion of Left Brigade These are to be handed over and work commenced on the 18th inst.	
	" 17		Orders for recall of 3 Canadian A.M.C. Officers on loan to the Division since APRIL. This makes 5 officers deficient.	
	" 18		Work on the new R.A.Ps commenced by Field Ambulances personnel under R.E. supervision. A.D.M.S. to see R.A.P. HYTHE TUNNEL.	
	" 19		Captain H. RUBIN, M.O.R.C. (USA) from 72nd Field Ambce. to 12th Sherwood Foresters. Captain G.L.LAWLOR, R.A.M.C. from 72nd Field Ambulance to 1st North Staffs. Proposed Medical Arrangements for the attack published.	

Army Form C. 2118.

WAR DIARY
or
INTELLIGENCE SUMMARY.
(Erase heading not required.)

Instructions regarding War Diaries and Intelligence Summaries are contained in F. S. Regs., Part II. and the Staff Manual respectively. Title pages will be prepared in manuscript.

Place	Date	Hour	Summary of Events and Information	Remarks and references to Appendices
SAINS-EN-GOHELLE.	1918. Sep 20		The new degassing chambersat A.D.S?.COLONELS POST - St. PIERRE and W.W.C.P. FOSSE 11 completed and N.C.Os. from each Field Ambulance instructed in their use.	
	" 21		D.A.D.M.S. to see progress of work on new R.A.Ps.. The two of the 72nd Brigade are practically completed and could be occupied any time. The R.A.P. Right Battalion 17th Brigade will take several days to complete.	
	" 22		A.D.M.S. and D.A.D.M.S. forward - inspected A.D.S. St. PIERRE and JUNCTION R.A.P.	
	" 23		R.A.P. in HYTHE TUNNEL completed with the exception of knocking down a sandbag wall at the entrance - this will be done only just previous to being taken into use.	
	" 24		R.A.P. in CATAPULT TRENCH completed. Al the forward R.A.Ps. now ready for occupation when required.	
	" 25		Warning Order received. Division will probably be relieved at an early date.	
	" 26		Orders received that the Division will be relieved by the 58th Division on 28-29-30th September, and will move to staging area CHATEAU DE LA HAIE.	
	" 27		Lieut. F.G. RILEY, M.O.R.C.,(USA) joined for duty. Attached to 72nd Field Ambulance. A.D.M.S., 58th Division called re taking over and all details arranged. R.A.M.C. Order No. 131 issued. Copy attached.	
	" 28		Destination changed to LUCHEUX Area (in Third Army.)	
	" 29		72nd Field Ambulance handed over and moved is from AIX NOULETTE to HERSIN. Captain G.H.B.BLACK, A.A.M.C. arrived as reinforcement - attached to 73rd Field Ambulance.	
	" 30	4 pm.	58th Division took over and D.H.Q. moved from SAINS-EN-GOHELLE to LUCHEUX in Third Army Area. 72 Field Ambulance moved to WARLUZEL. Handing over of 73 and 74 Field Ambulances completed 12 noon.	

30th September 1918.

[signature]

Colonel, A.M.S.

A.D.M.S., 24th Division.

147/3323

ADMS. 24th Do.

Oct 19 17

COMMITTEE FOR THE
MEDICAL HISTORY OF THE WAR
30 DEC. 1918
Date

WAR DIARY
or
INTELLIGENCE SUMMARY.

(Erase heading not required.)

Army Form C. 2118.

Place	Date	Hour	Summary of Events and Information	Remarks and references to Appendices
LUCHEUX	1.10.18		73 and 74 Field Ambulances arrived in new area.	
"	2.10.18		Ambulances intensive training commenced - Special attention is being paid to Marching - & Application of Thomas Splints. 3 Repair Kept patching & repairing ADS's etc.	
	3.10.18		} Routine	
	4.10.18			
	5.10.18		Division to move tomorrow to XVII Corps. Arrived and attached to H.Q. XVII Corps. 74 F Amb (Tent Division) ordered to take over Corps Main Dressing Station by 6 p.m. 6th inst.	
	6.10.18		Move by tactical train to MOEUVRES area.	
MOEUVRES	7.10.18		XVII Corps to attack tomorrow. The 24th Division is to be in support of 63rd and 57th Divisions. Orders issued for Bearer Divisions of Field Ambulances to work with their Brigades. 73 F Amb to be prepared to take over ADS MOYELLES from 63rd Div at 2.15.0 p.m. 74 ADS forward of (Tus). 72 F Amb open forward Corps Main Dressing Station F20a (FONTAINE) under orders of D.D.M.S. D.H.Q. organised into Forward and Rear H.Q. Arrived & started work 1600h (Cpt) to forward D.H.Q. CANTAING MILL. The remainder of A.D.M.S. office attached to the Cache Records Office at Col. D.S. to compile monthly refns & returns etc.	
CANTAING	8.10.18		Attack 0430 hrs completely unsuccessful. 63rd Divn gained objectives but considerable casualties owing to counter attack by enemy with tanks.	
		1600h	63rd Divn to be relieved by 24th Division who are to continue attack tomorrow. 73 F Amb took over ADS. NOYELLES. 74 F Amb prepared to move and open forward ADS.	
		1800h	Forward D.H.Q. to NINE WOOD. Relief of medical units complete.	

Army Form C. 2118.

WAR DIARY
or
INTELLIGENCE SUMMARY.
(Erase heading not required.)

Instructions regarding War Diaries and Intelligence Summaries are contained in F.S. Regs., Part II. and the Staff Manual respectively. Title pages will be prepared in manuscript.

Place	Date	Hour	Summary of Events and Information	Remarks and references to Appendices
NINE WOOD	9.10.18	0530 hours	Attack resumed 0530 hours. 72 I.B. leading. All objectives gained with little opposition, and troops pushing on. 74 ? Amb forward - ADS opposite to NIERGNIES. where they opened ADS at 2300 hours. Adv. DHQ to MONT SUR L'OEUVRE. (G 8 d 9.9.)	
MONT SUR L'OEUVRE	10.10.18		Some rain last night which has made roads very bad for Ambulance cars. 73 ? Amb leap-frogged and opened ADS at Factory B 5 6.88 on CAMBRAI - SOLESMES Road. Advance still pursuing though resistance stiffening. Divisional Amb cars now evacuating 12 miles to CADS, but MAC Relay post established at RUMILLY at 1600 hours to lessen a/c strain on Divl Cars. DHQ to CAMBRAI.	
CAMBRAI	11.10.18		Corps Main Dressing Station opened at B 7 a. (CAMBRAI - SOLESMES road). 74 ? Amb were to have relieved ADS. at AVESNES and taken over Enemy hospital, but were unable to often owing to shelling - our troops held up in front of ST AUBERT. our Divn on our left we cut up on Cauderville operations on left. Casualties (wounded only) approx 420. Capt TREN RANCE no 8 Plt Kents to England, Evacuated injured and Capt IRELAND 73 ? Amb Evac Sick 10 Casualties among RAMC bearers.	
"	12.10.18		Enemy retiring. 74 ? Amb opened ADS. in AVESNES-les-AUBERT. Cars por ST AUBERT.	
"	13.10.18		DHQ & AVESNES-LES-AUBERT	
AVESNES-LES-AUBERT	14.10.18		Enemy standing on line at LA SELLE RIVER. Our troops on N edge MONDICOURT and HAUSSY	
"	15.10.18		72. I.B. to attack tomorrow to Capture MONDICOURT, HAUSSY and river crossings there. About 600 civilians came down from HAUSSY 2200 hours. 73 F Amb moved to RIEUX.	
"	16.10.18		Attack 0530 hours. Completely successful on Rt on HAUSSY. Held up on left. About 400 prisoners.	
		1200hrs	Heavy Enemy barrage on river crossings and slopes W of HAUSSY.	
		1500hrs	Enemy Counter attacks and drive our troops back over river. Heavy shell fire (HE and gas) all day. Evacuation at Cauldrie from HAUSSY has been very difficult, but Cauldrie & dug out, DSRt, part taken softly to 72 F Amb beam. Cauldies for day approx 280 (wounded)	

Army Form C. 2118.

WAR DIARY
or
INTELLIGENCE SUMMARY.
(Erase heading not required.)

Instructions regarding War Diaries and Intelligence Summaries are contained in F. S. Regs., Part II. and the Staff Manual respectively. Title pages will be prepared in manuscript.

Place	Date	Hour	Summary of Events and Information	Remarks and references to Appendices
AVESNES LES AUBERT	17.10.18		24th Division to be relieved by 19th Divn. 73 F Amb moved to CAMBRAI. 74 F Amb to CANONCLES.	
"	18.10.18		Hands over to 19th Div. D.H.Q. moved to CAMBRAI.	
CAMBRAI.	19.10.18		Training programme for troops formulated. Division is expected to be in reserve for that period.	
"	20.10.18		G.O.C. 24 Division inspected 74 F Amb and Bearers of 72 F Amb.	
"	21.10.18		Routine and Training.	
"	22.10.18			
"	23.10.18			
"	24.10.18			
"	25.10.18		24 Division to move into support. 74 F Amb moved with 17th I Bde to CANDICLES.	
"	26.10.18		D.H.Q. to ST AUBERT. 73 F Amb to HAUSSY. 72 F Amb (less Bearers) running C.M.D.S. at AVES NET LES-AUBERT.	
ST AUBERT.	27.10.18		Conference of Ambulance commanders at CM.D.S. to discuss arrangements for next town in the line. Decided to have blankets and stretcher dump at Car Post. Bearer officer of Bde in line to have a Ford car, and Car in front of A.D.S. to be in charge of Bearer Officer working the line.	
"	28.10.18		At conference of ADsMS at CMDS.	
"	29.10.18		Routine.	
"	30.10.18			
"	31.10.18		Division to take over Rt sector of 61st Div Front at an early date. Amb Commanders ordered to reconnoitre.	

Note. Toll of casualties attached.

Cur/ari
Col Amd
A.D.M.S. 24th Division.

October 1918

Casualties – 24th Division

	SICK				WOUNDED			
	ADMITTED		EVACUATED		ADMITTED		EVACUATED	
	OFFICERS	O.R	OFFICERS	O.R	OFFICERS	O.R	OFFICERS	O.R
Oct 1								
2								
3								
4								
5								
6								
7								
8								
9	-	33	-	5	1	64	1	54
10	-	38	-	35	3	158	3	121
11	2	48	2	32	3	118	3	102
12	1	64	1	77	14	414	14	408
13	-	56	-	15	1	66	1	54
14	1	24	-	30	4	131	4	99
15	1	28	-	37	8	158	9	156
16	1	20	1	27	3	51	3	57
17	1	18	1	42	8	254	7	255
18	-	22	1	9	-	18	-	17
19	1	24	-	3	-	25	-	25
20	-	9	-	10	4	31	2	6
21	-	25	-	13	-	8	-	8
22	-	33	2	10	1	2	1	3
23	1	43	1	8	-	8	-	7
24	1	37	1	14	-	4	-	4
25	-	42	-	28	-	1	-	-
26	-	30	-	24	-	3	-	2
27	2	67	-	2	-	2	-	1
28	-	45	-	11	-	-	-	1
29	-	43	-	39	-	1	-	-
30	-	38	-	55	-	11	-	6
31	1	36	-	2	-	5	-	4
Totals 9/31 Oct	13	823	10	528	50	1533	48	1390

ORIGINAL

War Diary of A.D.M.S. 24th Divn
for Novr 1918.

Vol XXXIX

WAR DIARY
INTELLIGENCE SUMMARY
(Erase heading not required.)

Army Form C. 2118.

November 1918.

Place	Date	Hour	Summary of Events and Information	Remarks and references to Appendices
ST AUBERT	1st Nov	—	Advd. forward to 61st Divl Area — met Officers XVII Corps. Selected site for an A.D.S. in School BERMERAIN.	
"	2nd "		A fresh attack is to open on Nov 4th. The Division is to attack as before on a Brigade front. 73.F.Amb. to open A.D.S. at BERMERAIN on the 3rd and is to be prepared to push A.D.S. forward as early as possible.	
"	3rd "		B.H.Q. to BERMERAIN. 73. F.Amb. also to BERMERAIN to open A.D.S. 74. F.Amb moved up and is in reserve. 72. F.Amb continue to run the Corps Main Dressing Station. A small party from 72.F.Amb sent forward to SEPMERIES to hold a building for an ADS. tomorrow.	
		18.00hrs	Enemy is going back on Divl front, our troops following up.	
		23.00h	Our troops on line of first objective for tomorrow.	
BERMERAIN	4th "	05.20h	Attack from line of first objective. Very little resistance at first. Good progress made. About 200 wounded through. 73 F Amb opens A.D.S. at SEPMERIES by 10.30 hours and later pushed on and opens A.D.S. at VILLERS POL. afterward A.D.S. at VILLERS POL. Traffic on roads very bad and owing to distance of Corps M.D.S. some difficulty in clearing cases. B.H.Q. to SEPMERIES.	
SEPMERIES	5th "		Advance resumed. 74 F. Amb moves up and opens ADS. at JENLAIN last night and moved ADS. forward to Chateau WARGNIES-LE-PETIT in at 15.00 hours. An attempt was made to push out ADS. along main BAVAI Road, but this was not possible owing to heavy Enemy Shelling. (1900 hrs.)	

Army Form C. 2118

WAR DIARY
or
INTELLIGENCE SUMMARY.
(Erase heading not required.)

Instructions regarding War Diaries and Intelligence Summaries are contained in F.S. Regs., Part II and the Staff Manual respectively. Title pages will be prepared in manuscript.

Place	Date	Hour	Summary of Events and Information	Remarks and references to Appendices
	Nov 5th		Continued. DHQ. to WARGNIES-LE-GRAND. Captd AD M.C. bearer officer 74 F Amb Wounded and evacuated	
WARGNIES-LE-GRAND	Nov 6th		More resistance by the enemy. Considerable enemy shelling of back areas and roads. Few casualties	
"	7th		Advance continuing. New CM.D.S. opened at Chateau WARGNIES-LE-PETIT at 06 30 hrs. This considerably eased the strain on Divl ambulance cars. 73 F Amb opened ADS at ST WAAST. Enemy has blown bridges between road at ST WAAST - great difficulty in getting round these	
"	8th		Adv DHQ. to Chateau de RAMETZ BAVAI. Advance continuing. 73 F Amb opened ADS. in old German Hospital BAVAI. Still difficulty with blown bridges but roads good East of BAVAI.	
BAVAI.	9th		ADS. still at BAVAI with Cars running forward to MAUBERGE-MONS road. Enemy still retiring and hold up very little opposition. Casualties very light.	
"	10th		20th Division are to take over from 24th Division today - The VI Corps is forming an advance guard for the Third Army front. Relief of Brigade in line completed by 18 00 hrs. Genl 24 Division still in command of line. 1 other reinforcement reporter for duty.	
"	11th	0730 hrs	Wire received stating that hostilities cease at 11 00 hours. Division withdrawn to BAVAI area.	
"	12th		1 officer Reinforcement joined - 16 73 F Amb. Large numbers of returning civilians coming through from enemy lines. 73 F Amb opened Soup Kitchen in BAVAI Square.	
"	13th			

Army Form C. 2118.

WAR DIARY
or
INTELLIGENCE SUMMARY.
(Erase heading not required.)

Instructions regarding War Diaries and Intelligence
[Sum]maries are contained in F. S. Regs., Part II.
and the Staff Manual respectively. Title pages
will be prepared in manuscript.

Place	Date	Hour	Summary of Events and Information	Remarks and references to Appendices
BAVAI	Nov 14th		Corps Main Dressing Station closed. Divisions not to evacuate cases to M.A.C. at WARGNIES-LE-PETIT, who take them on to C.C.S. Lt RILEY M.R.C. 72 F Amb. Evacuated sick. Corps Rest Station closing down.	
"	15th		Division expected to move shortly, only cases likely to recover in 3-4 days are being retained. All other cases to C.C.S.	
"	16th		About 40 cases leave. Lt Col Cunningham too ill F Amb. acting A.D.M.S.	
"	17th		Move of Division commenced. Brigades moving to area SEMERIES - JENLAIN - WARGNIES-LE-PETIT. F Ambulances are moving with their Brigade Groups.	
"	18th		Further move to DENAIN area. D.H.Q. to MASNY.	
MASNY	19th		Brigades and Artillery to SOMAIN - ECAILLON - AUBERCHICOURT LEWAARDE area. 9 Amb - 72 at MASNY. 73. ANICHE 74 SOMAIN.	
"	20th		A/D.M.S. A/D.D.M.S. visit 9 Amb.	
"	22.-		Orders received that Capt DUTHIE 74 F Amb. is to report forthwith to W.O. for release. Apparent to see D/D.M.S. VIII Corps re medical arrangements.	
"	26 II		Division to move to TOURNAI AREA probably about the 30 - 1st Dec. Particulars of move today. F Amb. moves with Brigade Groups.	

Army Form C. 2118.

WAR DIARY
or
INTELLIGENCE SUMMARY.
(Erase heading not required.)

Place	Date	Hour	Summary of Events and Information	Remarks and references to Appendices
MASNY	Nov 26th		Further move today. F Amb now located —	
			72 & Amb. DUVIGNIES.	
			73 ". MOUCHIN.	
			74 ". RUMIGIES.	
			DHQ & Co SAMEON. The Division now comes under I Corps. & start to see	
			2nd and I Corps.	
SAMEON.	28th		Orders to replace Lt HELLER MRC 71 Labour Group. CAPT BARWICK RAMC sent	
			and Lt HELLER to 74 9 Amb.	
"	30th		17th) Bde move to their final area. 74 F Amb at GRUSON.	

Churchope Col.
April 2n Dr.

Original
Duplicate War Diary
ADMS 24th Division
December 1918.
Vol XL

WAR DIARY or INTELLIGENCE SUMMARY

Army Form C. 2118.

Instructions regarding War Diaries and Intelligence Summaries are contained in F. S. Regs., Part II. and the Staff Manual respectively. Title pages will be prepared in manuscript.

(Erase heading not required.)

Place	Date	Hour	Summary of Events and Information	Remarks and references to Appendices
SAMÉON			December 1918.	
	1st Dec	—	ADMS returned from leave to U.K.	
"	2nd Dec	—	—	
"	3rd Dec	—	Capt. Lowe RAMC proceeded to England on expiry of contract, and the Asst. Medical Officer to be demobilized. Capt. Robertson RAMC proceeded to 2nd Division having return from DMS and is struck off strength accordingly.	AP
"	4th Dec	—	Routine.	
"	5th Dec	—	17 Inf Bde now in final area but Niles Bdes still moving — Field Ambs with respective Bde groups.	
"	6th Dec	—	ADMS and DADMS to VALENCIENNES to visit DMS First Army just 7th Fd. Ambulances have commenced to be demobilized.	AP
"	7th Dec			
"	8th Dec			
"	9th "		Routine	
"	10th "			
"	11th "			
RONGY (BELGIUM)	12th Dec		Div HQ moved to RONGY just over the Belgian frontier. A small village — only Div troops billetted there. Field Ambulances unmoved. all cars to TOURNAI (3 CCS?) — pavé road particularly bad — causing several casualties to cars — broken frames etc.	AP

Army Form C. 2118.

WAR DIARY
or
INTELLIGENCE SUMMARY.
(Erase heading not required.)

Instructions regarding War Diaries and Intelligence Summaries are contained in F. S. Regs., Part II. and the Staff Manual respectively. Title pages will be prepared in manuscript.

Place	Date	Hour	Summary of Events and Information	Remarks and references to Appendices
RONCY	13th Dec	—	Major Silby DADMS, evacuated sick to 51 CCS (5 days fever) Capt R.A.H. Duttn Rame, 73 Field Amb, assumed duties of DADMS.	Ab
"	14th Dec	—	Col Mackenzie ADMS, also sick. 5 cases of clinical typhoid discovered amongst civilian at RONCY. DADMS visited these civilian cases, and recommended several sanitary precautions to be taken.	
"	15th Dec	—	Col Mackenzie still in bed sick. Draft of 23 OR arrived — all posted to 73 Field Amb.	
"	16th Dec	—	Civilian doctor supplied with T.A.B. Vaccine for inoculation of civilians at RONCY. Major Silby reported from 51 CCS as ENTERIC FEVER, and evacuated to 39 Stationary Hospital at LILLE.	Ab
"	17th Dec	—		
TOURNAI	18th Dec	—	Div HQ moved to TOURNAI. Fine town with many splendid buildings, including a famous Cathedral dating from 11th Century. ADMS Office 91 rue de Catherine. Education scheme is gradually being commenced to all units. Great difficulty is being experienced owing to lack of books, paper etc, but these are being overcome. (Menzies) Capt Dutton Rame, to 51 CCS sick. Capt J Cullen Rame, 73 Field Amb, to be a/DADMS.	Ab

WAR DIARY or INTELLIGENCE SUMMARY

Army Form C. 2118.

Place	Date	Hour	Summary of Events and Information	Remarks and references to Appendices
TOURNAI	20th Dec	—	All units now in territorial positions. 72 Field Amb. & TOURNAI, 73 Field Amb. at FLORENT (5 miles from TOURNAI) and 74 Field Amb. at GRUSON (9 miles from TOURNAI).	AD
"	21st Dec		Col Mackenzie evacuated sick to 51 CCS (10 days fever). Lieut El Cunningham 73 Field Amb. took over A.D.M.S.	
"	22nd Dec		ADMS Office moved to 27 Quai Jaillet-Pierre, TOURNAI beside the Canal de l'Escaut. Capt Cullen reported 73 Field Amb.	AD
"	23rd Dec		Col Mackenzie diagnosed Paratyphoid B.	
"	24th Dec		Col Mackenzie transferred to 39 Stationary Hospital, LILLE. Capt Dalton RAMC discharged from 51 CCS and to duty as a/DADMS.	
"	25th Dec		Xmas day.	
"	26th Dec		Visited Infantry Barracks, and both Hiram delousers had been condemned but owing to shortage of coal cannot be worked.	AD
"	27th Dec 28 " 29 " 30 "		Xmas festivities continuing. Several english ladies tell at 51 CCS in accordance with W.O. telegram permitting social functions of this character for the period 24th Dec – 5th Jan 3rd inclusive.	
"	31st Dec		ADMS and DADMS visited 73 Field Amb. also the 73rd & 74th Field Baths at RUMES.	

signature
ADMS 74 Div.

1841

ORIGINAL

War Diary of A.D.M.S.
24th Division.
for January 1919.

Box 1951

Vol XLI

Army Form C. 2118.

WAR DIARY
INTELLIGENCE SUMMARY.
(Erase heading not required.)

Instructions regarding War Diaries and Intelligence Summaries are contained in F. S. Regs., Part II. and the Staff Manual respectively. Title pages will be prepared in manuscript.

Place	Date	Hour	Summary of Events and Information	Remarks and references to Appendices
TOURNAI (BELGIUM)	January 1919			
	1st Jan.		A/ADMS visited Cavalry barracks and inspected sanitation of 12th Bn Sherwood Foresters and 24th Divisional Royal Engineers. Much improvement has been left by the Germans.	
	2nd Jan.		Lt Col J.W.M. Cunningham DSO RAMC, A/ADMS 24 Div, proceeded on leave to U.K. Lt Col C.H. Denys MC RAMC, 72 Field Ambulance to be A/ADMS. 1st Lieut H. Peck M.R.C. U.S.A. posted to 102nd M.G. Bn. and struck off strength. M/DADMS, Capt Fulton, visited Col MacKenzie & Major Selby in Hospital (39 Stationary) at Lille. Both doing well.	
	3rd Jan.		Routine.	
	4th Jan.		Owing to shortage of Medical Officers it was necessary to allot 2 Medical Officers to the 3 units of the Infantry Brigade, and 1 Medical Officer to the 2 Artillery Bdes.	
	5th Jan.		Routine.	
	6th Jan.		Major J.P.Cahir RAMC proceeded to England on expiry of contract, and is struck off the strength.	
	7th Jan.			
	8th Jan.		The no. of R.A.M.C. officers in the Division is now reduced to 25. Normal 39. Deficiency of 14.	
	9th 10th 11th		Routine.	

Army Form C.2118.

WAR DIARY
or
INTELLIGENCE SUMMARY.
(Erase heading not required.)

Instructions regarding War Diaries and Intelligence Summaries are contained in F.S. Regs., Part II. and the Staff Manual respectively. Title pages will be prepared in manuscript.

Place	Date	Hour	Summary of Events and Information	Remarks and references to Appendices
TOURNAI (BELGIUM)			January 1919 (Continued)	
	12th Jan		a/ADMS visited DDMS I Corps. Capt. G. S. MacConkey RAMC proceeded to 91st Wing R.A.F. vice Capt H. Mortimer RAMC who reported to Division, and is posted to 106 Bde R.F.A.	Auth DMS First Army PL 813/535 d/2.1.19.
"	13th Jan		Routine	
"	14th Jan		a/ADMS visited Infantry Barracks and inspected Sanitation, the Divisional Clothing Store was also examined, and the disinfection of undoclothing put to the test. Result, after incineration of eggs taken from clothing, absolutely satisfactory.	
"	15th Jan		a/ADMS visited Brigade Baths at RUMES. Delouser working. c/ADMS visited 73 & 74 Field Ambulances, and new baths at BAISIEUX.	
"	16th Jan		Routine	
"	17th Jan		a/ADMS visited Cavalry Barracks to inspect progress made as regards Removal of manure etc. Progress excellent.	
"	18th Jan		a/ADMS visited new baths being installed at Cavalry Barracks, and inspected billets of 104 Field Coy RE.	
"	19th Jan		a/DADMS visited TAINTIGNIES re 2 cases ? TYPHOID reported amongst civilian population. Sanitary precautions taken are considered sufficient.	
"	20 Jan		a/ADMS visited New Inspection Room of Divisional Royal Engineers	

WAR DIARY
or
INTELLIGENCE SUMMARY.

Army Form C. 2118.

Place	Date	Hour	Summary of Events and Information	Remarks and references to Appendices
TOURNAI (BELGIUM)	20 Jan		January 1919 Continued Lt. T.C. Mackenzie DSO. AMS. reported the Division for Hospital and assumed appointment of DMS. Major E.J. Selby RAMC reported from Hospital and resumes appointment of ADMS.	
"	21st 22nd		Routine	
"	23rd Jan		Capt Hopper RAMC proceeded to No 6 C.C.S. for duty and is struck off strength	
"	24th 25th Jan		Routine	
"	26 Jan		Sunbeam ambulance belonging to 74 Field Ambulance was reported stolen in streets of TOURNAI. Divisional Court of Enquiry to be held.	
"	27 28 29 Jan		Routine	
"	30 Jan		Major General H.N. Thompson AMS, DMS Second Army, visited the Division and inspected 74 Field Ambulance. Afterwards he addressed the men of the Ambulance on the subject of Demobilization.	
"	31 Jan		Routine	

Mackenzie Col.
ADMS 2nd Div

7/19

ORIGINAL

War Diary of A.D.M.S. 24th Divn
For February, 1919.

Vol XLII

Army Form C. 2118.

WAR DIARY
or
INTELLIGENCE SUMMARY.
(Erase heading not required.)

Instructions regarding War Diaries and Intelligence Summaries are contained in F. S. Regs., Part II. and the Staff Manual respectively. Title pages will be prepared in manuscript.

Place	Date	Hour	Summary of Events and Information	Remarks and references to Appendices
TOURNAI, (BELGIUM)	February 1919			
	1st	—	Demobilyation of R.A.M.C. now under direct control of Director General Medical Services — allotment of Other ranks daily = 20 men for for 1st Division. No officers R.A.M.C. to be demobilyed at present.	
	2nd		except in special cases. A.D.M.S. visited Divisional H.Q. billets.	
	3rd		A.D.M.S. and D/DADMS visited Divisional baths & delousers (Tournai).	
	4th		Routine	
	5th		A.D.M.S. visited Prophylactic Treatment Room of 24th Bn M.G.C. and Divisional R.E.	
	6th		Routine	
	7th		Ambulance car stolen during night from 72nd Field Ambulance, Tournai	
	8th		Routine	
	9th		Col. Mackenzie A.M.S., A.D.M.S. 24th Division, proceeds on 30 days' leave to U.K. Lt Col J.W.M. Cunningham D.S.O. R.A.M.C., 73 Field Ambulance, to be a/A.D.M.S. 24th Division	
	10th			
	11th 12th 13th 14th 15th		Routine	
	16th		Capt J.L.D. Burton R.A.M.C. (S.R.) proceeds to U.K. for release. Authority D.G.A.M.S.	

WAR DIARY
INTELLIGENCE SUMMARY
(Erase heading not required.)

Army Form C.

Place	Date	Hour	Summary of Events and Information	Remarks and references to Appendices
TOURNAI (BELGIUM)	February 1919			
	17		Routine	
	18		Presentation of colours to 3 battalions of 73rd Inf. Bde. Parade ground - Champ de Manoeuvres Tournai. G.O.C. 2nd Army and I Corps were present. Also G.O.C. 2nd Division, and staff. Maj. & Q. Selby Rame, DADMS of Division returned from leave UK and resumed duties as D.A.D.M.S. Capt R.A.H. Selby Rame 73 Field Ambulance, to regimental duty.	
	19th			
	20th		Routine	
	21st		Units of 17-21 Bde are now moving by Tournai.	
	22nd			
	23rd		Routine	
	24th			
	25th			
	26th		Capt W.A. Alexander RAMC proceeded to 4th Rhine to report to Dmys. Sent army. Maj. C.A. Burger RAMC	
	27th		No. of personnel (other ranks) RAMC presented to U.K. on styling (contract) for release (Sub Anklaws) Personnel (OR) not eligible for release — 183 Personnel (OR) eligible for release (Sub Anklaws) — 28 Request (OR) complete Cadres of 2 amb — 129 Total strength GR RAMC — 340	
	28th		Routine	

John Cunningham
Lt Col
ADMS

Apt 43
60/3553

Confidential
Mar 1919

War Diary for March 1919
24 DIV
VOL XLIII

17 JUL 1919

WAR DIARY

INTELLIGENCE SUMMARY

Army Form C 2118

Place	Date	Hour	Summary of Events and Information	Remarks and references to Appendices
TOURNAI	March 1919		**ROUTINE**	
	1st		Orders received for demobilization	
	3rd		Capt Norcock R.A.M.C. att 9th E Surveys to LANSER R.A.M.C. takes from 72 F.A.K to 9th E Surveys.	
	4th		9th E Surveys left to Armies for Army of the Rhine	
	8th		Capt Wallace R.A.M.C. and 20 O.R. R.A.M.C. sent to lorry camp for demobilization. This leaves 126 O.R. R.A.M.C. available for release	
	12th		L/Cpl Cunningham 800 R.A.M.C., O.C. 73 F Amb ordered to report for Army duty as Ot N°12 Stationary Hospital ST POL. Left train	
	13th		31 O.R. R.A.M.C. sent to Concentration Camp for demobilization. Instructions received to add 6% to above strength for sick wastage. This leaves 3 men for Field Amb.	
	14th		Capt T.C. Mackenzie 820. Attd returns from leave. A draft of 15 O.R. R.A.M.C. (reliable men and volunteers) despatched to Armies 29 Div. Divisional orders to concentrate in BAISIEUX area N Vehicle park by Ambulances instructed to send as much transport spare than today.	
	18th		Attend took over duties (Kempson) POSTED 1 Corps	
	21st		Orders for return to A.E.F. of Capt GREENWAY and Lt HELLER. (left 22nd)	

Army Form C. 2118.

WAR DIARY
INTELLIGENCE SUMMARY
(Erase heading not required.)

Instructions regarding War Diaries and Intelligence Summaries are contained in F. S. Regs., Part II. and the Staff Manual respectively. Title pages will be prepared in manuscript.

Place	Date	Hour	Summary of Events and Information	Remarks and references to Appendices
TOURNAI	Mch 21st	Cont'd	Capt TAYLOR Rouen to F. Amb. 1/3 Lon to 51 CCS. The Unit's B 18/1/1 and 3 American Officers supplies. 1st Reinforcement 1st N Staffords Moved to Cone concentration area of Mullen & 2 Field Coys. to Mullen & 2 Field Coys. New Gidge F. Amb (2 Echelons) received Ambulance orders to move of Amb & return to hand in surplus to S.A.D.O's for evacn. Capts CAMPBELL, ROBIN and MULLINS MC USA ordered to American Course.	
"	22nd			
"	25th			
"	26th		Div B.R. Rouen to Concentration camp for duty. Division Officials moved to Bde Gp H.Q, Sub orders Capts ANDREW and FRIER Rouen to Adam ROUEN. Lieut KENNEDY Rouen to Adam Ambulance Train ABBEVILLE. 72 F. Amb moves to GOSSON. The remainder of the cavalry Except Sub H.Q. Sub Train and 2 R.M. to H.Q. moves to concentration area.	
"	29th		All officers on F Amb except 1 per Amb'ce, and all Ambulance officers Rank of H.Q. Cops - Divisions struck off strength from (as a7) and some on the strength of N°1 Area.	

J. M. Clune Col. HDM5 24 Div

www.ingramcontent.com/pod-product-compliance
Lightning Source LLC
Chambersburg PA
CBHW080845010526
44114CB00017B/2373